The Pontificate of Benedict X

The Pontificate of Benedict XVI

Its Premises and Promises

Edited and with an Introduction by

William G. Rusch

WILLIAM B. EERDMANS PUBLISHING COMPANY

GRAND RAPIDS, MICHIGAN / CAMBRIDGE, U.K.

Published 2009 by
Wm. B. Eerdmans Publishing Co.
2140 Oak Industrial Drive N.E., Grand Rapids, Michigan 49505 /
P.O. Box 163, Cambridge CB3 9PU U.K.

Printed in the United States of America

15 14 13 12 11 10 09   7 6 5 4 3 2 1

Library of Congress Cataloging-in-Publication Data

The Pontificate of Benedict XVI : its premises and promises /
    edited and introduction by William G. Rusch.
        p.   cm.
    ISBN 978-0-8028-4868-0 (pbk. : alk. paper)
    1. Benedict XVI, Pope, 1927–   I. Rusch, William G.
    BX1378.6.P66   2009
    282.092 — dc22

                                    2009009680

www.eerdmans.com

Contents

Contents

Introduction

WILLIAM G. RUSCH

On April 19, 2005, late in the afternoon, white smoke issued from the chimney of the Sistine Chapel. This was a clear sign to an awaiting and expectant crowd gathered in Saint Peter's Square in Rome that the conclave of cardinals had elected a successor to the much-beloved Pope John Paul II. Now in a real sense the long and influential pontificate of the first Polish Pope was ended. The Roman Catholic Church in the opening years of a new century and millennium was in new hands.

In Rome and around the world, there was anticipation as to who would succeed John Paul II. The formal announcement soon came that Joseph Cardinal Ratzinger, Prefect of the Congregation for the Doctrine of the Faith, and a 78-year-old German theologian and archbishop, had been elected Pope and taken the name of Benedict XVI.

The choice in a number of ways was not surprising. Cardinal Ratzinger was Dean of the College of Cardinals. He had been a close collaborator with John Paul II. Since the days of the Second Vatican Council, he had become a major theological voice in Roman Catholic and broader academic circles. He had played a major role in an impressive way in the events around the funeral of his predecessor.

Nevertheless, whether accurately or not, Joseph Ratzinger in the international media was often portrayed as an extreme conservative — rigid, and even stringent. Because of his age, many wondered if the cardinals had chosen an "interim" Pope after the many years of John Paul II. His election seemed to confirm that Italian cardinals no longer had a lock on the papal office.

Speculation began almost at once about what kind of papacy Benedict XVI would shape. He is probably the first Prefect of the Congregation of the Doctrine of the Faith to be elected Pope. He is the first world-class theologian to enter this office in centuries. Would his closest rivals be Leo the Great and Gregory the Great? He is also, most likely — and certainly in recent history — the most prolific theological writer to become pope.

In addition, he assumed the papacy at a time of profound global changes and intense internal pressures within the Roman Catholic Church itself. How is the Roman Catholic Church, with declining membership and vocations in many parts of the world, to relate to the twenty-first century and at the same time remain faithful to Catholic Christianity? How is it to position itself vis-à-vis the ecumenical movement and other major world religions? How is it to overcome the failure of some of its pastoral leadership? These are just some of the questions that anyone elected Pope in the year 2005 would have to encounter.

But the intriguing and enigmatic question from the outset was: How would *Joseph Ratzinger,* now Benedict XVI, confront these challenges and what would his handling of these issues mean? Also present from the beginning, for Catholics and non-Catholics around the world, were the wider implications of the answer to that question.

Could a clue to answering this inquiry be the continuity, or its lack, between Joseph Ratzinger and Benedict XVI? A number of persons across the ecumenical spectrum were asked by the editor of this volume to reflect independently on the question: *How will the life experiences and theological reflections of Joseph Ratzinger influence the pontificate of Benedict XVI?* The group included men and women theologians from the Baptist, Episcopalian, Lutheran, Methodist, Orthodox, Pentecostal, Reformed, and Roman Catholic traditions. Each of them addressed the question of continuity or discontinuity in a Benedict XVI pontificate and what might be expected of such a pontificate. The result is the ensuing chapters with a postscript by a preeminent Roman Catholic theologian and commentator on the world scene.

Many books have been written about the central figure of this volume, and many more will no doubt follow. At the conclusion of four years of Benedict XVI as Pope of the Roman Catholic Church, this collection has some claim to distinctness, if not uniqueness. It seeks not only to contribute to a greater understanding of this Pope but to offer respectfully an encouragement for him in some of the significant paths he has already explored. It will be apparent, though, that some of Cardinal Ratzinger/Pope

Benedict's ideas and actions have raised concerns, doubts, and even rejection by some of the authors in this collection — not surprisingly, for such issues reflect the reality of the time when Joseph Ratzinger of Bavaria became Benedict XVI of Rome.

Dale T. Irvin (Baptist) in chapter one takes up the topic of Benedict's views of European Christianity and how these perspectives fit into the global context of Christianity in the twenty-first century. Irvin examines the now-famous lecture that the Pope delivered in Regensburg on September 12, 2006. He concludes that in spite of all the media attention and subsequent reaction in the Muslim world, Benedict's main point in that academic lecture was to argue that Christianity achieved a decisive synthesis of revelation and reason by a joining of biblical faith and Greek philosophy. Irvin declares that Benedict in this lecture insists that Christianity is related to Europe's history in a unique way that is not true of any other culture. According to Irvin, Benedict views the contemporary uncoupling of Christian faith from the history of Western Europe as a "dehellenization" that will cut faith from reason and encourage violence. The author of this first chapter also sees in other remarks of Cardinal Ratzinger/Pope Benedict a recognition that the way forward for the Roman Catholic Church is a greater embrace of pluralism and diversity than presented in the Regensburg lecture. Irvin concludes that if the pontificate of Benedict develops ideas he uttered in Turkey in November 2006, a new era for world Christianity could be possible.

In chapter two, Ephraim Radner (Episcopalian) explores the question of providential pluralism as an ecumenical gift. He suggests that the adaptive, conciliar character of Anglicanism could provide a gift to the universal church. Referring to an essay of Cardinal Ratzinger in 2004, "Europe: Its Spiritual Foundation," he notes that Ratzinger is drawing on a long tradition of the dualism between church and state. Radner illustrates how Anglicanism has been concerned with the maintenance of a religious conscience within a developing pluralistic society and shows how some features of Anglicanism have allowed it to do precisely this. Radner concludes this chapter by showing how these issues have remained a longstanding matter of concern to the Cardinal, now Pope.

In chapter three, Harding Meyer (Lutheran) from his perspective as a German ecumenical theologian looks at Cardinal Ratzinger/Pope Benedict in terms of three roles: theologian, philosopher of religion, and ecumenist. In all three cases, Meyer sees the life experiences of Joseph Ratzinger as critical to understanding Pope Benedict XVI. He notes especially Rat-zinger's participation in the Second Vatican Council, his experience with student unrest in Germany in the 1960s, and his appointment as Prefect of the Congregation for the Doctrine of the Faith by John Paul II in 1981. Ac-cording to Meyer, the twenty some years that Ratzinger spent as a univer-sity professor of doctrine and dogmatics will deeply influence his papal thinking, notably his insistence on the personal God who comes to hu-mankind in the person of Jesus of Nazareth. Meyer also suggests that these years contributed to Ratzinger/Benedict's views of the synthesis of reason, faith, and life as the power that allowed Christianity to become a major world religion. Like Irvin in an earlier chapter, Meyer views Benedict as concerned about the destruction of this synthesis and what it could mean for the future of Christianity in Europe and elsewhere. Unlike much cover-age in the media, Meyer regards Benedict in harmony with Ratzinger as a committed ecumenist. The key question will be: How does Benedict un-derstand and plan to exercise his ministry of unity? It can be anticipated, according to Meyer, that in ecumenical dialogue the basic convictions of the Church will be maintained. Dialogue will not become mere diplomatic negotiations. Another likelihood is that preference may well be given to di-alogue with the Orthodox churches. Yet Meyer concludes that there is enough evidence in the career of Joseph Ratzinger to suggest that Lu-theran–Roman Catholic dialogue could be a priority for this German Pope.

Geoffrey Wainwright (Methodist) in chapter four explores the topic of continuity in the thought of Cardinal Ratzinger and Pope Benedict by exam-ining his first two encyclicals, *Deus Caritas Est* and *Spe Salvi*. The main focus of the chapter is on the first encyclical. Wainwright looks at how the Cardinal and then Pope deals with the question of death in the context of a concern to demonstrate how faith and reason can serve the one Truth proclaimed by Christianity. Wainwright pursues this examination by a discussion of six themes: the essential constitution of the human being (The Being of Man), the existential vocation of humankind (The Human Vocation), the human need for redemption and its divine provision (Redemption, or the Retrieval of the Lost), the ethical challenge of faith (The Ethical Challenge), the qual-ity and direction of society and culture (The Quality of Culture), and the fi-nal prospect of the human person and the race (The Future and the Final Prospect). In each of these sections Wainwright shows by a careful compari-son of Cardinal Ratzinger's earlier writings and sermons how the first encyclical of Pope Benedict incorporates ideas that were present in his earliest reflections. The Methodist writer of this chapter notes a common attitude about death held by both Cardinal Ratzinger and Charles Wesley by reference to two quotations.

This fourth chapter concludes with some comments on Benedict's second encyclical, *Spe Salvi.* Wainwright points out the continuity between the two encyclicals in their concern for the meaning and conduct of life, especially in view of the final question of human existence posed by death. He sees this concern emerge in three interrelated areas: that of each and every human person, that of the social constitution of humankind, and finally, that of the human race as a whole and its history.

The fifth chapter, authored by Metropolitan Maximos (Orthodox), addresses the topic: Will the ecclesiology of Cardinal Ratzinger influence the pontificate of Pope Benedict XVI? Maximos begins by discussing the basic ecclesiological problems of Roman primacy and universal jurisdiction between East and West, problems recognized by Cardinal Ratzinger himself. He notes that the *Letter to the Bishops of the Catholic Church on Some Aspects of the Church Understood as Communion* and the Declaration, *Dominus Iesus,* have been responsible in recent years for special problems between the Orthodox churches and the Roman Catholic Church. The author then offers some possible resolution to these ecclesiological problems, based on an examination of some of Cardinal Ratzinger's own writings. Maximos believes that this ecclesiology, articulated by Cardinal Ratzinger, may well influence in a positive manner the pontificate of Benedict. If this does occur, Maximos concludes a rapprochement could take place between the Orthodox churches and the Roman Catholic Church and even the possibility at some point in the nearer future of full communion between Eastern and Roman Catholic Christianity. He views the visit of Pope Benedict in 2006 to the Ecumenical Patriarchate, the visit of Cardinal Kasper to the Patriarchate in the following year, and the *Common Declaration* of Pope Benedict XVI and Ecumenical Patriarch Bartholomew as all positive signs of what may come out of the present pontificate.

Cheryl Bridges Johns (Pentecostal) in chapter six presents an evaluation of Cardinal Ratzinger/Pope Benedict XVI as a conservative in regard to the issues of faith but one who is open to dialogue. She sees this as being of special importance for the Global South, where both Pentecostals and Roman Catholics form the largest blocks of Christians. According to Johns, Pentecostals and Roman Catholics should acknowledge a common passion for Christ, for the Church, and for the truth of the gospel. She examines each of these passions in the thought of Ratzinger/Benedict. She notes how, for the Cardinal and now Pope, this passion for Christ is closely connected with his thought about the Logos and the Eucharist. Here Johns speaks of Ratzinger/Benedict's thinking about the Trinity. Pentecostals should be appreciative of his approach, but they will seek a more prominent pneumatology. In a discussion of the passion for the Church, the author of the chapter also comments on liberation theology and the role of Cardinal Ratzinger in critiquing it. She shows how Pentecostalism has made contributions, e.g., in appreciation of the role of women, in places where liberation theology has flourished. She believes that Benedict's passion for the Church can be a significant corrective in the North American context to the individualization in the Pentecostal tradition. Ratzinger/Benedict's passion for the truth of the gospel is related to his understanding of the Logos as the source of reason. Johns notes the Pope's appreciation of human reason and also his caution about its limits, and compares this with the way that Pentecostals view reason. The chapter ends with the suggestion that a reformed Catholicism and a mature Pentecostalism may hold the key to the future of Christianity.

Joseph D. Small (Presbyterian) provides in chapter seven a Reformed appreciation of Joseph Ratzinger as professor, Prefect, and Pope. He urges Reformed Christians to give careful attention to the theological reflections of this Cardinal, now Pope, because many of the questions of Benedict's concerns are issues that have been central to the Reformed tradition. Small observes that many of Benedict's positions will not be congenial to Reformed faith and life, but these different conclusions may serve to focus Reformed questions and even lead to an enrichment of Reformed answers. He cautions that there may not be a straight line from the professor by way of the Prefect to the Pope. Yet the thought of Ratzinger through the years has been quite consistent. The chapter addresses questions of "truth and the church" and "the church as communion," and shows how Ratzinger/Benedict's views on these topics can be, in fact, in dialogue with the writings of John Calvin and the Reformed tradition.

Small closes the chapter with a section on the present ecumenical situation. He is sympathetic to Benedict's views of the need to maintain truth in ecumenical dialogue and a primacy of action over issues of truth. Small notes that if Benedict continues Ratzinger's passion for the truth of the faith with an openness to the presence of faith's truths in other churches, his contribution could be significant. As this Reformed author states, the Bishop of Rome is uniquely placed to engender deep ecumenical engagement in the doctrine of the faith.

Sara Butler (Roman Catholic) takes up in chapter eight the question of what clues Joseph Ratzinger's personal experience and theological reflection can give to Benedict's pontificate. She focuses on Benedict's first encyclical, *Deus Caritas Est*, whose culmination is an invitation to gaze upon "the pierced heart of Jesus on the cross." Butler sees in this admonition a desire on the part of Benedict to have the Catholic faithful increase in their devotional knowledge and love of Jesus Christ as Savior. By an examination of earlier writings and preaching of Cardinal Ratzinger, Butler documents how he has expressed this concern since the 1970s and 1980s. Long before his papal election Ratzinger placed himself in the tradition of Pope Pius XII's encyclical of 1956, *Haurietis Aquas*, which urged devotion to the Sacred Heart of Jesus. Thus already, early in Benedict's pontificate, it is possible to see him returning to this theme to confront a Catholic crisis in faith and devotion, which Benedict views as a crisis in devotion to the Sacred Heart of Jesus. According to Butler, it is clear to Cardinal Ratzinger, and now Pope Benedict, that this devotion can lead to an understanding and expression of the church's faith in Christ and Christ's free self-surrender in love. Thus it is able to provide a needed doctrinal context to face new questions. Butler indicates that the hints of this position can be found in the Christological chapter of the *Catechism of the Catholic Church*, where Ratzinger as Prefect of the Congregation for the Doctrine of the Faith had a major influence. The chapter concludes by showing how the pierced heart of Jesus as an icon of God's love has become a major part of the argument of *Deus Caritas Est* and a hermeneutical key to Benedict's book, *Jesus of Nazareth*. Butler believes that Benedict in the coming years will continue to encourage Christians to renew their faith with a devotional knowledge of Jesus Christ, shown forth in this icon of love, "the pierced heart of Jesus."

The final word in this collection of essays is given to the late Richard John Neuhaus. During his life, Neuhaus highly admired Cardinal Ratzinger/Pope Benedict. From his Roman Catholic perspective, in this postscript written in September of 2008, Neuhaus makes some observations on the insightfulness of the chapters in this volume in offering a key to fathom the life and thought of Benedict XVI. Neuhaus thus engages in a task that will occupy theologians, church leaders, and ecumenists during this pontificate and well beyond.

William G. Rusch

The composition and publication of this volume would not have been possible without the support and participation of a number of colleagues and friends who saw the ecumenical potential of such a collection of essays. This group obviously includes but is not limited to the contributors. Special gratitude is owed to William B. Eerdmans Jr., who constantly demonstrates his commitment to the visible unity of Christ's Church in the publishing program of the William B. Eerdmans Company. My close friend Norman A. Hjelm has journeyed with this project from the earliest days of my conception of it. His advice has been invaluable. In the last phase of production, he was willing to accept responsibilities which I was unable to perform. A word of mere thanks hardly adequate.

1 Benedict XVI, the Ends of European Christendom, and the Horizons of World Christianity

DALE T. IRVIN

On September 12, 2006, Pope Benedict XVI delivered a lecture before some 1500 students and faculty at the University of Regensburg, in southern Germany. The event quickly made unexpected headlines around the world, igniting anger and outrage throughout the Islamic community in particular. Early in his lecture the Pope quoted from an obscure fourteenth-century Byzantine text a statement that appeared in effect to say the Prophet Muhammad had brought evil and Islam had been spread by the sword. The Holy Father did not say he agreed with this sentiment, but his inclusion of the reference in his lecture, coupled with his later seeming inability to distance himself sufficiently from the assertion or clarify adequately why he even included it at all, further fanned the fires of anger that raged across the world.

The University of Regensburg was an unlikely location from whence to ignite such an interreligious storm. The city of Regensburg is located in the southern German region of Bavaria, where Benedict had been born and raised. Both religiously and culturally the region is characterized by the continuity of its traditional German Catholic identity.[1] By all accounts Benedict considers these northern foothills of the Alps to be as much his spiritual as his cultural homeland.[2] The decision to journey home seven-

---

1. "The practice of the Catholic religion was, indeed, more consistent in Bavaria than in any other part of Germany," writes Aidan Nichols, OP, in the opening chapter of *The Thought of Benedict XVI: An Introduction to the Thought of Joseph Ratzinger* (New York: Burns & Oates, 2005), p. 17.

2. "Joseph Ratzinger is very much a Bavarian theologian," says Nichols in the opening line of *The Thought of Benedict XVI*, p. 5.

teen months after his elevation to the papacy and deliver an academic lecture in the Aula Magna of the university where he had served as an early faculty member, dean, and then vice president before being appointed Archbishop of Munich-Freising in 1977, had much to do with his overall vision for his papacy.[3]

Benedict opened the lecture by remembering his experience as a professor at the University of Bonn in the late 1950s. Historians, philosophers, and theologians on the faculty had regularly gathered for lively discussion in those days, he recalled. Despite the difficulties that representatives of the various academic disciplines had in communicating with each other from time to time, "we made up a whole, working in everything on the basis of a single rationality with its various aspects and sharing responsibility for the right use of reason," he said. Referring to the university's two theological faculties (Protestant and Catholic), the Pope noted:

> by inquiring about the reasonableness of faith, they too carried out a work that is necessarily part of the "whole" of the *universitas scientiarum,* even if not everyone could share the faith which theologians seek to correlate with reason as a whole. This *profound sense of coherence within the universe of reason* was not troubled, even when it was once reported that a colleague had said there was something odd about our university: it had two faculties devoted to something that did not exist: God. That even in the face of such radical scepticism it is still necessary and reasonable to raise the question of God through the use of reason, and to do so in the context of the tradition of the Christian faith: this, within the university as a whole, was accepted without question (emphasis added).

It was the loss of this "profound sense of coherence within the universe of reason" that was the main concern of the Pope's lecture at Regensburg on that September afternoon in 2006. His lecture was titled "Faith, Reason and the University: Memories and Reflections." The statement about Islam being a religion of violence was made in reference to its supposed separation of reason from religion. The text from which Benedict drew the reference was written by the fourteenth-century Eastern Roman emperor, Manuel II Palaiologos, on a dialogue that the em-

3. The University of Regensburg was founded in 1962. The School of Theology opened its doors in 1968. Joseph Ratzinger, now Benedict XVI, joined the faculty in 1969.

peror had with a Persian Muslim scholar. Benedict referred to that text almost in passing. He was reminded of the main topic of his lecture, he said, when he had been recently reading a new scholarly work on the dialogue edited by Theodore Khoury. The Pope then quoted the emperor who, in the course of the dialogue in 1391, had said, "Show me just what Mohammed brought that was new, and there you will find things only evil and inhuman, such as his command to spread by the sword the faith he preached."

"What was the Pope thinking?" asked headline writers and bloggers alike as reports of the statement raced around the globe. It is a valid question. At first glance the reference to Islam in the text appears to be random and arbitrary at best. It bears little direct reference to the rest of the lecture that followed. Nothing more about Islam was said. The main point that the pontiff drew from the emperor's remarks was that there is an inherent connection between unreasonable religion and violence. But the point could have easily been made in any number of other ways without referring to Islam, and certainly without referring to the works of one of the last Christian emperors in the East Roman (or Byzantine) Empire, or what is now the modern nation of Turkey.

A number of commentators suggested that the Holy Father was simply reverting to the ways of an academician. Being back in the Bavarian countryside, speaking before the faculty and students in the familiar setting of the small university of Regensburg, he was demonstrating his intellectual range. Perhaps he was simply seeking to demonstrate that he was keeping up on his academic reading. Perhaps he even forgot for a moment that he was the Pope, and that papal pronouncements, even in the context of an academic lecture, are closely scrutinized and can often have unexpected consequences around the world.

One hesitates, of course, to suggest that the Holy Father would be so haphazard in his thinking. A more careful reading of the lecture that the Pope delivered that day in fact dispels such a notion. The reference to the Byzantine emperor, Islam, and the construction of a reasonable faith had very much to do with the overall point of the lecture. They make a great deal of sense when located within the wider horizon of Joseph Ratzinger's intellectual world.

To see this it is necessary to look at the fuller section from the lecture that touched off the storm in September 2006. I quote the passage at length:

In the seventh conversation (διάλεξις — controversy) edited by Professor Khoury, the emperor touches on the theme of the holy war. The emperor must have known that surah 2.256 reads: "There is no compulsion in religion." According to some of the experts, this is probably one of the surahs of the early period, when Mohammed was still powerless and under threat. But naturally the emperor also knew the instructions, developed later and recorded in the Qur'an, concerning holy war. Without descending to details, such as the difference in treatment accorded to those who have the "Book" and the "infidels," he addresses his interlocutor with a startling brusqueness, a brusqueness that we find unacceptable, on the central question about the relationship between religion and violence in general, saying: "Show me just what Mohammed brought that was new, and there you will find things only evil and inhuman, such as his command to spread by the sword the faith he preached." The emperor, after having expressed himself so forcefully, goes on to explain in detail the reasons why spreading the faith through violence is something unreasonable. Violence is incompatible with the nature of God and the nature of the soul. "God," he says, "is not pleased by blood — and not acting reasonably (σὺν λόγω) is contrary to God's nature. Faith is born of the soul, not the body. Whoever would lead someone to faith needs the ability to speak well and to reason properly, without violence and threats. . . . To convince a reasonable soul, one does not need a strong arm, or weapons of any kind, or any other means of threatening a person with death. . . ."

Several observations are in order regarding this extraordinary passage. First, Benedict is not as ignorant of Islam as the news media in the days following the Regensburg episode too easily tended to portray him to be.[4] He acknowledged in the lecture the inappropriateness of the emperor's assertion that Islam was intrinsically violent, calling the "startling brusqueness" of the emperor "unacceptable." The Pope's assertion that Surah 2.256 is from the earlier period of the Prophet's life is probably incorrect, but this is not enough to disqualify him of being reasonably well informed of

4. For a fuller explication of his understanding of Islam, see Joseph Cardinal Ratzinger, *Salt of the Earth: The Church at the End of the Millennium: An Interview with Peter Seewald* (San Francisco: Ignatius, 1997); Joseph Cardinal Ratzinger, Marcello Pera, and Michale F. Moore, *Without Roots: The West, Relativism, Christianity, Islam* (New York: Basic Books, 2004); Benedict XVI, *Europe Today and Tomorrow* (San Francisco: Ignatius Press, 2007).

Islamic faith and practice. Nor is he opposed to interfaith dialogue or to fostering a more positive environment for interfaith relations. Two months after the Regensburg speech the Pope journeyed to Turkey. During one of his speeches there he is reported to have said, "I would like to recite a few sentences from Pope Gregory VII from the year 1076, which he directs at a Muslim prince from North Africa. . . . Gregory VII spoke of the special love ('caritas') that Christians and Muslims owe each other, for 'we both believe in and attest to the one God, if in different ways, every day we praise Him and revere Him as the creator of the centuries and ruler of this world.'"[5] The reference to Gregory may well have been an intentional effort on the part of Benedict to repair the damage done to Christian-Muslim relations worldwide by the Regensburg lecture, but even if it was, it helps quell the notion that the Pope is entirely insensitive to Muslim concerns.

Second, the choice of this particular emperor, Manuel II Palaiologos, seems to have been important. Benedict recognized that Manuel II would most likely have known the Qur'an. The emperor was indeed acquainted with Islamic belief and practice as he had spent time as a hostage in the Ottoman court. It was under his later rule that the Byzantine Empire was finally reduced to paying tribute to the Ottoman Empire, thereby in effect making the Byzantine Empire a vassal to the Ottoman state. Manuel II's son, Constantine XI, was the last Byzantine emperor, for under his rule Constantinople fell in 1453 to the Ottoman armies. The Ottomans were Muslims, and although the modern nation of Turkey that emerged from their empire is constitutionally defined as a secular state, Benedict had already noted on at least several occasions his belief that Turkey had Islamic cultural roots. It was on these grounds in part that the Pope had earlier opposed Turkey's accession into the European Union.[6] Yet upon his visit to

5. Reported by Alexander Smoltczyk, "In the Shadow of Muhammad," *Spiegel On Line International,* November 28, 2006; accessed at http://www.spiegel.de/international/ 0,1518,451250,00.html.

6. See Joseph Cardinal Ratzinger, *Christianity and the Crisis of Cultures* (San Francisco: Ignatius Press, 2006), p. 36. Barbara Kralis, in an article titled "Benedict XVI — 'Ubi Petrus, Ibi Ecclesia,'" that was posted on the webpage of the conservative political organization "Renew America" at http://www.renewamerica.us/columns/kralis/050420, quotes the Pope as saying: "The roots that have formed Europe, that have permitted the formation of this continent, are those of Christianity. Turkey has always represented another continent, in permanent contrast with Europe. There were the [old Ottoman Empire] wars against the

Turkey in November of 2006, in the aftermath of his Regensburg lecture, the same visit during which he quoted the irenic statement of Gregory VII, Benedict reversed his earlier opposition and stated his support of Turkey's admission into the European Union.

The reason Benedict had earlier opposed Turkey's entrance into the Union was closely related to his argument for inserting a statement in the proposed European Constitution that recognized what he has repeatedly called Europe's "Christian roots." On numerous occasions he has stated in various ways that Christianity is "the foundations on which Europe rests" and that "Europe once was the Christian continent."[7] In his September 2006 lecture before the faculty and students at Regensburg University, the Holy Father argued that Christianity was able to achieve a decisive synthesis of transcendence (or revelation) and reason by joining biblical faith and Greek philosophy. He continued:

> This inner rapprochement between biblical faith and Greek philosophical inquiry was an event of decisive importance not only from the standpoint of the history of religions, but also from that of world history — it is an event which concerns us even today. Given this convergence, *it is not surprising that Christianity, despite its origins and some significant developments in the East, finally took on its historically decisive character in Europe. We can also express this the other way around: this convergence, with the subsequent addition of the Roman heritage, created Europe and remains the foundation of what can rightly be called Europe.*[8]

Here we find a remarkable convergence of two very different ideas. On the one hand, the Pope is arguing that in Europe Christianity took on its historically decisive character, which one might say is its ultimate historical shape or form, or the closest to being its fullest historical expression and essence. Christianity is related to Europe's history in a way that it is related to no other cultural history. In other words, Christianity is European

Byzantine Empire, the fall of Constantinople, the Balkan wars, and the threat against Vienna and Austria. It would be an error to equate the two continents. . . . Turkey is founded upon Islam. . . . Thus the entry of Turkey into the EU would be anti-historical."

7. Ratzinger, *Christianity and the Crisis of Cultures*, p. 29.

8. Benedict XVI, "Faith, Reason and the University: Memories and Reflections," accessed at http://www.vatican.va/holy_father/benedict_xvi/speeches/2006/september/documents/hf_ben-xvi_spe_20060912_university-regensburg_en.html (emphasis added).

and Europe is Christian in ways that are historically decisive, and one might even say are now historically essential or immutable, for both.

But still the question lingers, why go to a Byzantine emperor to find this quotation to make this particular point? The answer to this lies in the main idea that the Regensburg lecture sought to develop. It was the heritage of Greek philosophy, the Pope said, that gave rise to the form of reason that then in turn became joined together with biblical revelation in such a way that the fullness of faith could be ultimately expressed and achieved. The encounter and eventual rapprochement between biblical revelation and Greek philosophy that took place in Europe was not happenstance. It was divinely ordained, said the Pope. In the Regensburg lecture Benedict refers to it as an "intrinsic necessity."

By citing a Byzantine emperor on the matter, referring specifically to the Greek biblical and philosophical notion of acting according to "reason" or the "word" (σὺν λόγω), Benedict was perhaps offering an olive branch to that portion of the Christian world, a significant portion of the Eastern Orthodox community, that continues to look toward Constantinople for spiritual guidance and regards the bishop of Constantinople as the Ecumenical Patriarch. But even more importantly, Benedict was able to invoke the Greek philosophical heritage of Hellenism that is considered to be a primary feature of the more general Greco-Roman civilization of antiquity. This particular statement of Manuel II lent itself to supporting Benedict's claim for the compatibility between true Christian faith and true human reason. The synthesis of these two in turn is tied essentially in his thinking to the historical form Christianity took in the Latin world of the West.

Benedict highlighted in his lecture the emperor's assertion that spreading the faith by violence is unreasonable. "Violence is incompatible with the nature of God and the nature of the soul," said the Pope in what I gather are his words, not those of Manuel II. The Pope continued, saying that for Islam, God is utterly transcendent, and not even bound by reason. The Byzantine emperor, on the other hand, believed God is not pleased by acting contrary to reason. God acts "σὺν λόγω." Reason, in other words, is given to temper transcendence and is the antidote to violence. Where Islam teaches (according to Benedict) that God can act unreasonably, the Christian West was able to challenge this by synthesizing Greek notions of reason with biblical notions of transcendence. The point he was trying to make comes clearer when he states, "I believe that here we can see the profound harmony between what is Greek in the best sense of the word and the biblical understanding of faith in God."

The fact that he qualified this convergence and harmony of faith and reason with "the subsequent addition of the Roman heritage" ties this synthesis more closely specifically to the history of Western European culture. In doing so, however, it also betrays a deep anxiety that has characterized Western European Christendom for centuries. Western Christendom after the fourth century conducted its theological affairs in Latin, not Greek. Its cultural form was not in direct continuity with classical Hellenism, but a hybrid of Greco-Latin-Germanic formation. Western Europe's inheritance of the classical Greek heritage was indirect and by way of translation. Judith Herrin has argued that between the fifth and eighth centuries the ancient Greco-Roman world broke up into three distinct political-cultural entities. Each of these three civilizations — the Latin West, Byzantium, and the Islamic empire — claimed a direct and unbroken religious and cultural line of inheritance with the philosophical foundations of the ancient Greco-Roman civilization that preceded them. But only the Greek-speaking Byzantines could demonstrate direct linguistic and cultural continuity with the classical Greek heritage as they continued to use the ancient language of Plato and Aristotle. Both the Latin-speaking Franks to the West and the Arabic-speaking Muslims to the East consequently faced a fundamental challenge regarding their claims to direct inheritance of this legacy.[9]

Benedict addressed this challenge, and the anxiety it produces, by arguing that it was only with "the subsequent addition of the Roman heritage," a heritage that was essentially political even when it concerned matters of ecclesiology, that Christianity came to achieve its historically decisive form. The Roman addition achieved a level of synthesis between biblical faith and Greek reason to a degree that Constantinople and the Byzantine civilization in general did not. The history of Western Europe and true Christianity in turn become mutually defining at an essential level in the Pope's worldview. The synthesis of faith and reason is historically achieved in its truest form in the synthesis of Western European cultural life and Christian faith that we generally call Western Christendom, or the *Corpus Christianum*.

9. Judith Herrin, *The Formation of Christendom* (Princeton: Princeton University Press, 1989).

This harmonious synthesis was threatened, in Benedict's view, in the modern era by the program of "dehellenization." Dehellenization has come in three distinct historical stages or instances, he argued in the Regensburg lectures. The first emerged in the sixteenth century in the program of the Protestant Reformation and its commitment to *sola scriptura*. The second took shape in the nineteenth-century project of liberal theology, best represented in the work of Adolf von Harnack. This nineteenth-century liberal project introduced a new form of reason that in effect reduced it to its mathematical and empirical dimensions. Religion was thereby excluded methodologically from being at the center, which was now occupied alone by reason. Religion was relegated to a marginal position of practical reason (in the case of Kant) or a subcultural rank. The third stage Benedict perceived to be currently under way and can be described as that of cultural pluralism. "In the light of our experience with cultural pluralism, it is often said nowadays that the synthesis with Hellenism achieved in the early Church was an initial inculturation which ought not to be binding on other cultures. The latter are said to have the right to return to the simple message of the New Testament prior to that inculturation, in order to inculturate it anew in their own particular milieux." Benedict rejected this argument, however, as being too simplistic. The New Testament already bears a considerable imprint from the Greek spirit, and the manner in which biblical faith and Hellenistic reason developed historically in the early Christian experience is fundamentally consonant with the nature of the faith, he argued. The early Christian synthesis of Hellenistic reason and biblical revelation remains binding for all who profess Christian faith, and this synthesis is threatened by the emerging cultural pluralism in Christianity today.

Benedict returned at the end of the lecture to the argument that a full embrace of this ancient synthesis of Hellenistic reason and biblical faith is necessary for the modern age in order for theology to again be given its proper place at the university's table of knowledge. At the end of his lecture he quoted again from the fourteenth-century emperor: "'Not to act reasonably, to act with *logos,* is contrary to the nature of God,' said Manuel II, according to his Christian understanding of God, in response to his Persian interlocutor. It is to this great *logos,* to this breadth of reason, that we invite our partners in the dialogue of cultures."

By the end of the lecture it is clear that Benedict was not trying to say something about Islam at all. The Pope's interlocutors, the ones he called "our partners in the dialogue of cultures," were clearly not those of Manuel II, a Persian Muslim. The rhetorical move that the lecture made was to link Islam, which the emperor said was violent, with dehellenization of Christian theology through its three stages of the sixteenth-century Protestant Reformation, nineteenth-century liberalism, and twentieth-century cultural pluralism. The implications are that dehellenization, from Benedict's perspective at least, is irrational (σὺν λόγω) and thus capable of fostering evil and violence. Furthermore, dehellenization and de-Europeanization (or Christian cultural pluralism) are one and the same, for the fullest synthesis of Hellenization and Christian faith was achieved in the history of Western Europe. Benedict has stated without equivocation his belief that Christian faith is tied to the history of Western Europe in ways that are historically definitive and essential to its practice. Cultural pluralism threatens this synthesis, and thereby threatens the fullest expressions of the faith itself. Those who would seek to uncouple Christian faith from the history of Western Europe at an essential level, or who regard the synthesis as but one authentic contextual formation among potential others, are charged with fostering "dehellenization," and are thereby in danger of cutting faith from reason, giving rise to unreasonable forms of religion that promote evil and violence under the umbrella of transcendence.

The Pope's interlocutors in this conversation, the ones to whom he was appealing in what he considered to be "partners in the dialogue of cultures," are those who inhabit the Western European intellectual community. Throughout his intellectual career one of his main concerns has been to bring the Western European intellectual community, and by extension Western European culture, back to an integrated, living experience of Christian faith. Events he lived through in Western Europe in 1968 were especially formative in this regard.[10] Consequently Benedict's horizons to date have remained almost exclusively limited to Western Europe. But what does the future, of his papacy and of the faith itself, look like from the wider

10. John Allen, Jr., *Pope Benedict XVI: A Biography of Joseph Ratzinger* (New York and London: Continuum, 2000, retitled and republished 2006), p. 49, writes: "In 1968, Ratzinger watched a wave of student uprisings wash across Europe, and they were especially strong at Tübingen [where he was teaching at the time]. Marxism seemed poised to replace Christianity as the unifying system of meaning in Europe, and even Ratzinger's own students were chanting 'accursed be Jesus!' as a revolutionary motto. The experience shocked him and helped to stimulate his more conservative stance."

horizons of world Christianity? What if the future of Christian faith were not tied to the past of European history? In the remaining pages of this essay I want to look at the future of both Benedict's papacy and of the church more generally from a perspective situated on the wider horizon of world Christian experience and even world religious experience. Benedict himself indicated he was capable of occupying such a horizon in his comments on Islam and Christianity in his November 2006 trip to Turkey, during which he invoked the irenic words of Gregory VII. For the sake of the church that is truly universal, these horizons must continue to be expanded.

The first step in this direction is to reconsider the dehellenization thesis. Benedict has argued that the particular synthesis of Hellenism and Christian faith that took place in the early centuries of the Christian movement and came to full fruition in Latin Christendom can be said to be essential for the Christian faith. This historic achievement remains necessary for any full expression of the faith today, because without the tempering of transcendence with Greek reason, religion is in danger of giving rise to evil and violence (which are by definition unreasonable). The fullest expression of this synthesis is found in the historical achievement of Western Christendom, which in turn means its history is necessary to any full expression of Christian faith in the world today. The challenges to it, brought about by Islam, the Protestant Reformation, nineteenth-century liberal theology, and contemporary cultural pluralism, have all thus threatened not only the integrity of Western Christendom but the vitality of Christian faith.[11]

There are two major problems with this thesis. The first is that Benedict's historical reconstruction hides the problems that Hellenization brought about, and the losses to Christian faith and practice that were incurred especially in Western theology. Second, it avoids the fact that Christian faith did not from the beginning take root only in Greek culture, and that there are alternatives (then and now) to Hellenization that offer alternative paradigms for the integration of faith and reason. Concerning both points, I find the analysis offered in the pages of Robert W. Jenson's landmark work in Trinitarian theology, *The Triune Identity,* to be quite helpful.

11. Since September 2006 the Pope has reiterated the challenge to Islam regarding, in his view, the need for Muslim intellectuals to engage in a greater embrace of reasoned reflection. See the online article by Sandro Magister, "Why Benedict XVI is So Cautious with the Letter of the 138 Muslims," at *Chiesa* at http://chiesa.espresso.repubblica.it/articolo/178461?eng=y.

I offer Jenson's reading of the Hellenization of Christian faith as an alternative to Benedict's not because Jenson argues for dehellenization or offers a non-Western perspective, but precisely because Jenson is able to work through his thesis from a perspective inside the same Western and even Hellenistic theological horizon that Benedict occupies, arriving at a carefully nuanced different location.

Jenson begins his work with the observation that "Trinitarian discourse is Christianity's effort to identify the God who has claimed us."[12] "Father, Son, and Holy Spirit" is Christianity's way of naming God, occupying in Christian life the place that the Divine Tetragrammaton (YHWH) occupies in the life of the people of Israel. The main purpose of Jenson's book is to seek to help bring about a renewal of this Trinitarian naming of God for the churches of the West in order precisely to renew their life and mission. Along the way his historical recounting of the reasons for the diminishment of Trinitarian understanding in the West brings him into direct interaction with the Hellenization thesis.

Jenson argues that the "key steps of the trinitarian logic" made in the pages of the New Testament and proclaimed in the Good News of Jesus Christ are derived from and fully consonant with the understanding of God found in the Hebrew Scriptures.[13] The message of the Good News was proclaimed in the first centuries mostly (although not exclusively) within a cultural context dominated philosophically by Hellenism. The result was confrontation and a clash, not an easy synthesis. "Hellenic theology was from the beginning an exact antagonist of biblical faith."[14] What took place over the next several centuries in Christian intellectual life in the Mediterranean world can best be described as an incomplete Christianization of Hellenism. The fullest achievement of Christianization, according to Jenson, came in the works of Athanasius and the Cappadocians in the fourth century. The theologians of the Latin-speaking West from the late fourth century on, such as Boethius but especially Augustine, on the other hand, failed to understand this achievement. The result in the West was the return and triumph of Hellenism, and a concomitant diminished or even defective Trinitarian understand-

---

12. Robert W. Jenson, *The Triune Identity: God According to the Gospel* (Philadelphia: Fortress Press, 1982; reprinted Eugene, OR: Wipf & Stock, 2002), p. 4.

13. Jenson, *The Triune Identity,* p. 38.

14. Jenson, *The Triune Identity,* p. 57.

ing of the identity of God.[15] Thus Jenson does not argue for dehellenization, but its transformation.

> Throughout I have insisted on the clash of the gospel's and Hellenism's
> interpretation of God and have blamed Western theology's trinitarian
> enfeeblement on defeat in this battle. It is time to reiterate that I do not
> intend thereby to decry the "Hellenization" of Christianity or to pro-
> pose termination of the metaphysical reflection in which the confronta-
> tion with Hellenism has involved the gospel. On the contrary, the fault
> of Western trinitarianism was precisely a failure to carry on the meta-
> physical creativity begun by the Cappadocians, and so long as the West-
> ern church endures, it must be Hellenic.[16]

The answer Jenson offers is to complete the metaphysical project of thinking through the Cappadocian revisions of Hellenistic thinking regarding
God, and renewing trinitarianism for the contemporary world.

But what about the possibilities of the gospel's encounter with metaphysical systems other than Hellenism? Jenson does not deny either the
possibility or actuality of such an encounter.

> If the gospel had not met an incompatible identification of God in the
> Greek interpretation of deity, it would have met one in some other —
> and indeed it did and does in those branches of the mission that lead to
> great culture areas other than that in which our narrative is set. . . . The
> gospel's initial history in the non-Hellenic world was terminated by Is-
> lam, and its new history in them is, theologically, just beginning.[17]

He then hints at the implications of this for cultural pluralism in the conclusion of the book:

> If it should turn out that trinitarianism has definitely ceased in the West,
> the gospel will nevertheless continue elsewhere, and so will the gospel's
> interpreting of God. In the life and reflection of the African and Asian
> churches, the immediate trinitarianism described in Chapters 1 and 2

15. Jenson, *The Triune Identity,* pp. 114-17.
16. Jenson, *The Triune Identity,* p. 161.
17. Jenson, *The Triune Identity,* p. 57.

plays and will play much the same role as in the story we have told. The developed reflection of the remaining chapters, dependent as it is on the particular partner which our culture-religion sets for the gospel, will not be reproduced in other branches of the gospel's history. But analogues must surely appear. Perhaps in the struggle for and about these, the Western church's trinitarian history, including such efforts as we now make, could — even in the worst case of their own vitality — play a final exemplary and cautionary role.[18]

Jenson's argument in the end brings us to the possibility of a legitimate pluralism of reasons and histories. Without denying the significant historical achievements of Western Christendom in the past, we are not necessarily bound to them historically as essential for Christian faith and practice in the future. The history of the West is indeed definitive in the sense that it has taken place and has indeed affected Christian faith throughout the world, but its effect is as much cautionary as it is exemplary. Christian faith is in fact not bound to any historical cultural formation. Quite the contrary is true: Christian faith is inherently transcultural. It comes to its fullest expression in and through its passage across historical and cultural boundaries. What emerge across these boundaries to make the connections that are catholic are what Jenson in the passage just quoted calls "analogues."

Translation is the key to this movement of faith across cultural boundaries, as Lamin Sanneh has so brilliantly argued in his magisterial work, *Translating the Message*.[19] Sanneh, who is a Roman Catholic, offers an important qualification of Benedict's observation regarding the New Testament. While the New Testament undeniably was written in Greek (although it should be immediately noted it was written in *koinē*, not classical Greek, thereby tapping in to a more transcultural form of first-century Hellenism than that which later informed theology in the Greco-Roman context), it was in many ways already itself a translation. Jesus did not teach in Greek as far as we can tell. The language of his day-to-day ministering was most likely Aramaic. The Gospels, which purport to represent the words of Jesus, are therefore already a translation of the message into a new cultural context, that of *koinē* Greek.

18. Jenson, *The Triune Identity*, pp. 186-87.
19. Lamin Sanneh, *Translating the Message: The Missionary Impact on Culture* (Maryknoll, NY: Orbis Books, 1989).

The process of the translation of Christian faith across historical cultural boundaries, then, predates the actual composition of the New Testament texts. Furthermore, the process was not unidirectional, but was multidirectional and polycentric. Christianity did not just synthesize biblical faith with Hellenism in the first several centuries. Christianity moved in several cultural directions, east as well as west. Its dominant cultural expressions came to be those of the Greco-Roman world, the Greek and Latin civilizations. But these were not Christianity's exclusive home. A significant portion of Christians developed their faith and practice in a Syriac-speaking context, in the Persian world for instance. Strands of Hellenism still found their way into the religious life of Christians in the east, mostly in Aristotelian form after the fifth century, through exegetes such as Theodore of Mopsuestia. Nevertheless, the liturgical life of these churches and their theological formations can hardly be said to be guided by the reasoning grounded in a Greek notion of *logos*. With their strong commitments to exegetical theology, guided in part by Theodore of Mopsuestia, the churches of the east were much more likely to allow biblical patterns of reasoning to shape their theology, interpreting John's notion of *logos* in light of the reasoning that guided the Hebrew Bible.[20] And however much they may have been interrupted and in many cases cut off by the historical developments of Islam in this part of the world, as Jenson notes, they nev-

---

20. It is interesting in this regard to note the Vatican's 2001 publication, "Guidelines for Admission to the Eucharist between the Chaldean Church and the Assyrian Church of the East." At one point the document states: "In the first place, the Anaphora of Addai and Mari is one of the most ancient Anaphoras, dating back to the time of the very early Church; it was composed and used with the clear intention of celebrating the Eucharist in full continuity with the Last Supper and according to the intention of the Church; its validity was never officially contested, neither in the Christian East nor in the Christian West.

"Secondly, the Catholic Church recognises the Assyrian Church of the East as a true particular Church, built upon orthodox faith and apostolic succession. The Assyrian Church of the East has also preserved full Eucharistic faith in the presence of our Lord under the species of bread and wine and in the sacrificial character of the Eucharist. In the Assyrian Church of the East, though not in full communion with the Catholic Church, are thus to be found '*true sacraments, and above all, by apostolic succession, the priesthood and the Eucharist*' (U.R., n. 15)" [emphasis in the original]. Implied by this statement is the recognition of the validity of the Syriac liturgy, and thus of the larger cultural and linguistic theological framework in which the liturgy took place and which it in turn informed. The document was accessed at http://www.vatican.va/roman_curia/pontifical_councils/chrstuni/documents/rc_pc_chrstuni_doc_20011025_chiesa-caldea-assira_en.html.

ertheless continue to provide an alternative model of cultural synthesis and engagement.

Challenging the exclusive claims of European history to being the privileged historical carrier of Christian faith, and opening up our understanding of Christian faith to see other cultural formations, is vital to the future of the movement. It is especially important to see how the forms of reasoning that are found in other religious traditions and faiths can become more than mere dialogue partners. Benedict's assertion, however much wrapped it might have been in the words of a fourteenth-century Byzantine emperor — that the religion of Muhammad brought evil and violence — begs the question of what Christianity has brought. Through the centuries Christians have regularly sought to spread their faith by the sword. However much one might want to assert qualifiers in regard to the authenticity or faithfulness of their expressions, it is historically undeniable that men and women claiming to be acting in the name of Jesus Christ have through the centuries carried out horrendous acts of violence across the face of the earth in the name of their religion.[21] On the other hand, there is much in the history of Islam in its rich and diverse exegetical and legal traditions that offers viable alternative modes of reasoning that can help shape Christian faith in the future.

The failure to appreciate fully the violence associated with the Western Christian past, and the historical entanglement of the church with such violence through past colonial conquests in Asia, Africa, and especially Latin America, has arguably been a major factor in the confrontation between Ratzinger and proponents of various strands of liberation theology over the past several decades. The confrontation characterized much of the work of the Congregation for the Doctrine of the Faith (CDF) during the 1980s and 1990s when it was headed by Cardinal Ratzinger. Ratzinger's main charge leveled against Latin American liberation theology was that it had adopted Marxist views of history and class conflict which were antithetical to Christian faith. Ratzinger criticized the notion of the theology's making a "special option" for the poor as weakening the universal promise of grace. Liberation theology, he said, overemphasized the social nature of sin. By applying a historical critique to the institutional life of the church, liberation theol-

21. See Dale T. Irvin, "The Terror of History and the Memory of Redemption: Engaging the Ambiguities of the Christian Past," in *Surviving Terror: Hope and Justice in a World of Violence,* ed. Victoria L. Erickson and Michelle Lim Jones (Grand Rapids: Brazos, 2002).

ogy was undercutting its authority and sacraments.[22] Throughout the controversy Ratzinger refused to grant the validity of one of the fundamental methodological shifts enunciated by Gustavo Gutiérrez. European theologies since the European Enlightenment, argues Gutiérrez, have overwhelmingly taken as the interlocutor for their theological conversations the modern "non-believer." Latin America liberation theology, on the other hand, has taken as its primary interlocutor the "non-person." The shift is critical for determining what form of reasoning one determines to employ as a dialogue partner in articulating the faith in practice.[23]

Toward the end of Ratzinger's tenure at CDF, theologies of religious pluralism, especially ones that had emerged from Asia and that appeared to grant other religions as having a degree of salvific value independent of the Catholic Church, came under severe criticism as being dangerous to the faith. Ratzinger decried what appeared to him to be the relativism that placed Jesus Christ on the same level as other great religious figures of the world and thus did not seem to acknowledge clearly enough his unique, supernatural character. Christological exclusivism has been repeatedly linked to the exclusive nature of salvation through the Catholic Church in Ratzinger's theology, with an accompanying denial of independent salvific value being found in other religions. The most controversial (some would say notorious) document to emerge from CDF during this period, *Dominus Iesus,* while by all accounts not directly authored by Cardinal Ratzinger, nevertheless was published in 2000 over his signature as Prefect of the Congregation.[24] One of the most striking characteristics of *Dominus Iesus* is that for a document seeking to address the challenge posed by religious pluralism to Christian faith, there is a complete lack of sensitivity to the concerns of Christians living as minority religionists in religiously pluralistic contexts, especially in Asia. *Dominus Iesus* continues to employ a language and reflect cultural experiences and modes of

---

22. See Allen, *Pope Benedict XVI,* chapter 4, "Authentic Liberation," pp. 131-74; Joseph Cardinal Ratzinger, *Instruction on Certain Aspects of the "Theology of Liberation"* (Washington, DC: United States Catholic Conference, 1984) and archived online at http://www.vatican.va/roman_curia/congregations/cfaith/documents/rc_con_cfaith_doc_19840806_theology-liberation_en.html.

23. See Gustavo Gutiérrez, *The Power of the Poor in History* (Maryknoll, NY: Orbis Books, 1983).

24. The document is found on the Vatican's website at http://www.vatican.va/roman_curia/congregations/cfaith/documents/rc_con_cfaith_doc_20000806_dominus-iesus_en.html.

reasoning that may be historically appropriate to Western theological contexts, but it has little that reflects sensitivity to the unique challenges posed by languages, cultures, and modes of reasoning that are grounded in the diverse life and experience of Christians living in Asia.

The question of language, culture, and modes of reasoning is not peripheral to the meaning of Christian faith. It reaches to the very heart of what is at stake for world Christianity in the future. Without question Benedict is right when he claims that Europe's history is inextricably tied to the history of Christianity. Christian concepts, and not just Hellenistic ones, are buried deep in the languages and cultures that trace a European descent. Europe is not just Christian of course. One finds ample evidence in European culture and life of other religious influences, of Muslim and Jewish as well as older Celtic, Latin, and Germanic religious concepts and practices. But Europe is Christian insofar as Christianity dominated its cultural formations for long centuries in the past.

Where Benedict is wrong is in the implication that Christianity can only have a European past, or that the Christian faith is inextricably or essentially tied to its European history, or to a period in its history when Europe dominated. Christian faith can and indeed must engage the language, culture, and modes of reasoning beyond those of Europe and its Hellenic-Latin past. But this means that Christianity will be articulated through language, concepts, and modes of reasoning that have derived from religions and philosophies that are other than those of Europe's past. Christians in Thailand, notes Mark Tamthai, director of the Institute for the Study of Religion and Culture at Payap University in Thailand, live their Christian faith and express their Christian faith through the medium of a language and culture that are deeply Buddhist. The Thai language, he notes, has Buddhist concepts embedded deeply within it, so that talking about Christianity in Thailand requires one to use Buddhist concepts. Thinking through Christian faith in the Thai language requires one to use forms of reasoning that have been shaped by a Buddhist, not a Christian, historical intellectual past. One is nevertheless fully able to do Christian theology in the Thai language, and thus to do Christian theology from within a Buddhist linguistic and cultural thought-world, argues Tamthai. But it is a theology that does not belong to Europe.[25]

25. Comments made at the inaugural editorial board meeting of the *Journal of World Christianity* at the Harvard Center for World Religions, May 5, 2006.

The quest for a profound sense of coherence such as what Benedict re-called from his days in Bonn need not be set aside in the future of world Christianity. But the quest cannot be for a coherence that is grounded only in the history of a European Christian past. Cultural pluralism is not a threat, but the answer to the problems of Christian faith being ideologi-cally narrowed to the history and culture of a Western European past.[26] Furthermore, such pluralism is not only for the Christian world outside Europe. The history of European Christianity itself is far more diversified and pluralistic that Benedict's representation of it would tend to make it appear. The concept of pluralism and diversity is not alien even to Catholic history in Europe. Yves Congar notes that the Council of Trent, the sixteenth-century Catholic council which met at the time that Benedict says the first wave of "dehellenization" was taking place, acknowledged the validity of multiple traditions by which Christian faith was historically communicated. According to Congar, Trent recognized that these ecclesi-astical traditions, while not identical with the original apostolic tradition, could not be separated from it either and gained their authority from it. Trent, says Congar, acknowledged these multiple forms of tradition as modes in which the totality of faith was contained.[27]

The way forward for Benedict, for the Catholic Church, and for world Christianity is a greater embrace of the pluralism and diversity that are manifested in the Christian past and will continue to proliferate in the Christian future. But there are signs that Pope Benedict XVI himself recog-nizes this. The statement made during his visit to Turkey in November 2006, regarding the "special love" the Christians and Muslims owe one an-other, is a critical indicator of this direction. Love in effect replaces reason-ing as the means by which the incoherence of our age can be addressed and overcome. Love addresses the incoherence of violence and inhumanity

---

26. Ernst Troeltsch almost a century ago noted the manner in which European histori-cal consciousness located Europe at the center of history and universalized its effects, result-ing in an ideology he called "Europeanism" *(Europäismus)*. Troeltsch admitted that all of this could be little more than naïve European pride at work, reinforced by a history of Euro-pean Christian dogmatics that located Europe at the center of the universe. See Ernst Troeltsch, *Gesammelte Schriften III, Der Historismus und seine Probleme: Erstes Buch, Das logische Problem der Geschichtsphilosophie* (Tübingen: J. C. B. Mohr [Paul Siebeck], 1922), p. 707.

27. Yves M. J. Congar, *Tradition and Traditions: An Historical and a Theological Essay* (New York: Macmillan, 1967), p. 160.

through its embrace of the other,[28] including the Christian other whose history, language, and culture cannot be reduced to the European past and will not be confined by a European future. Should the Holy Father continue in this direction in his thinking — should the embrace of the other become as central to his papacy as the embrace of tradition and the embrace of truth — I have no doubt that we will finally see a new era opening up and the day when Christianity will truly be able to embrace the world.

---

28. See Miroslav Volf, *Exclusion and Embrace: A Theological Exploration of Identity, Otherness, and Reconciliation* (Nashville: Abingdon, 1996).

2 Providential Pluralism: An Ecumenical Gift?

EPHRAIM RADNER

Why might God wish Anglicanism and the Catholic Church of Rome to live side by side at this time for the sake of his kingdom in Christ? I shall tentatively offer a response to this question in terms of the providential *political* demands of our world in this era. I shall suggest that the adaptive conciliar character of Anglicanism may yet prove a gift to the universal church as it struggles within evolving pluralisms, even as this universality of the church of Christ must fasten Anglicanism to and transform her into something to which she must give way.

To pose the question again: Why might God wish Anglicanism and the Catholic Church of Rome to live side by side at this time for the sake of his kingdom in Christ, rather than allow one or the other to dissipate or merge? This is not strictly a question of systematic theological interest; it does not touch directly on the ecclesiological issues that have confronted our communities and dialogues. It goes more immediately to the reality that, as the Vatican can call us, we are in fact "brothers and sisters in Christ," and therefore our lives side by side do in fact, on a fundamental level, reveal our being as brethren in the Lord. But how might this be so?

I wish to pose this question in the context of the concrete situation of Christian life within an increasingly (and in some cases completely) non-Christian West, and its globally extended dynamics. In doing so, I take up Pope Benedict's discussions, shortly before his election, on the place of the Christian church in contemporary Europe in particular. Thus I intend to look at some comments of Cardinal Joseph Ratzinger and suggest their relevance to the thought of Pope Benedict XVI. These discussions, and in particular the Cardinal's highly provocative essay on "Europe: Its Spiritual

Ephraim Radner

Foundation," presented to the Italian Senate on May 13, 2004,[1] move into an area of reflection that is explicitly couched in providentialist terms. Through his explication of the shape of Europe's history and the meaning this might have in informing the particular vocation of Christians within the present social context, Ratzinger calls us to discern God's leading.

It might seem that this very topic would preclude, *prima facie,* placing Anglicanism at the center of divine Providence's overarching direction of the universal church. That is, one might well pose, on purely historical grounds and by observing the conflict and fragmentation currently besetting Anglican churches, the following question: Does the Anglican Communion (and therefore Anglicanism itself as a more general reality) demonstrate the inadequacy, *tout court* and without further analysis, of any positive evaluation of "ecclesial communities" (as Anglicanism is identified by the Vatican) in the face of secularism? And if this is so, are such communities fundamentally irrelevant to the general problem of Christian witness and vocation in contemporary society? What could Anglicanism, then, offer to Catholic Christianity except a cautionary tale of what can happen when one strays from the ordering authority of a divinely upheld ecclesial *magisterium?*

And posing such a question does indeed point to some larger ecclesiological implications. Some touch on the nature of the church in general, as in the public debate of late 1999 through 2001 between Cardinal Kasper and then Cardinal Ratzinger on the relation of particular churches and the universal church, especially in terms of the interaction of discernment and direction.[2] Others touch on central ecumenical questions: For instance, if certain Christians, given the character of their ecclesial

1. These thoughts were later elaborated in terms of the particular anti-theism of Enlightenment rationalism, in his talk of April 1, 2005, "Europe's Crisis of Culture."

2. The debate began with an article by Cardinal Kasper, "On the Office of Bishop" ("Zur Theologie und Praxis des bischöflichen Amtes"), in *Auf neue Art Kirche Sein: Wirklichkeiten-Herausforderungen-Wandlungen,* ed. Werner Schreer and Georg Steins (Munich: Bernward bei Don Bosco, 1999), pp. 32-48. Subsequent essays in the debate included: J. Ratzinger's "Ecclesiology of the Constitution on the Church, Vatican II, 'Lumen Gentium,'" in *L'Osservatore Romano,* Sept. 19, 2001; "The Local Church and the Universal Church: A Response to Walter Kasper," by Cardinal Ratzinger, *America,* Nov. 19, 2001; and "On the Church: A Friendly Reply to Cardinal Ratzinger," by Cardinal Kasper, *America,* April 23-30, 2001 (trans. Ladislas Orsy, S.J.; originally published in the journal *Stimmen der Zeit* [December 2000]). An overview and analysis, with Kasper's views in mind, is provided in Kilian McDonnell, "Walter Kasper on the Theology and the Praxis of the Bishop's Office," *Theological Studies* 63, no. 4 (2002): 711-29.

existences, cannot provide effective, that is, faithful witness in the midst of the context of a non-Christian West, what then is the nature of the witness actually given and how might it indeed reflect that character of the church's integrity or lack of it?

The argument I will offer here rejects the *prima facie* judgment noted above, but without necessarily assuming conclusions regarding the ecclesiological issues also mentioned. I will suggest, however, that there *is* something that the Anglican Communion is doing that bears directly on the providential calling of Christians in general. It is something, in fact, that both speaks into the shape of that calling for the Church Catholic as Ratzinger/Benedict has laid out its environing historicity, and into the relation of the Catholic Church and particular ecclesial communities.

In his 2004 talk, as elsewhere, Ratzinger concluded that the contemporary European state, understood in its multiple forms and in its emerging union, has suffered a foundational loss of moral perception, through its rejection, in particular, of its specifically Christian religious origins and cultural formation. The need for a renewed Christian moral witness within Europe, he then argued, is an essential demand for the sake of society's common life and integrity.

The conclusion itself is premised on some particular historical arguments, that, in themselves, do not engage in the systematic details and distinctions of Catholic ecclesiology — indeed, they rely on a broader identification of Christianity that includes the realm of particular churches and ecclesial communities as they have emerged through time. For instance, Ratzinger/Benedict argues that there has been at work in the West a fundamental dualism between church and state, grounded in Jesus' own teaching and affirmed early on by, e.g., Pope Gelasius I.[3] It is a dualism, furthermore, that has beneficially separated the two for the sake of the growth of human freedom. Granted a long period of vying and adaptive relations between ecclesial and civil powers, it is this dualism that has generated many of the basic political structures and expectations of human liberty we now take for granted.[4]

---

3. He cites Gelasius's *Letter to Emperor Anastasius,* which, however, is slightly ambiguous in the relations it draws between the "two powers"; the selection noted from the *Patrologia Latina,* 59, 108c speaks more directly to the call for humility between the two spheres of authority.

4. See also J. Ratzinger, *Kirche, Ökumene und Politik* (Einsiedeln: Johannes Verlag, 1987), p. 151.

There have been multiple adjustments and reorientations of relations between church and state that have extended across major ecclesial-political shifts over time. The Cardinal particularly identified the migration of Europe's power-center to the north, the expansion outward finally to America of European cultural influence, and the French Revolution's establishment of a dynamic movement towards atheistic secularism. The latter included within its wake not only the woeful legacy of Fascism and materialistic communism, but also the embedded and lingering relativist dogmatism of contemporary European society, expressed in aspects of the proposed European Constitution. Through all of this, there has been a converging evolution of modern views of the state as a pluralistic entity. This has proved a phenomenon that has brought benefits for both individual freedom and security. But it has also, paradoxically, supplied the basis for the exclusion of God from common discourse and decision-making, and has erected a society in which the church's own life has been both qualitatively and quantitatively constrained and diminished.

In response, Ratzinger has taken up a voluntaristic aspect of Arnold Toynbee's sense that Western societies need more deliberately to reintegrate religious witness into their mix. And so the Pope has called for Christians to take on the role of "creative minorities" who are willing to provide to European society the foundational moral witness that its own evolution has eliminated from its structures, to the great danger of its human integrity. This view is shared, *mutatis mutandis,* by non-Christian students of European society like Jürgen Habermas, who has recently reached similar conclusions from a non-religious direction, by observing not so much the diminishment of religious commitment, as its intractability within European society, and hence its demanded recognition.[5]

But the challenge here is precisely how moral witness, to the end of providing foundational conscience to a basically atheistic civil society, can be given to a state whose pluralistic framework is perhaps opposed to moral (let alone religious) foundationalism itself. Benedict has pointedly underlined this informing contradiction on numerous occasions: it is not simply that Christianity is no longer at the center of the state's identity;

5. Jürgen Habermas, "Notes on a Post-Secular Society," available in English at www.signandsight.com. The original text appeared in German as "Die Dialektik der Säkularisierung" in *Blätter für deutsche und internationale Politik,* April 2008, from a lecture of March 15, 2007, at the Nexus Institute of the University of Tilburg, Netherlands.

Christianity is actually denied as a legitimate shaper of acceptable public, and perhaps even publicly expressed, consciousness.[6]

Here, alternative details to the broad historical outline that Ratzinger/ Benedict has presented are necessary, ones that quite precisely place Anglicanism in a particular and possibly constructive providential role. We can approach this under two historical rubrics:

First, there is the history of failure in Christian witness, especially during the re-establishment of the church-state dualism of the early modern era. It is on this score that some have taken particular aim at Ratzinger/ Benedict's outline, claiming that it ignores the deep *resistance* of Roman Catholic and (less so) Reformation churches to the separation of spheres, one that was furthermore built on a previously long history of Christian efforts to elide the difference, thus giving rise to untold suffering. However one wishes to characterize this history, its reality must be taken into account as one attempts to locate Christian witness within a civil arena that today simply mistrusts religious commitment of all kinds, most particularly Christian conviction, on the basis of a real reading of her "fruits," however one-sided.

Second, one must note the peculiarities of Anglo-American (and not just American) adjustments to this reality. Despite erecting a state church, as in many other parts of Europe, Britain in a unique way became the crucible of development for religious and political pluralism that was only then transferred to America. The arguments and ideologies of Locke and his followers, and others of related interests, cannot be underestimated, both in their influence and in their innovating response to the grievous contemporary burdens of religious violence and oppression. This response, of the seventeenth and early eighteenth centuries, has proved far more significant and formative than the conflicted and debated origins of the Church of England in the sixteenth century.[7] To a large extent it ought

---

6. See the 2005 lecture, "Europe's Crisis of Culture."

7. The complex interaction, during the late seventeenth and eighteenth centuries of the Anglican Establishment, its powerfully formative religious context, its appropriation of a theology of toleration, its ordering of political and Christian pluralism, and finally its struggle to maintain its role as a national "conscience" have all been the object of recent study by historians like W. M. Jacob, Ian Green, and David Hempton. See, with wide references, Hempton's summary essay "Established Churches and the Growth of Religious Pluralism: A Case Study of Christianisation and Secularization in England Since 1700," in Hugh McLeod, ed., *The Decline of Christendom in Western Europe, 1750-2000* (Cambridge: Cambridge Uni-

to inform the character of Anglicanism itself in modern study as much as the more narrowly theological categories of the Reformation and its immediate adjudication. The debate between Gladstone and Newman in the nineteenth century, however one wants to evaluate its particulars, is a witness to this.

In any outline of Europe's and the West's politico-religious history, then, Anglicanism needs to be viewed as an odd or "outlying" element that attempted, quite deliberately, to maintain the role of the foundational "religious conscience" — an established but increasingly politically deferring church within a developing pluralistic society. Furthermore, in Anglicanism's expansion into geographical areas where it could no longer maintain its political establishment, however bound in many instances to colonial power, Anglicanism has in fact maintained versions of this identity in different forms, from Africa and Asia, Canada (more obviously), and (in a very ambiguous way) even in the United States.

How has Anglicanism done this? The question and its response are obviously pertinent to filling out Ratzinger/Benedict's outline of Europe's providential history.

But before answering the question, one must revisit the shape of religious conviction within a pluralism that evolved, in large part, to escape the poison of such conviction cruelly imposed. And in doing this, one will have to confront the fact that being a religious "minority" has not proven an easy or consistent vocation for Christians, precisely because, in the modern Western state's suspicion of the church's claim to respect the duality of separate spheres, it has raised up a *contradictory* monopoly of moral claims that logically attack the foundations of the church's own self-understanding. Pluralistic co-existence, of a normative kind, represents in practice an ongoing assault upon Christian claims.

Social scientists, like Habermas, have noted the need in the modern pluralistic state for a kind of "constitutional patriotism" on the part of all citizens, such that Christians, for instance, must be committed to the final efficacy, socially speaking, of a certain framework of laws that stands outside their own personal convictions. Rawls has said something analogous. But in practice this is not easy when the framework itself either protects or,

versity Press, 2003), pp. 81-98. The more strictly ecclesiological implications of these kinds of studies are only now being grappled with, in a positive manner, by theologians like Bishop Stephen Sykes and Archbishop Rowan Williams.

through the deliberations of the democratic process, imposes elements that contradict Christian moral commitments. How could it be easy when these Christian commitments, as the Pope has articulated with greater and greater force in the past few years, depend upon often non-negotiable and absolute truths bound to the being and revelation of God in Christ Jesus? Benedict has listed several areas of foundational Christian moral commitment that the church must announce to society and embody herself, but each has in fact been contradicted by the laws of most European and Western nations. The moral truth of "human dignity" has been contradicted by widespread social neglect of children and the poor, by the permission and support of abortion, and by the use of fetuses for research and fertilization purposes. The fundamental human ordering of marriage and family has been legally contradicted by the provision of no-fault divorce, social incentives for single-parent families, and the legal recognition of homosexual unions. One might also note problems facing the third "constituent moral element" that Christianity ought to provide its host society, according to the Pope: respect for that which others consider "sacred." In the realm of a pluralistic society, one that includes religious pluralism, the contradictory and sometimes openly opposing religious convictions of groups are never neutral articulations, as we know from the missionary habits of more Christianly marginal (but highly successful) groups like Mormons and Jehovah's Witnesses, not to mention Muslims. Religious articulations actually *alter* social configurations; and multiple articulations provide often-conflicting dynamics to such change.

In the face of such social contradictions to their moral commitments, religious minorities have only a few options. They can adopt postures of sectarian withdrawal, relying on the state to protect a space for survival. Or — a more common form of religious adaptation — minorities can simply embrace a compartmentalized life: they can, at best, speak to the moral demands that would oppose blatant immoralities (on their own terms), but permit their continuance through an acceptance of the political process that upholds them. The evolution of "privatized" religion is an inevitable outflow of this. Yet are not the extreme consequences of National Socialism, which the Pope so pointedly describes — as well as the culture of death in the United States — also related to such compartmentalization? What Benedict does not distinguish, then, is how creative minorities are not, within an accepted pluralistic and privatizing religious sphere, necessarily or at least probably corrupted. The "keeper" of the moral foundation of the state has — in fact often, and very recently, and even today — proven the accomplice to the state's or its various groups' morally destructive campaigns. Plural "dualisms" are intrinsically difficult to sustain.

It is in light of this challenge that we can perhaps see how Anglicanism, not only ideally through its historical reshaping but also in practice (if often dismally), has attempted to work within this sphere of plural contradictions in a peculiar way, both adaptive and demanding at once. Anglicanism in Britain, as we noted, adopted the role of moral conscience on the basis of an accepted and protected pluralism. She did not simply have it forced upon her in the wake of an evolved state that had surpassed the church's own development. And it is just this historical positioning that has led Anglican churches, beginning most foundationally with the Church of England, to order their witness in certain practical ways, not without theological significance. The way this has happened — and again we raise the ecclesiological question of Providence — has included the following features.

First, Anglicanism has accepted the fundamental criterion of authority outside of her own structures, that is, the Scriptures. This is obviously an element directly derivative of her Reformation origins. But it should be understood as an element apprehended and applied in a peculiar way that was more and more ordered to the demand for political restraint and humility in the midst of a shared social arena where authority was to be discerned and not simply claimed and imposed.

The result, second, has been an ever-relativized, although not evacuated, hierarchy — an ordering of human authority that has demanded justificatory evidence for its trustworthiness and persuasive evidence for its reasoning.

This has led, thirdly, to structures that have evolved, if unevenly and haltingly, towards ever more open deliberation in decision-making. It would be wrong to understand this in terms of democratic deliberation. But, within the setting of plural convictions, the need for trust and persuasion calls forth mechanisms of prayer, discussion, and discernment.

Indeed, and fourthly, both scripturally and pragmatically these structures have tended towards a conciliar ordering, in a manner that moves laterally, from one area and sphere of representation to another, rather than vertically, up or down rungs of discernment. It is the *ongoing* character of conciliar discernment and the formation of consent over time that have finally emerged as Anglicanism's moral posture before the vying claims of a pluralistic world. The foundation of ecclesial life in a necessary order of consent, in fact, has been at the center of conciliar understandings of the church since the later Middle Ages; and it is just here that we find peculiar overlappings of Anglican ecclesiology and the new realities of the pluralistic state.

So that, finally, rather than simply being open-ended, such ongoing conciliar operation becomes more and more bound by the shape of its history, its formative bequests. The round of consensual counsel and discernment under Scripture, in a way that (in theory) tethers the *sola scriptura* Reformation commitment to a temporal and communal form, in the end proves that form to be one of traditioned stewardship.

Some of these features end up providing overlap with Catholic realities, but others clearly do not, and those that do (as Ratzinger himself has noted in the past)[8] may not mean quite the same things. However, in practice again, these elements in fact embrace the reality of *multiple consciences,* always persuasively, and with an eye to an ordered and articulated resolution that is nevertheless always bound both to a history and a higher truth. The features just mentioned undergird political engagement and conscientious opposition in a particular way that can potentially overcome the compartmentalization of faith that has so morally stunted Christian witness in pluralistic societies. Instead, in this configuration, the Christian takes hold of the same evangelical vocation on the two levels of church and civic society at once, in a fashion that is procedurally analogous and sometimes even parallel.

If there is a moral advantage to this Anglican self-ordering within a pluralistic society, it is the relative avoidance of that double-mindedness that has so corrupted the Christian church's attempt to deal with the secular contradictions of her life. If there is a danger — and a great one it is! — to this kind of self-ordering, it is the subtle but relentless appropriation of the Christian life by the simple processes and dynamics of pluralistic political methods and energies. But in either case, it is important to see the current travails of the Anglican Communion in these terms, however one evaluates their outcome: they represent a genuine Christian response to the realities of the historical situation, not only of Europe obviously, but of a developed and changed political ordering on a global scale. Within the

8. J. Ratzinger, "Anglican-Catholic Dialogue: Its Problems and Hopes," in *Insight: A Journal for Church and Community* 1 (1983): 2-11.

currents of historical development that Ratzinger/Benedict has himself laid out, Anglicanism appears to have reordered itself — or been reordered by the forces of social change and according to the uncertain contours of its recent Communion character — as a Christian witness within a setting of (often only theoretically) protected religious *competition* that plays by the rules of pluralistic persuasion and consent.

There are obvious weaknesses to this reordering, demonstrated through the fractures and contradictions of the present Anglican experience. But the calling is also obvious, given the very details of the story Benedict has retold on several occasions, thereby elucidating the vocation of all Christians. Is there here, therefore, some providential weight for Rome as well? There is such a thing as a modern "catacomb Christianity," one that, in Chateaubriand's image, marked the late eighteenth-century French church as it survived, in pursued faithfulness, the violence of those who would drive God out of the world. And perhaps this Christianity of faithfulness-on-the-run will prove the ultimate calling of Christians in our day, as societies of secular "rationalism" progressively drive the church from their precincts of civic life. But it is not a fate to be sought so much as received when the open witness of the evangelical truths of Christ are not only rejected but attacked. At such a time — but not before — being "creative," for the Christian minority, will mean something different than Ratzinger/Benedict clearly intended in taking up Toynbee's terms for our present vocation. For now, at least, we are not so much running and hiding, with whatever love and courage, but engaging openly the pluralistic society that has granted space even to the church for her witness while, it must be admitted, protecting her from her own worst excesses. And this has its own heavy burdens, particularly on the shape of our common life.

Despite the resolutely "political" character of this description of providential calling — and I do not hesitate in calling Anglicanism "political all the way down" — it is a politics that has in view the corporate nature of the Christian calling in the world of historical demand. And from this, theological realities and truths have not been banished. Returning, therefore, to the deeper ecclesiological and ecumenical dimensions of this more simply historical-political reflection, I can end with two sets of questions:

a. If there is a providential ordering to the reality of "ecclesial communities," vis-à-vis the universal church, even conceived of in Catholic terms — and this has been affirmed in part by the Catholic Church — it may lie in this reordering of Christian moral witness, with respect not only to Anglicanism, but with respect to the way separated brethren in general are being asked to relate to the whole. Could it be that God is using these separated communities to draw the church into a posture of deliberative counsel? Could this counsel be one that bespeaks the general constraints of humility spoken of by Gelasius I now placed at the center of the *church's* life, and not only in terms of her posture towards the state? And could it be that this constraining humility, as it informs the intra-ecclesial life of the church, will also inform the church's adaptive ability to engage the life of a world where the Christian witness is both without the power of majority commitment, but also demands her utmost persuasive efforts to provide that moral foundation necessary for the life of humankind to flourish in God's will?

b. There is a question here to the Catholic Church that comes as a humble challenge to the meaning of the church's interior ordering. But there is also an open admission of weakness on the part of Anglicans like myself in posing this question. The question therefore constitutes a kind of prayer that the providential gifts of Rome's (right) understanding of the priority of the universal church over the particular churches — let alone over ecclesial communities — be offered us in return. And if offered, it can only be in just the kind of persuasive and openly deliberative ways that might finally draw back together separated Christians into a unity that will in fact provide new historical shapes that are no longer distorted images of the universal. Instead, they may yet prove newly integral within the societies that have now emerged as protecting yet also sapping the moral truths of the gospel.

If, as Ratzinger/Benedict has properly argued, the full scope of history's promises for the church lies outside of the church's own temporal grasp,[9] that does not mean that the thrust of God's time for us will not permit the receiving of such challenges as servants of his Word in the midst of a world thirsting to hear.

---

9. He began to underline this already in 1959 with his study of St. Bonaventure, translated into English as *The Theology of History in St. Bonaventure* (Chicago: Franciscan Herald Press, 1971), and brought it to a universal audience with the "Instruction on Certain Aspects of the 'Theology of Liberation'" of 1984, from the Sacred Congregation for the Doctrine of the Faith, that ends with the resounding quote from Paul VI's *Profession of Faith of the People of God* on the "Kingdom of God, begun here below in the Church of Christ, [yet] not of this world."

3 Pope Benedict XVI as Theologian, Philosopher of Religion, and Ecumenist

HARDING MEYER

It was in many respects a very special election of a Pope, when the College of Cardinals on April 19, 2005, elected Cardinal Joseph Ratzinger as the successor of John Paul II. It consumed the media, and we all shared in it. Two peculiarities were especially prominent.

First, for the first time in several centuries a German was again elected the successor of the Apostle Peter. "Wir sind Papst!" (We are the Pope), proclaimed the *Bildzeitung*. When was the last time that a German sat on the papal throne? is not an easy question to answer. The usual answer is that it happened five centuries ago, or more exactly, when Hadrian VI was Pope. He was one of the Popes of the Reformation period. His pontificate comprised only two years (1522-1523). His sarcophagus can be visited in the choir of the German church of Santa Maria dell' Anima in Rome. But to be more specific, Hadrian VI was Dutch, born in Utrecht.

Second, and this is without a doubt much more important than the German nationality of the Pope — he was the Prefect of the Congregation for the Doctrine of the Faith, thus the leader of that important Vatican authority, which since the Middle Ages has had to watch over the purity of the Catholic doctrine of the faith. That this person, the *highest guardian* of the Catholic Church, above all others, was elected as Pope can only mean that the College of Cardinals was convinced without a long hesitation that exactly *such a man* was needed in the present situation as its visible head,

---

This essay was translated by William G. Rusch.

this brilliant thinker and theologian, who for about twenty-five years with great gifts and competence had fulfilled his official responsibility, viz. "to promote *sound doctrine,* to correct *errors,* and to lead *erring persons* back to the right road."

I do not know if and when in earlier centuries such a Prefect of the Congregation for the Doctrine of the Faith has been elected Pope. But I myself do have the impression that this event in the case of Benedict XVI was indeed an important and very significant peculiarity, which can tell us something of what is to be expected from Benedict XVI.

The Life Journey of Joseph Ratzinger

Certainly the life journey of Benedict XVI is also interesting. Much has been said and written since his enthronement about his origin in a small, rural Bavarian community, about his good Catholic parents and family, about his deep rootage in Catholic piety, about his youth, about his quiet, reserved nature, his love of music, his great talent, and his study of theology. All this certainly may have an influence on his future conduct of the papacy. But this is not the place to go into his private life journey with its partially idyllic details.

It is more important that on this life journey Benedict XVI had certain experiences that can be considered as *crucial experiences,* experiences that were determinative for him and certainly will also influence his future effects as Pope. I would like in any case from *my* perspective to stress three such crucial experiences.

1. his participation in the Second Vatican Council, 1962 to 1965
2. his experience with the student unrest in the years 1968 to 1969
3. his appointment and service as Prefect of the Congregation for the Doctrine of the Faith, 1981-2005.

His Participation in the Second Vatican Council (1962-1965)

Pope John XXIII had called this council in the year 1959. According to the wish of the Pope, it was to be a "council of renewal." The Italian word, *aggiornamento,* became at that time a key word. It designated the wish to open the Catholic Church for the contemporary world. "Push open the doors," John XXIII had demanded at that time. The Pope and many others wanted a modern church with a modern doctrine of faith.

As with every council of the Catholic Church, this council too was a council of *bishops*. But many of the more influential bishops had a theologian as an advisor, a theological expert ("peritus") at their side, whom they especially held in high regard. Hans Küng, for example, or Karl Rahner were such council-advisors, and the Archbishop of Cologne, Cardinal Frings, had brought along the young Professor Joseph Ratzinger of Bonn and later Münster as his advisor. Thus Ratzinger for the first time entered the great ecclesial and theological stage. Here can be seen a *first crucial experience* in his life.

These theological advisors had an enormous influence on the course and results of the council. Many of these advisors were what could be described as "progressive" theologians, and contributed decisively to the council's really becoming a "council of renewal" and not only moving in the old ways. Thus Ratzinger at that time is said to have written the sensational council speech of Cardinal Frings, which made a decisive contribution with the result that the original, declared traditional and conservative plan of the council was considerably changed and yielded to a *new, reform-oriented* plan. Also, Ratzinger had an important influence on the theological decisions of the council, for example, on the important constitution on revelation (*Dei Verbum*).

This shows how ecclesially and theologically open and progressive a thinker Ratzinger was at that time, who — like Hans Küng and Karl Rahner — criticized the encrusted structures of the Church and was deeply convinced of the necessity of ecclesial renewal.

His Experiences with Student Unrest (1968-1969)

But — and this was the *second crucial experience* in the life of Benedict XVI — only a few years after the end of the council a clear change in Ratzinger's attitude appeared, a change that for many who knew him as a theologian of the council was surprising and also disappointing.

It was at that time — beginning with the famous year 1968, the time of the student unrest with its radical criticism of the existing situation, not only in society and politics, but also in the Church — that Ratzinger was a professor in Tübingen, where his colleague and council-companion, Hans Küng, had specially attracted him.

And now it happened, that Ratzinger became a target of the student unrest. He had been celebrated in overflowing lecture halls as a star theologian and a forerunner of the council, and yet the criticism of students now fell on him. His lectures became tumultuous scenes. Blasphemous interjections interrupted him. Student "bully-boys" snatched the microphone from him and shouted him down.

Ratzinger experienced this unrest, in part caused by Marxist thinking, as an expression of "atheistic piety." He could state later in his autobiography (*Aus meinem Leben,* 1997): "I have seen the cruel face of this atheistic piety unveiled, the psycho-terror, the lack of restraint, with which one could relinquish every moral reflection as bourgeois relics."[1]

Ratzinger gave up his professorship at Tübingen and went in 1969 to the quieter University of Regensburg. His Tübingen colleague Hans Küng, who also lived through that situation, wrote later: "He [Ratzinger] was rightly shocked and withdrew himself. That he had the call to Regensburg, he had concealed from us. He had still said, we will speak about it, but then only a letter arrived."

One could say this traumatic "Tübingen experience" caused Ratzinger at the deepest level to become critical of a society to which, he believed, the Church had opened itself and involved itself in its trends and values, viz., egalitarianism, the principle of majority rule, democratization, religious relativism, and moral populism and decadence. Ratzinger said later: "In these years I learned when a discussion must cease, because it changes into lies and must support resistance in order to preserve freedom."

And still Ratzinger later has always said — I think correctly — he had been no "traditionalist" who only would have liked to value and preserve the past, the "yesterday." Rather, he remained true to the Second Vatican Council and the thought of the renewal of the Church. For the Church *needs* constant reform. But the "renewal of the Church" has its limits. If Pope John XXIII had demanded "Push open the doors," the present Ratzinger would probably add: "Yes, indeed! — *but not too wide!*"

Especially for him the "renewal of the Church" is not simply and foremost the openness of the Church to the contemporary world — to mod-

---

1. See Joseph Ratzinger, *Milestones: Memoirs 1927-1977* (San Francisco: Ignatius Press, 1998).

ern thought, to the present *Zeitgeist*. Ratzinger says that by such means the Church finally becomes a merely "human-Church." To understand the method and means of the Second Vatican Council with its renewal vigor in this way would be false. According to his conviction, this view does not comprehend the "real" council. Rather, such an interpretation of the council leads to a "process of decline."

On the contrary, *real* renewal of the Church is for him in the first place and basically a "renewal of the Church *from its origin*." This permanent origin of the Church lies in Jesus Christ. It was very impressive when Benedict XVI in his sermon at his installation (April 24, 2005) again took up the words of John XXIII, "Push open the doors," but the words were supplemented with: "Yes, open, fling the doors open *for Christ!*"

"Erneuerung vom Ursprung her" ("Renewal from the Origin") — that is the title of one of his essays (1991). And he uses it for an illustrative comparison: When Michelangelo was once asked how he created his glorious statues, he is said to have answered: "I knock off what does not belong there." This means: I set free what this marble block already hides within itself. This always new "uncovering of the origin and the being of the Church" is for Ratzinger the *true* "renewal of the Church, of which the Church always stands in need." I think the evangelical Reformers would have been able to speak in the same manner. Indeed they have also spoken and acted thus.

His Appointment as Prefect of the Congregation for the Doctrine of the Faith (1981-2005)

Paul VI made *even this* professor of theology the Archbishop of Munich and Freising in 1977, and named him one month later a cardinal. Four years later John Paul II called him to Rome as Prefect of the Congregation for the Doctrine of the Faith.

This was the *third crucial event* in the life of Ratzinger before he became Benedict XVI. Thus his *papal* appointment as the "highest guardian" of the faith of the Church was for him the decisive confirmation that he had done with his thought and convictions exactly what this high office expected of its holder, namely "to promote *sound doctrine,* to correct *errors,* and to lead erring persons back to the right road."

Cardinal Ratzinger carried out this task for the following twenty-four years. In this period of time there occurred numerous official reports of the Congregation for the Doctrine of the Faith and also pronouncements of the Pope in which Cardinal Ratzinger had a clear role. In progressive Catholic circles these reports and declarations often caused disappointment and even resulted in protest. One thinks of the process against his former colleague and council-companion, Hans Küng, which indeed was not initiated by Ratzinger but was carried to completion by him. One also thinks of the sharp condemnation of Latin American liberation theology, of the rejection of the ordination of women, of the critical response to the question of contraception, of the declaration *Dominus Iesus,* in which the full ecclesial nature of the evangelical church was denied.[2] And there are many more examples. I think especially of the enormous, more than 700-page comprehensive Catholic "World Catechism" of 1992/93.[3] Its execution lasted six full years. This monumental "World Catechism" was, and indeed is, organized "to preserve the content of faith" as it states, and to protect "the precious content of Christian teaching" against all trends of popularity and relativism, the great signs of intellectual history of our time — of "postmodernism" as it is usually named.

In brief: all this, which occurred in the last two decades in the Roman Congregation for the Doctrine of the Faith, clearly bears the stamp of the conviction of the theologian and Cardinal Ratzinger. His every controlling concern is that the Christian faith not lose its clear certainty and contours and not lose itself in a cloud of uncertainty. *Relativism* — that is the word that turns up again and again with him. *Relativism* — which designates for him the contemporary crisis of Christianity.

And this great concern Ratzinger takes with him into his pontificate as Benedict XVI. One day before his selection on April 18th, he gave a sermon at the mass before the entrance of the cardinals into the conclave. I would like to quote from this sermon an extremely typical and much-noted section. He states there: "With how many opinions of faith have we become acquainted, how many ideological streams, how many ways of thinking? . . . To have a clear faith according to the credo of the Church often is branded as fundamentalism, wherein relativism, which itself is allowed to be driven here and there by the gust of any opinion of teaching [cf. Eph.

---

2. Http://www.vatican.va/roman_curia/congregations/cfaith/documents/rc_con_cfaith _doc_20000806_dominus-iesus_en.html.

3. *Catechism of the Catholic Church,* 2nd ed. (New York: Doubleday, 2003).

4:14], appears as the contemporary individual modern attitude. A *dictator-ship of relativism* arises, that recognizes nothing as final and as the final measure only that which I . . . allow properly to be of worth."

These are words of warning that the Protestant churches too should hear. For this spirit of "relativism" for a long time has also made itself at home in Protestant circles. One shrinks, where it is necessary, from opposing clearly and decisively the spirit of the time. One shrinks from stating a clear "no." The noble word *tolerance* is misused in order to tolerate all possible opinions and trends, even if the basics of the Christian faith, of Christian worship, and of Christian morals are placed in question. The great slogan "pluralism" serves to blur the clear boundaries between the Christian faith and other religions and to suggest that the different religions at their core are all the same and all differences are of equal value. And where nevertheless a decisive "no" is stated in order to protect the substance of the Christian faith, then one is ready to swing as a great club the judgment of "discrimination." This is the spirit of boundless "popularity" that dominates our time, the time of the "postmodern." "Anything goes," as the spirit of popularity and relativism has been summarized by one of its representatives.

Already the theologian and Cardinal Ratzinger had clearly opposed this, and as Benedict XVI he will continue to oppose it.

Still, it would be completely missing the point to see him as a rigid tra-ditionalist, a "Panzer-Cardinal," as he was named in his early Roman years by the Italians, someone who on the basis of the pure power of his office simply pushed through his convictions. As a brilliant thinker and theolo-gian he did not have to do that. He knew where a discussion must cease be-cause it was flogging things to death and leading into a fog; he did not wear himself out in debate, conversation, or in matter-of-fact argumentation. Someone once said of him: "Of all the conservatives in the church, he is the one with the greatest capacity for dialogue." I myself have repeatedly experienced this and can only confirm it.

Thus my overview of the life journey of Joseph Ratzinger with its three stages or crucial experiences. And this life journey leads him finally — at the death of John Paul II — to a conclave, which he leaves as Benedict XVI. But in no way does he leave behind him the experiences of his life journey. They will be part of the pontificate that lies before him.

This glance at Joseph Ratzinger's life journey already says much about his thought and his convictions. Nevertheless it is important to go into greater detail, however briefly.

Joseph Ratzinger as Dogmatist, Philosopher of Religion, and Ecumenist

The Dogmatist

For a good twenty years, Ratzinger was a university professor of doctrine and dogmatics. He has written much. Among his books could especially be stressed his *Introduction to Christianity (Einführung in das Christentum)* of 1968.[4] This work is a summary of the lectures he gave in the summer of 1967 in Tübingen, thus at the time of the outbreak of student unrest. The influence of this event has already been mentioned. That this work, translated into many languages, was much read (even though it is not easy to read), is shown by the fact that it had to be continually reprinted, for the last time in the year 2000.

This book discloses what the "renewal of the Church from its origin" is for Ratzinger. It is the recollection of, and the concentration on, the *testimony of God and Christ*, as it is contained in the Holy Scriptures, in which "God himself speaks," and how the *Church*, especially the church of the first Christian centuries, developed this testimony in its doctrine and in its dogma. It is therefore an exploration of the early church's *Apostolic Creed*, the basic Christian confession, and its "heart of the matter" is, as it is stated there, "the question of *God* and of *Christ*."[5]

Who or what *God* is, Ratzinger determines with the opening words of the Gospel according to John: "In the beginning was the *Word*." This means: God is not merely a higher power, the highest principle, a reality of the hereafter, the abstract impersonal origin of all being. As such, God is revered in the great Eastern religions, e.g., Buddhism and Hinduism. Philosophers have also viewed God in a like manner. But not only philosophers thus see God. This is also the current idea of God, which is constantly encountered today, as far as one still speaks of God and reckons with a "God."

"In the beginning was the *Word*," on the contrary, states: God is *a person*, a person who speaks, hears, and answers, a person whom we meet, with whom we also speak, whom we call upon and hear, to whom we can answer. God is nothing abstract, no mere basic cause of all things, who does not and cannot care about humankind. "Deus neminem amat" (God

---

4. Joseph Ratzinger, *Introduction to Christianity* (San Francisco: Ignatius Press, 1969).
5. *Introduction to Christianity*, Foreword.

loves no one); thus states philosophy. No, Christians believe in a God *of humankind.* In a God who turns to humankind and takes care of human beings. When the Israelites speak of God, they speak always about God as the God turning to human beings. They call God "the God of Abraham, the God of Isaac, the God of Jacob," the God who led them "from Egypt" and out of Egyptian slavery. God has a *name:* "I believe in God *the Father*"; thus begins the Christian creed.

And this *personal* God, the Father, takes care and concerns himself with humankind, so much that he himself comes to humankind in the form of a human being in the *person* of Jesus of Nazareth, the "Christ." God takes on human form and enters into human history.

Incarnation of God — this presentation of God is definitely strange and contrary to human perception. Constantly and especially in contemporary thought with its constricted understanding of reason, there are attempts to interpret away this miraculous event. It is not that the historical existence of this Jesus of Nazareth is simply denied. Not that! But there is a satisfaction with the *human person* Jesus, with the so-called "historical Jesus." One sees in this "historical Jesus" only a great, perhaps even the greatest representation of humankind: a great interpreter of God, a charismatic teacher of wisdom, an advocate of the poor and weak, the proclaimer and model of a fellow-humanity, a noble person who remained true to his convictions until death.

Such and similar modern interpretations of Jesus and pictures of him are also encountered among theologians and in the Church. Ratzinger opposes them decisively with the witness of Holy Scripture and the confession of the Church. He states and shows that for the New Testament all the deeds and effects of Jesus — also his proclamation and preaching — have their own, complete meaning, solely on the basis of who this Jesus *is:* namely Christ, the Son of God. *Of this,* from whom and what Jesus *is,* the Christian confession of faith speaks. It does not simply enumerate what Jesus proclaimed, did, and suffered. *First of all* the confession of faith says who this Jesus *is,* who preached, worked, and suffered: "I believe in Jesus Christ, God's only-begotten Son." Also here — in reference to Christ — it is a question for Ratzinger of the renewal of faith and of the Church "from its origin."

The core of his book, *Introduction to Christianity,* was — as Ratzinger said — "the question of *God* and of *Christ.*"[6] Still one can say that in the

6. See *Introduction to Christianity.*

further development of his thought, the question of the *Church* is increasingly pronounced.

Without a doubt, and as mentioned earlier, his "Tübingen experiences" have decisively contributed to this. He encountered at that time an eminently *critical* attitude toward the Church. "Critical Church," "Church from below" — these were at the time the great and dominant slogans. The "hierarchical" structures of the Church were especially criticized: the priority-ranking structures of ecclesial office, highly esteemed in the Catholic Church, of priests and especially of bishops, vis-à-vis the people of the faithful, the "laity." Against this view there was demanded a "democratization" of the Church and a push for the recognition of the majority principle in the Church.

Now Ratzinger has always seen that the Church with all who belong to it — priests, bishops, and laity — is "the people of God." In his early period he had even written a book, given much attention, with the title: *The New People of God (Das neue Volk Gottes).*[7] Also the Second Vatican Council again restored to a place of honor the biblical concept of "people of God" as a description of the Church.

But that does not in any way mean that the Church is to be thought of as a "democracy" in which the people are sovereign. For human beings do not make the Church by gathering together. It is *God* who calls human beings to himself and from them creates the Church, *his people,* the "fellowship of the faithful." The Church is therefore an endowment of *God,* a divine fact. And only by that fact is the Church, as the creed confesses, "the *holy* Church," the space of a real meeting between God and humankind. It is, as it is stated in the Holy Scriptures, the "body of Christ," into which persons are received by baptism, and in which Christ alone — not the people of the faithful — is the head and sovereign.

But under him and "in his place" Christ has instituted the *apostolic office* and has given it authority to lead the Church in its visible existence and to keep it in truth. And this office of the apostles, which in the strict sense belongs to the Church, resides in the *bishops and their successors in office.* Without this episcopal office, existing in apostolic succession and standing in a chain of laying-on of episcopal hands that goes back to the apostles, there is no Church in the full sense.

Here, in this doctrine of the "hierarchical," i.e., episcopal, structure of

7. Joseph Ratzinger, *Das Neue Volk Gottes* (Wien/Düsseldorf: Patmos-Verlag, 1969).

the Church — not in the doctrine of God and of Christ — lies the point that for Ratzinger reveals the clearest distinction between the Catholic Church and Protestant churches. For this episcopal structure of the Church is missing on the Protestant side. And therefore in the declaration *Dominus Iesus* (2000) of the Congregation for the Doctrine of the Faith, led by Ratzinger, this means that the Protestant churches are not churches "in the proper sense."

The Philosopher of Religion

We all know that in our contemporary thought, thus in the thinking of the modern era, "faith" and "reason" have fallen apart; indeed they have become opponents. This view of the *basic conflict* between "faith" and "reason" the philosopher of religion Ratzinger would like to examine and overcome.

In a manner similar to the dogmatist Ratzinger, the philosopher of religion Ratzinger takes as his departure point the prologue of John's Gospel: "In the beginning was the *Word*" (in Greek: "In the beginning was the *Logos*"). And "logos" means at the same time both "Word" and "reason." Thus from the beginning — so Ratzinger concludes — there is a *basic and close connection* between Christian faith and reason.

It is this that distinguishes the Christian religion from all other religions of that time. Ratzinger can even advocate the thesis that Christianity is not at all a religion beside others. Rather, Christianity has "its predecessors and its internal preparation" not in religions, but "in the *philosophical Enlightenment*" of antiquity. While the other religions of that time with their myths arose from "poetry" or from "politics," Christianity is based on "cognition" *("Erkenntnis")*. It appeared — with its Old Testament-Jewish roots — at that time as "a religious form of philosophical monotheism," and thus as a "synthesis of reason and faith." This has bestowed on Christianity its attraction and its power. The victory of Christianity over the pagan religions was not possible except by its claim to "reasonableness," according to Ratzinger.

But there is still a third aspect to be added: the "moral seriousness of Christianity." This coincided with the "philosophical morality" of that time and its conviction that "the cognition of the Good is written in the heart of each human person."

This "synthesis of reason, faith, and life," this connection of faith with reason and the alignment of action to *caritas,* to the loving care of the suffering, the poor, and the weak, was the power of Christianity that allowed it to become a world religion — as stated by Ratzinger.

And he asks: "Why does this synthesis (faith, reason, and ethics) *today* no longer bear conviction?" He sees the reason for this in the European Enlightenment of the seventeenth and eighteenth centuries. This European Enlightenment led to an enormous *narrowing of the concept of reason.* Only the cognition of exact, empirical knowledge, only physics, the cognition of the visible, of the established, the measurable, and the verifiable are now "reasonable." Metaphysics, God, and faith no longer belong in the area of the "reasonable."

This narrowing of the concept of reason that is the elimination of faith leads finally to a destructive use of reason and to a "cruel ethic," as we experience it, for example, in the technology of war — but not only there. Goethe's Mephistopheles from *Faust* can say, "One names it reason and uses it, only to be more bestial than any beast." Above all, this reason, narrowed to the visible and measurable, is incapable of answering the question of the meaning of life.

Only the regaining of that original synthesis of "reason, faith, and ethics" — this is Ratzinger's conviction — will be able to overcome the crisis of the modern age: *Faith* can help reason again "to come to reason," to see its ethical limits and to retain a human measure. And *reason* can help faith so that it is not darkened by superstition, by esoteric intellectual games and human opinions, thus losing its clarity.

The Ecumenist

Benedict XVI has already emphasized in his first papal statement that the effort for the unity of the Church, that is, the "ecumenical effort," belongs to the priorities of his pontificate. From the Protestant side, this is very much noted and welcomed. But actually this effort for the unity of the Church belongs to the position-description of *each* Bishop of Rome. Here lies the *central core* of the papal office. Its ministry *is* a "ministry to the unity of the Church." Even the First Vatican Council with its disputed dogma of papal infallibility makes this point in all clearness.

But it will depend on *how* Benedict XVI understands and exercises his "ministry to unity."

It is clear that Ratzinger as a theologian and cardinal has never represented the thought of a so-called "return-ecumenism," the old notion that the churches separated from the Catholic Church must "return" to the bosom of that church. He has even rejected this thought. For him the sought-for unity of the Church is a "unity in diversity" or in "reconciled diversity." For diversity "does not affect the being of the Church." Already in 1964, at the time of the Second Vatican Council, he had used the interesting formulation "the unity of the Church" as a *unity of the Churches, which remain churches and still become one Church."*[8] This will most certainly also be valid for Benedict XVI.

But the concern is always met in Ratzinger, that "ecumenical dialogue" could become trivial. It could — as with political and diplomatic negotiations — become a mere attempt at compromise, where each side makes concessions and in this way reaches a superficial agreement. Ratzinger thus fears that also in the ecumenical dialogues the postmodern spirit of "relativism" will invade, the spirit of popularity, of mere "tolerance . . . which rests on indifference to truth." Therefore he demands that in ecumenical dialogue too, *the basic convictions* of the Church — its "basic decisions," as he likes to say — are not diminished, but remain preserved.

How does Ratzinger see now the relations of the Catholic Church to the other churches? One thing is clear: the Orthodox Church of the East stands closest to the Roman Catholic Church. What binds it to the Catholic Church are not only the common faith and sacraments, but also the apostolic episcopal office. Even if the churches of the East do not recognize the Roman Pope as the visible head of the Church, they still have the episcopal structure. Therefore they are from the Catholic view churches in the full sense. Everything seems to indicate that Benedict XVI has firmly decided to intensify the dialogue with these churches.

It could be the case quite possibly that the dialogue with the Protestant churches will be more and more overshadowed under Benedict XVI. Here the distinctions are greater, especially in the understanding of the Church — as I have already mentioned — on the question of the episcopal office with all the consequences that this unresolved question has, for instance, for the understanding of the Lord's Supper and for the problem of Catholic-Protestant Eucharistic sharing.

8. Joseph Ratzinger, "Die Kirche und die Kirchen," *Reformatio: Evangelische Zeitschrift für Kultur und Politik* XIII, Jahrgang, Heft 2 (February 1964): 105.

Nevertheless it must be said, and should not be forgotten, that the theologian and Cardinal Ratzinger has done important things for Catholic-Protestant rapprochement. I give three examples:

- Ratzinger was the first important Catholic theologian to offer the idea that the Catholic Church could "recognize" the Lutheran Confession, the "Augsburg Confession" of 1530 as a "proper form of the fulfillment of the common faith." This idea was taken up in the years between 1976 and 1980 in numerous Catholic/Protestant conversations and publications, which led to important ecclesial declarations. The pastoral message of the German Catholic bishops of January 20, 1980, said, for example: "It is time, with thanks to God to affirm everything, which is found in this (Protestant) confession as in the present witness of our Protestant brothers to Christian substance. We rejoice that we cannot only discover a partial consensus in some truths, but an agreement on the central truths of the faith." John Paul II in his address in Mainz on November 17, 1980, took this word of the Catholic bishops and made it his own.
- It must have been at the beginning of the 1990s that Cardinal Ratzinger, in a letter to the regional bishop of the Evangelical Lutheran Church in Bavaria, wrote a sentence regarding the Lutheran Lord's Supper, which had never been heard before or after from the Vatican. It read: Also "an ecclesiology focused on the concept of succession, as it is held in the Catholic Church, need in no way deny the saving presence of the Lord in a Eucharist celebrated by Lutherans." This sentence was even taken up in an official Catholic/Lutheran dialogue document.[9]
- And when it was a question about the *Joint Declaration on Justification* in the years 1995 to 1999, Ratzinger, as the Prefect of the Congregation for the Doctrine of the Faith, made a decisive contribution, so that on October 31, 1999, the official signing of this important declaration occurred.

Nevertheless Ratzinger held to and holds a concept that there is between Catholicism and Protestantism a deep "basic difference" *(Grund-*

---

9. Lutheran–Roman Catholic Joint Commission, *Church and Justification: Understanding the Church in the Light of the Doctrine of Justification* (Geneva: Lutheran World Federation, 1994), § 203 (p. 100) .

differenz). He especially locates this difference in the fact that in Protestant thinking the *Church* is less important. Belief, or more exactly, the *act* of faith, on the Protestant side is left to the individual Christian, so he thinks. Ratzinger speaks of a radical personalization, indeed a subjectivization of the act of faith with Protestants, and of a questionable "glorification," a hypostatization, of the (biblical) word. On the contrary for Catholic thought, the canon of Holy Scripture arose *in the Church*. Therefore faith always means according to the Catholic understanding faith *with the Church* and *with the apostolic teaching office* of the bishop, which interprets revelation in a binding manner.[10] Here it is a question of different "basic decisions" on the Catholic and Protestant sides, which still unreconciled stand in opposition.

Ratzinger set this forth in all its sharpness in the Luther-year (1983). Whether and to what degree the theologian Ratzinger is really correct with this view must for now remain open. But I hope that the Lutheran–Roman Catholic dialogue will go further into this matter and that it will lead to a clarification on this important question. It would be of the greatest importance for the Lutheran–Roman Catholic dialogue if the theologian who occupies the Chair of Peter would reconsider this harsh judgment, with which the Lutheran side of the dialogue cannot under any circumstances agree.

---

10. Joseph Ratzinger, *Principles of Catholic Theology: Building Stones for a Fundamental Theology* (San Francisco: Ignatius Press, 1985); *Theologische Prinzipienlehre,* p. 204.

4 The Sting of Death: The Unavoidable Question and the Response of Faith

GEOFFREY WAINWRIGHT

In a 1984 essay of Joseph Ratzinger entitled "Faith, Theology and Philosophy" occur these striking lines:

> Both faith and philosophy confront the primordial question which death addresses to man. Now the question of death is only the radical form of the question about how to live rightly. It asks whence man comes and whither he is going. It seeks an origin and a destination. Death, the one question which it is impossible to ignore forever, is thus a metaphysical thorn lodged in man's being. Man has no choice but to ask what might be the meaning of this final limit.[1]

The general purpose of the 1984 essay is to stake out a proper relationship between theology and philosophy. In the earliest centuries of our era, Christian apologetics and iconography could present Jesus — the Logos incarnate — as "the Philosopher." At its best, secular philosophy provided categories which — subject to transformation — could aid the confession of Christ and the proclamation of the gospel. In modern times, the relationship, both from the philosophical and from the theological side, has become more adversarial. Ratzinger wants to see philosophy as helping to frame the provocative questions, to which theology, on the basis of the

1. Joseph Ratzinger, *The Nature and Mission of Theology: Essays to Orient Theology in Today's Debates,* trans. Adrian Walker (San Francisco: Ignatius Press, 1995), pp. 13-29: "Faith, Philosophy and Theology," here p. 23; originally *Wesen und Auftrag der Theologie: Versuche zu ihrer Ortsbestimmung im Disput der Gegenwart* (Freiburg: Johannes Verlag, 1993), pp. 11-25: "Glaube, Philosophie und Theologie," here pp. 19-20.

gospel and the Christian faith, seeks to offer answers that in turn will stimulate philosophy in its search for truth. Death raises questions that can be philosophically formulated and that require theological response. Ratzinger sees faith and reason — in their respective and related ways — as serving the one Truth; and in this he matches the encyclical of Pope John Paul II, *Fides et Ratio* (1998), issued while Cardinal Ratzinger was Prefect of the Congregation for the Doctrine of the Faith.

Returning, then, to the primordial and unavoidable problem of "death": death sharply poses a complex set of questions concerning both the very being of man and also humankind's concrete existence — as particular persons and as a race with a social constitution and a history. In the words of a Lenten antiphon that can be traced back to Notker of St. Gall and has found its way into traditional English and German liturgical use: "Media vita in morte sumus"; "In the midst of life we are in death"; "Mitten wir im Leben sind mit dem Tod umfangen." Pope Benedict XVI's programmatic first encyclical, *Deus Caritas Est*, can be seen as offering, at least in outline, this pontificate's answer to the question of death; and the very title of the encyclical — its opening phrase, "God is Love" — will prove to be of the greatest significance.[2] A cluster of six themes will be noted, and a series of flashbacks will show how these components in the answer were presaged in the earlier writings — both scholarly and pastoral — of the theologian Joseph Ratzinger (professor at the Universities of Bonn, Münster, Tübingen, and Regensburg, 1959-1977; Archbishop of Munich and Freising, 1977-1981; and Prefect of the Congregation for the Doctrine of the Faith, 1981-2005). Besides showing the consistency in Joseph Ratzinger's thinking, recourse to the previous texts will provide richer materials from which the necessarily brief hints in the encyclical can be filled out. Quotations will permit readers to catch the flavor of Ratzinger's style in various modes, and references will then permit the more substantive pursuit of his thoughts. With each of the six sub-topics, we shall at least mention some of the contemporary ways in which the question of death comes to expression and the (inadequate) answers that are advanced from outside the Christian faith (and sometimes from within theology). The six themes may be provisionally formulated as follows: first, the essential con-

2. Pope Benedict's first encyclical was "given in Rome, at Saint Peter's, on 25 December, the Solemnity of the Nativity of the Lord, in the year 2005, the first of [his] Pontificate." For a brief initial comment of mine on *Deus Caritas Est*, see *Pro Ecclesia* 15 (2006), pp. 263-66.

stitution of the human being; second, the existential vocation of humankind; third, and crucially, the human need for redemption and its divine provision; fourth, the ethical challenge of faith; fifth, the quality and direction of society and culture; sixth, the final prospect of the human person and the race. The emphasis in this exposition will fall on Pope Benedict's first encyclical, *Deus Caritas Est,* but towards the end of the chapter we shall note how some, at least, of these themes were amplified in his second encyclical, *Spe Salvi.*

The Being of Man

In an initial comment on the semantic range of the word "love" at the human level, Pope Benedict singles out "love between man and woman, where body and soul are inseparably joined and human beings glimpse an apparently irresistible promise of happiness" (*Deus Caritas Est,* 2). The phrase "body and soul" might almost appear off-hand in this context, although it is interesting that the writer seems confident that this near-colloquialism will be immediately understood by the readers he is seeking to captivate. By the time of paragraph 5, he is ready to bring out the theological import of "body and soul": Christian faith "has always considered man a unity in duality, a reality in which spirit and matter compenetrate, and in which each is brought to a new nobility":

> Man is a being made up of body and soul. Man is truly himself when his body and soul are intimately united. . . . Should he aspire to be pure spirit and to reject the flesh as pertaining to his animal nature alone, then spirit and body would both lose their dignity. On the other hand, should he deny the spirit and consider matter, the body, as the only reality, he would likewise lose his greatness. . . . Only when both dimensions are truly united . . . is love — *eros* — able to mature and attain its authentic grandeur.

In his reading of contemporary society, Pope Benedict finds "the erotic" assuming what amounts to a character of morbidity:

> [T]he contemporary way of exalting the body is deceptive. *Eros,* reduced to pure "sex," has become a commodity, a mere "thing" to be bought

and sold, or rather, man himself becomes a commodity. This is hardly man's great "yes" to the body. On the contrary, he now considers his body and his sexuality as the purely material part of himself, to be used and exploited at will. Nor does he see it as an arena for the exercise of his freedom, but as a mere object that he attempts, as he pleases, to make both enjoyable and harmless. Here we are actually dealing with a debasement of the human body: no longer is it integrated into our overall existential freedom; no longer is it a vital expression of our whole being, but it is more or less relegated to the purely biological sphere. The apparent exaltation of the body can quickly turn into a hatred of bodiliness. (*Deus Caritas Est*, 2)

In reference to our main question of death, it seems that contemporary people may indeed be quite close to confirming Sigmund Freud's theory of the "death-wish" (*Todeswunsch*) as a universal instinct — where *eros* and *thanatos* finally coincide. For the Christian faith, the two remain polar opposites — until resolved in and through the divine *agape*.

The constitution of the human being as "a unity in duality," "a unified creature composed of body and soul" (*Deus Caritas Est*, 5), was insistently expounded by the theologian Ratzinger in his *Eschatologie* — the one volume that he himself contributed to the *Kleine Katholische Dogmatik* undertaken with his Regensburg colleague Johann Auer.[3] The vital importance of an ontology in any Christian answer to the inescapable question posed by death is clear. That Joseph Ratzinger, now as Pope Benedict, still believes that to be the case is shown by his allowing *Eschatologie* to be reprinted — and indeed with a confirmatory new preface, signed "Joseph Ratzinger — Benedikt XVI" and significantly dated on the Feast of All Saints 2006.[4]

In his *Eschatology*, Ratzinger refutes the view of some twentieth-century exponents of an allegedly "biblical theology" that saw an irreducible dichotomy between "Hebrew" and "Greek" understandings of man, in

---

3. *Eschatologie: Tod und ewiges Leben* (Regensburg: Verlag Friedrich Pustet, 1977); the sixth, expanded edition of 1990 will be used here. An intermediate English translation was *Eschatology: Death and Eternal Life*, trans. M. Waldstein and A. Nichols (Washington, DC: The Catholic University of America Press, 1988).

4. Joseph Ratzinger/Benedikt XVI, *Eschatologie* (Regensburg: Verlag Friedrich Pustet, 2007). The American publisher also reissued *Eschatology*, with the author's new preface now included. Both in the German and in the English-language versions of 2007, the pagination in the body of the book remains the same as in the editions cited in note 3.

which the "corporeality" and "total death" of the former are set against the "dualism" and "the soul's release" in the latter.[5] Exegetically, historically, and systematically, Ratzinger shows that both the Old Testament and Plato are more complex than that, while both find their correction, completion, and transformation in the life, teaching, passion, death, and resurrection of Jesus Christ. It was the presence of the crucified and now risen Christ to faith — coupled with the availability of eternal life and yet the persistence of earthly death on this side of the Parousia — that constituted the real foundation on which Christian theological thinking could gradually develop a corresponding anthropology. Needed was "an anthropology which in the first instance recognized that man is, in his unified totality, the creature of God, conceived and willed by him. But at the same time, this anthropology was also obliged to distinguish between an element that perishes and an element that abides — though in such a way that the path towards the resurrection, the definitive reunification of man and creation remained open."[6] It took until Thomas Aquinas to formulate precisely that "the soul belongs to the body as 'form,' but that which is the form of the body is still spirit. It makes man a person and opens him to immortality."[7] This "strictly Christian" idea of the soul — "as found in Catholic liturgy and theology up to the Second Vatican Council"[8] — is not "substantialistic" but rather "the vehicle of a 'dialogical' concept of humanity: man is defined by his intercourse with God."[9] That capacity for relatedness to

5. On the "Greek" side in particular, "the frequently encountered notion of a Hellenic-Platonic dualism of soul and body, with its corollary in the idea of the soul's immortality, is something of a theologian's fantasy" (*Eschatologie,* p. 123; *Eschatology,* p. 145).

6. *Eschatologie,* p. 125; *Eschatology,* pp. 147-48.

7. *Eschatologie,* p. 126; *Eschatology,* p. 149.

8. *Eschatologie,* p. 126; *Eschatology,* p. 150. Ratzinger may here be hinting at a lamentable feature of postconciliar liturgical revision: "Even the Missal of Paul VI dared to speak of the soul only here and there, and that in timorous fashion, otherwise avoiding all mention of it where possible. As for the German rite of burial, it has, so far as I can see, obliterated it altogether" (*Eschatologie,* p. 216; *Eschatology,* p. 246). Ratzinger notes (*Eschatologie,* p. 209) that at least one Methodist theologian "begründet in präziser Gedankenführung die Notwendigkeit von 'Seele' und 'Zwischenzustand' vom biblischen Zeugnis her" — referring to my chapter "The Last Things" in Geoffrey Wainwright, ed., *Keeping the Faith* (Philadelphia: Fortress Press, 1988), pp. 341-70, in particular pp. 356-58.

9. *Eschatologie,* pp. 127-29; *Eschatology,* pp. 150-53. "Soul is nothing other than man's capacity for relatedness with truth, with love eternal" (*Eschatologie,* p. 233; *Eschatology,* p. 259). And that truth and eternal love reside, of course, in the God who is "not a God of the dead but the God of the living (cf. Mark 12:26-27)" (*Eschatologie,* pp. 99-100; *Eschatology,* pp. 113-14).

God implies no "escape" from the concrete reality of creation but rather the very opposite:

> [I]t is the man who makes himself open to all being, in its wholeness and in its ground, and becomes thereby a "self," who is truly a person. Such openness is not a product of human achievement. It is given to man; man depends for it on Another. But it is given to man to be his very own possession. That is what is meant by creation. . . .

> [F]rom belief in creation there follows the integral character of Christian hope. What is saved is the one creature, man, in the wholeness and unity of his personhood as that appears in embodied life. . . . This does not mean that nothing in man is transient. But it does mean that in the transfiguration of the transient, what takes shape is the abiding. Matter as such cannot provide the underpinning for man's continuing identity. Even during our life on earth it is changing constantly. . . . Hence the indispensability of the body-soul distinction. Nevertheless, the Christian tradition . . . has conceived this duality in such a way that it is not dualistic but rather brings to light the worth and unity of the human being as a whole. Even in the continuous "wasting away" of the body, it is the whole man in his unity who moves towards eternity. It is in the life of the body that God's creature grows in maturity in expectation of seeing God's face.[10]

As to the resurrection at the end of earthly history: the biblical witness — itself grounded in the Resurrection of Jesus Christ — is encapsulated in the phrase "pneumatic realism"; in the doctrinal tradition, help was afforded by the Thomistic insight into "the unity of body and soul, a unity founded on the creative act and implying at once the abiding ordination of the soul to matter and the derivation of the identity of the body not from matter but from the person, the soul"; systematically, Ratzinger declines to speculate much beyond "the certainty that the dynamism of the cosmos leads towards a goal, a situation in which matter and spirit will belong to each other in a new and definitive fashion."[11] The Incarnation and continuing bodiliness of Christ mean that history in all its concreteness retains its

---

10. *Eschatologie*, pp. 130, 133; *Eschatology*, pp. 155, 158-59.
11. *Eschatologie*, pp. 137-60; *Eschatology*, pp. 165-94.

eternal seriousness for each and every person amid the complex network of human relationships in time and the purposes of God for creation.[12]

In contemporary secular philosophy, the basic anthropological question is posed, for example, in terms of consciousness or even cybernetics. According to the American sociobiologist E. O. Wilson, "[a]ll tangible phenomena, from the birth of stars to the working of social institutions, are based on material processes that are ultimately reducible, however long and tortuous the sequences, to the laws of physics," and the arts are described by Wilson as embracing "not only all physically possible worlds but also all conceivable worlds innately interesting and *congenial to the nervous sys-*

---

12. *Eschatologie,* pp. 152-57; *Eschatology,* pp. 184-90. On the question of immortality and the possibility of eternal separation from God, Ratzinger writes: "As a created being [man] is made for a relationship [with God] which entails indestructibility" (*Eschatologie,* p. 130; *Eschatology,* p. 154). "Man as we know him wants to generate his own immortality. He would like to fabricate it out of his own stuff. . . . But in this attempt to manufacture eternity, the vessel of man must, at the last, founder. What endures after one is not oneself. Man falls headlong into the unreal, yielding up his life to unreality, to death. The intimate connection of sin and death is the content of the curse we read of in the book of Genesis [Gen. 3:3]. An existence in which man tries to divinize himself, to become 'like a god' in his autonomy, independence and self-sufficiency, turns into a Sheol-existence, a being in nothingness, a shadow-life on the fringe of real living. This does not mean, however, that man can cancel God's creative act or put it into reverse. The result of his sin is not pure nothingness. Like every other creature, man can only move within the ambit of creation. Just as he cannot bring forth being of himself, so neither can he hurl it back into sheer nothingness. What he can achieve in this regard is not the annulment of being, but lived self-contradiction, a self-negating possibility, namely 'Sheol.' The natural ordination towards the truth, towards God, which of itself excludes nothingness, still endures, even when it is denied or forgotten" (German, p. 131; English, p. 156). "And this," says Ratzinger further, "is where the affirmations of christology come into their own. What happened in Christ was that God overcame this self-contradiction from within — as distinct from destroying human freedom by an arbitrary act from without. The living and dying of Christ tell us that God himself descends into the pit of Sheol, that in the land of absolute loneliness he makes relationship possible, healing the blind [John 9] and so giving life in the midst of death. The Christian teaching on eternal life takes on, once more, a thoroughly practical character at this point. Immortality is not something we achieve. Though it is a gift inherent in creation it is not something which just happens to occur in nature. . . . Immortality rests upon a relationship in which we are given a share, but by which, in sharing it, we are claimed in turn. It points to a *praxis* of receiving, to that model for living which is the self-emptying of Jesus, as opposed to the vain promise of salvation contained in the words 'Ye shall be as gods,' the sham of total emancipation. If the human capacity for truth and for love is the place where eternal life can break forth, then eternal life can be consciously experienced in the present" (German, pp. 131-32; English, pp. 156-57). See further *Eschatologie,* pp. 176-79; *Eschatology,* pp. 215-18.

tem."[13] Those who, like Wilson, wish totally to remove any residue of metaphysics will see human judgment as the spurious exercise of an illusory self within a consciousness that is merely *epi*-phenomenal. In old-fashioned philosophical terms, that is materialism — which remains alive and well despite the difficulties inherent in the notion of matter *understanding itself* as material. The questions currently take form: Is the brain a computer? Can machines think? A recent two-volume "history of cognitive science" by Margaret A. Boden bears the title *Mind as Machine*.[14] Much is at stake in the Christian ontology of man as body and soul, Ratzinger recognizes, in face of "a modern anthropology, worked out on the basis of natural science, and identifying the human being with his or her body, without any remainder that might admit a soul distinct from that body."[15]

The Human Vocation

According to our opening quotation from the essay of 1984, death raises the questions of "whence man comes, whither he is going"; it is looking for "an origin and a destination." Where the English translation reads "Man has no choice but to ask what might be the meaning of this final limit," the German original makes a clearer echo of Martin Heidegger: "Der Mensch muss danach fragen, was es mit diesem Ende auf sich habe." For Heidegger, human existence was an "existence unto death" ("Dasein zum Tode"). According to Pope Benedict's encyclical, the Christian faith — through its "image of God and the resulting image of mankind and its destiny" — offers for human existence a different possibility: "[T]he encounter with an event, a person," namely Jesus Christ, "gives life a new horizon and a decisive direction" (*Deus Caritas Est*, 1).

13. Edward O. Wilson, *Consilience: The Unity of Knowledge* (New York: Knopf, 1998), pp. 266 and 268 (emphasis added).

14. Margaret A. Boden, *Mind as Machine: A History of Cognitive Science* (Oxford: Clarendon Press, 2006), two volumes, 1631 pp.

15. *Eschatologie*, p. 94; *Eschatology*, p. 106. In the preface to the edition of 2007, Ratzinger recommends an article by Tobias Kläden, "Die aktuelle Debatte um das Leib-Seele-Problem," in *Theologische Revue* 102 (2006), cols. 183-202, and a review by F. A. Peters, in the same issue (2006, no. 3, cols. 201-4), of a book by Ewald Richter, *Wohin führt uns die moderne Hirnforschung? Ein Beitrag aus phänomenologischer und erkenntniskritischer Sicht* (Berlin: Duncker & Humblot, 2005).

In four sermons delivered as adult catechesis in the Liebfrauendom in Munich during Lent of 1981, Archbishop Ratzinger made it clear that "the story of creation and the fall" is not to be "demythologized" — even in a benevolent sense — and thus reduced to an "existential*ist*" interpretation.[16] Rather, human existence is to be grounded in creation realistically understood. The Genesis stories — when read in light of the Torah and the New Testament to which they were leading — teach that "only if [and because] it is true that the universe comes from [divine] freedom, love, and reason, and that these are the real underlying powers, can we trust one another, go forward into the future, and live as human beings" (p. 22; p. 18): "God created the universe in order to enter into a history of love with humankind, . . . to be able to become a human being and pour out his love upon us and to invite us to love him in return" (pp. 29-30; p. 30).

Temporality belongs to creation, and speaks to us of "the passage from a beginning to an end" (p. 25; p. 22). To be formed from the dust of the ground [Gen. 2:7a] means being, like all earthly creatures, "destined for death" (p. 37; p. 43). But to "bear God's breath" [Gen. 2:7b] is to be "God's image" [Gen. 1:26f.]; to be "addressed by him" (p. 38; pp. 44-45) and to be, in turn, "capable of addressing God" (p. 40; p. 47f.). In Jesus Christ, the "definitive Adam" (pp. 40f.; p. 48), "we can discern what the human being, God's project, is, and thereby our own status" (p. 46; p. 57). But Christ's entry into the world needed to occur in redemptive mode on account of the Fall.

According to Ratzinger's interpretation of Genesis 3 in the fourth of the Munich sermons of Lent 1981, the story of Adam reveals the nature of human guilt and thus concerns the existence of us all. The Fall consists in the refusal to recognize "the boundary of good and evil," the moral order

16. Joseph Ratzinger, *Im Anfang schuf Gott* (Munich: Erich Wewel Verlag, 1986); *In the Beginning: The Catholic Understanding of the Story of Creation and the Fall,* trans. Boniface Ramsey, with an appendix (Grand Rapids: Eerdmans, 1995). In the preface to the published version of the Munich sermons, dated from Rome on the Feast of St. Augustine 1985, Cardinal Ratzinger declared that his new responsibility as Prefect of the Congregation for the Doctrine of the Faith had further persuaded him of the urgency of bringing the doctrine of creation to the fore in Christian proclamation. The point against demythologization is made in a note to the preface (pp. 60-61 in the German; pp. x-xii in the English). In the next couple of paragraphs I cite page references in parentheses (first the German, then the English editions). Into my brief quotations I have sometimes introduced — within brackets — phrases from the context for the sake of clarity; and in further citing this work I have occasionally adapted the published translation in other ways also.

that the God of the covenant has built into creation as its "inner standard or norm *(das innere Mass)*." The Fall is thus a denial both of the proximity of God and of our own creaturehood. Whatever death might have been, had Adam not sinned, death now holds negative sway:

> [S]in is, in its essence, a renunciation of the truth. Now we can also understand the mysterious meaning of the words: "If you eat of it [that is, if you deny the boundary, if you deny your creatureliness], then you will die" (cf. Gen. 2:16f.; 3:1-5). This means that human beings who deny the boundary of good and evil, which is the inner standard of creation, deny the truth. They are living in untruth and in unreality. Their lives are mere appearance; they stand under the sway of death. We who are largely surrounded by a world of untruths, of unlife, know how strong this sway of death is, which even negates life itself and makes it a kind of death. (pp. 54-55; p. 71)[17]

The story of God's "project" for humanity, its frustration, its retrieval, its promised triumph, is the comprehensive content of the Scriptures. The biblical structure is what grounds Ratzinger the systematic theologian's exposition of the origin and destination of human existence — of human history and of each person — as a movement of *exitus* and *reditus,* begin-

17. The contemporary Orthodox theologian and hierarch John Zizioulas, in *Communion and Otherness: Further Studies in Personhood and the Church* (London and New York: T. & T. Clark/Continuum, 2006), also views death as *the* ontological and existential problem (for example, pp. 40-41, 226-29, 257-58, but in fact often). Zizioulas locates the fallenness of humankind in its perversion of the particularity of "personhood" (which resides in being made "in the image of God"; cf. Gen. 1:26-27) in favor of an "individualism" that is in fact absorbed into an undifferentiated "nature" (which, as creatureliness, is inherently mortal). According to Zizioulas, there is no "natural immortality" for the creature, and certainly not for fallen humankind; but eternal life can be freely and graciously given by the Father of the risen Christ (pp. 265-69). A negative outcome also is allowed by the freedom that properly goes with personhood: "A man remains eternally free to aspire after the destruction of himself and others. However, being unable to attain it, . . . he will be eternally tormented by the non-accomplishment of his freedom. . . . Hell is the existential space where all those who desire the loss of others — and cannot obtain it, because of the Resurrection [of Christ] — are held. Hatred is, *par excellence,* the foretaste of hell" (p. 268). Thus Zizioulas holds in check the quasi-universalism fashionable among other admirers of Gregory of Nyssa: "Hell is the place of the dead precisely because what is absent is the personal identity which personhood gives, the positive relationship with God, our being recognized as beings by God. It is the condition of 'I do not know you' (Mt. 25:12)" (p. 281).

ning in God's free and loving act of creation and ending in a free and lov-ing response of the finally perfected creatures to God the consummator. Within the great "arc from *exitus* to *reditus*," the "great historical process by which the world moves towards the fulfillment of God being 'all in all,'" the smaller units "carry within themselves the great rhythm of the whole, give it concrete forms that are ever new, and so provide it with the force of its movement"; these units include not only "the lives of the different cul-tures and communities of human history, in which the drama of begin-ning, development, and end is played out," but also "the many small circles of the lives of individuals."[18] Because of the Fall — humankind's self-assertive refusal of God's gracious offer in creation — the "return" can take place only by the way of the Cross, a "death to self." In *The Spirit of the Lit-urgy*, Ratzinger puts this in staurological and sacramental terms that antic-ipate what he will say in *Deus Caritas Est:*

> The great gesture of embrace emanating from the Crucified has not yet reached its goal; it has only just begun. Christian liturgy is liturgy on the way, a liturgy of pilgrimage toward the transfiguration of the world, which will only take place when God is "all in all."[19]

In sum, death belongs to our concrete human existence both as histor-ical creatures and as sinners. The gospel proclaims the possibility of death's transformation under both those aspects by the redeeming and renewing work of God. We thereby return to the "encounter" that "gives life a new horizon and a decisive direction" (*Deus Caritas Est,* 1).

---

18. *Der Geist der Liturgie: Eine Einführung* (Freiburg im Breisgau: Herder, 2000), pp. 25-29, cf. p. 52; *The Spirit of the Liturgy,* trans. John Saward (San Francisco: Ignatius Press, 2000), pp. 29-34, cf. p. 59. I have drawn heavily on that book in my essay "A Remedy for Rela-tivism: The Cosmic, Historical, and Eschatological Dimensions of the Liturgy according to the Theologian Joseph Ratzinger," in *Nova et Vetera,* English edition, vol. 5, no. 2 (2007), pp. 403-30; also to be found in Geoffrey Wainwright, *Embracing Purpose: Essays on God, the World and the Church* (Peterborough, UK: Epworth, 2007), pp. 265-90, 351-52.

19. *Der Geist der Liturgie,* p. 43; *The Spirit of the Liturgy,* p. 50. For the exitus-reditus theme, Ratzinger himself directs his readers (*Der Geist der Liturgie,* p. 195; *The Spirit of the Liturgy,* p. 227) to his own habilitation-thesis *Die Geschichtstheologie des heiligen Bonaventura* (Munich and Zurich: Verlag Schnell & Steiner, 1959; 2nd edition, St. Ottilien: Eos, 1992); *The Theology of History in St. Bonaventure,* trans. Zachary Hayes (Chicago: Fran-ciscan Herald Press, 1971). See especially pp. 140-48 in the German (1st edition), pp. 138-48 in the English.

Redemption, or the Retrieval of the Lost

Invoking Hosea 11:8-9 and God's refusal to abandon adulterous Israel, Pope Benedict notes that "God's passionate love for his people — for humanity — is at the same time a forgiving love. It is so great that it turns God against himself, his love against his justice. Here Christians can see a dim prefigurement of the mystery of the Cross: so great is God's love for man that by becoming man he follows him even into death, and so reconciles justice and love" (*Deus Caritas Est*, 10). With the Incarnation, God's engagement with the world "now takes on dramatic form when, in Jesus Christ, it is God himself who goes in search of the 'stray sheep,' a suffering and lost humanity. . . . His death on the Cross is the culmination of that turning of God against himself in which he gives himself in order to raise man up and save him. This is love in its most radical form. By contemplating the pierced side of Christ (cf. John 19:37), we can understand the starting-point of this Encyclical Letter: 'God is love' (1 John 4:8)" (*Deus Caritas Est*, 12).

In the strongly Trinitarian paragraph 19, Pope Benedict summarizes the first half of the encyclical through a configuration of images that frequently recur in his theological writings as Joseph Ratzinger:

> In the foregoing reflections, we have been able to focus our attention on the Pierced one (cf. John 19:37; Zechariah 12:10), recognizing the plan of the Father who, moved by love (cf. John 3:16), sent his only-begotten Son into the world to redeem man. By dying on the Cross — as Saint John tells us — Jesus "gave up his Spirit" (John 19:30), anticipating the gift of the Holy Spirit that he would make after his Resurrection (cf. John 20:22). This was to fulfill the promise of "rivers of living water" that would flow out of the hearts of believers, through the outpouring of the Spirit (cf. John 7:38-39). The Spirit, in fact, is that interior power which harmonizes their hearts with Christ's heart and moves them to love their brethren as Christ loved them, when he bent down to wash the feet of the disciples (cf. John 13:1-13) and above all when he gave his life for us (cf. John 13:1; 15:13).

At least four elements figure in this sketch, and they are all characteristic of Ratzinger the theologian. First, the strictly redemptive and unique character of Christ's death: it was "the death of death," or, as the Orthodox liturgy puts it, "by death he trampled down death, and gave life to those in the tomb," and the anaphoral acclamation in the Missal of Paul VI: "Dying, you destroyed our death. Rising, you restored our life. Lord Jesus, come in glory." Joseph Ratzinger finds "the origin of the Eucharist in the paschal mystery," that is, in "the turning point of the Cross and the Resurrection, . . . the basis for Christianity in all its novelty, . . . the very center of the mystery of Christ."[20] The fundamental Christological and soteriological themes of Pope John Paul II's first encyclical *Redemptor Hominis* (1979) and his later *Redemptoris Missio* (1990) were, of course, taken up in the declaration *Dominus Iesus* from the Congregation for the Doctrine of the Faith in 2000. That last-named document bears the matching imprint of the then Cardinal Prefect Joseph Ratzinger in these crucial matters.

Second, we find in paragraph 19 of *Deus Caritas Est* the "attractive" power of Christ's saving death: we are drawn to him by the contemplation of his wounded side. In *The Spirit of the Liturgy* we find it said that "[i]n the pierced heart of the Crucified, God's own heart is opened up — here we see who God is and what he is like."[21] Already in an address to the Congress on the Sacred Heart of Jesus held at Toulouse in 1981, Joseph Ratzinger had invoked Hosea 11:8-9 and found in "the pierced Heart of the Crucified . . . the literal fulfillment of the prophecy of the Heart of God, which overturns its righteousness by mercy and by that very action remains righteous." In contrast with the Stoic view, where "the task of the heart is self-preservation, holding together what is its own," Ratzinger finds that "[t]he pierced Heart of Jesus has truly 'overturned' this definition":

> This Heart is not concerned with self-preservation but with self-surrender. It saves the world by opening itself. The revolution of the opened Heart is the content of the Easter mystery. The heart saves, indeed, but it saves by giving itself away. Thus, in the Heart of Jesus, the

---

20. From Archbishop Ratzinger's four Lenten sermons delivered at the Michaelskirche in Munich in 1978, first published in *Eucharistie: Mitte der Kirche* (Munich: Erich Wewel Verlag, 1978). These sermons were later republished, together with other pieces, in Joseph Ratzinger, *Gott ist uns nahe: Eucharistie, Mitte des Lebens,* ed. S. O. Horn and V. Pfnür (Augsburg: Sankt Ulrich Verlag, 2001); English in *God Is Near Us: The Eucharist, the Heart of Life,* trans. Henry Taylor (San Francisco: Ignatius Press, 2003). Here *Gott ist uns nahe,* pp. 25-39, 64; *God Is Near Us,* pp. 27-41, 65.

21. *Der Geist der Liturgie,* p. 40; *The Spirit of the Liturgy,* p. 48. The theme of "the pierced heart of Jesus" returns in *Deus Caritas Est,* 39.

center of Christianity is set before us. It expresses everything, all that is genuinely new and revolutionary in the New Covenant. This Heart calls to our heart. It invites us to step forth out of the futile attempt of self-preservation and, by joining in the task of love, by handing ourselves over to him and with him, to discover the fullness of love which alone is eternity and which alone sustains the world.[22]

In another of Ratzinger's favorite images, the outstretched arms of the crucified Christ are ready to embrace us and all men (cf. John 12:32).[23] In the Munich catecheses of 1981, he said this:

> Christ is the new Adam, with whom humankind begins anew. The Son, who is by nature relationship and relatedness, re-establishes relationships. His arms, spread out on the Cross, are an open invitation to relationship, which is continually offered to us. The Cross, the place of his obedience, is the true tree of life. . . . From this tree there comes not the word of temptation but that of redeeming love, the word of obedience, which an obedient God himself used, thus offering us his obedience as a context for freedom. The Cross is the tree of life, now become approachable. By his passion Christ, as it were, removed the fiery sword, passed through the fire, and erected the Cross as the true pole of the earth, by which it is itself once more set aright. Therefore the Eucharist, as the presence of the Cross, is the abiding tree of life, which is ever in our midst and ever invites us to take the fruit of true life. . . . To receive it, to eat of the tree of life, thus means to receive the crucified Lord and consequently to accept the parameters of his life, his obedience, his "yes," the measure of our creatureliness. It means to accept the love of God, which is our truth — that dependence on God which is no more an imposition

22. See "The Mystery of Easter: Substance and Foundation of Devotion to the Sacred Heart," in Joseph Ratzinger, *Behold the Pierced One: An Approach to a Spiritual Christology,* trans. Graham Harrison (San Francisco: Ignatius Press, 1986), pp. 47-69, here pp. 64 and 69 (slightly altered). German in *Schauen auf den Durchbohrten: Versuche zu einer spirituellen Christologie* (Einsiedeln: Johannes Verlag, 1984; 2nd edition 1990), pp. 41-59, here pp. 54-55 and 58-59.

23. He quotes Lactantius from the fourth century: "In his Passion God spread out his arms and thus embraced the globe as a sign that a future people, from the rising of the sun to its setting, would gather under his wings" (*Div. Inst.* IV, 26; CSEL 19, 383); cf. *Der Geist der Liturgie,* p. 157; *The Spirit of the Liturgy,* pp. 182-83.

from without than is the Son's sonship. It is precisely this "dependence" that is freedom, because it is truth and love.[24]

Third, Christ's death and resurrection released the Spirit, whose special work is to join and conform us to Christ. Elsewhere — and without, of course, any contradiction — Ratzinger will again highlight the role of the sacraments in this regard:

> In this connection, the Fathers always had at the back of their minds the conclusion of the Passion narrative according to St. John: blood and water flow from the opened side of Christ; Baptism and Eucharist spring from the pierced heart of Jesus.[25]

> Jesus is the New Adam, who goes down into the darkness of death's sleep and opens within it the beginning of a new humanity. From his side, that side which has been opened up in loving sacrifice, comes forth a spring that brings to fruition the whole of history. From the self-sacrifice of Jesus in death stream blood and water, Eucharist and baptism, as the source of a new community.[26]

Fourth, the benefits of Christ's saving death take shape among believers as an imitative participation. Another favorite image of Ratzinger's is that of the grain that must die in order to produce fruit. In paragraph 6 of *Deus Caritas Est*, Pope Benedict writes:

> Love is indeed "ecstasy" [*ek-stasis*], not in the sense of a moment of intoxication, but rather as a journey, an ongoing exodus out of the closed inward-looking self towards its liberation through self-giving, and thus towards authentic self-discovery and indeed the discovery of God:

---

24. *Im Anfang schuf Gott* (as in note 16 above), pp. 58-59; *In the Beginning* (as in note 16 above), p. 76.

25. *Der Geist der Liturgie*, p. 191, cf. p. 73; *The Spirit of the Liturgy*, p. 222, cf. p. 84.

26. "The Wellspring of Life from the Side of the Lord, Opened in Loving Sacrifice," in Joseph Ratzinger, *God Is Near Us: The Eucharist, the Heart of Life* (as in note 20 above), pp. 42-55, here pp. 42-43 (slightly altered); *Gott ist uns nahe,* pp. 41-54, here pp. 41-42. Ratzinger notes that "for the side of Jesus, when it is pierced, John has chosen exactly the same word as is used in the creation story to tell of the creation of Eve, where we normally translate it as Adam's 'rib.'"

"Whoever seeks to gain his life will lose it, but whoever loses his life will preserve it" (Luke 17:33), as Jesus says throughout the Gospels (cf. Matthew 10:39; 16:25; Mark 8:35; Luke 9:24; John 12:25). In these words, Jesus portrays his own path, which leads through the Cross to the Resurrection: the path of the grain of wheat that falls to the ground and dies, and in this way bears much fruit. Starting from the depths of his own sacrifice and of the love that reaches fulfillment therein, he also portrays in these words the essence of love and indeed of human life itself.

In a Munich sermon of 1978, Archbishop Ratzinger had preached this:

It was alone that [Christ] died, as the grain of wheat, but he does not rise alone, but as a whole ear of corn, taking with him the communion of the saints. Since the Resurrection, Christ no longer stands alone but is — as the Church Fathers say — always *caput et corpus:* head and body, open to us all. Thus he makes his word come true: "I, when I am lifted up from the earth, will draw all men to myself" (John 12:32). . . . The magnitude of Christ's achievement consists precisely in his not remaining separate, over and against us, which might thus relegate us once more to a merely passive rôle; he does not merely bear with us; rather, he bears us up; he identifies himself with us to such an extent that our sins belong to him and his being to us: he truly accepts us and takes us up, so that we ourselves cooperate and join in the sacrifice with him, participating in the mystery ourselves. Thus our own life and suffering, our own hoping and loving, can also become fruitful, in the new center *(Mitte)* he has given us to our existence.[27]

In his firm insistence on the saving death of Christ, the Pope in his encyclical is offering no facile theodicy. Recalling Job's "complain[t] before God about the incomprehensible and apparently unjustified suffering in the world" (Job 23:3, 5-6, 15-16), Benedict confesses:

Often we cannot understand why God refrains from interfering. Yet he does not prevent us from crying out, like Jesus on the Cross: "My God, my God, why have you forsaken me?" (Matthew 27:46). We should con-

---

27. "The Wellspring of Life" (as in note 26 above), p. 50 (slightly altered); *Gott ist uns nahe,* p. 49.

tinue asking this question in prayerful dialogue before his face: "Lord, holy and true, how long will it be?" (Revelation 6:10). It is Saint Augustine who gives us faith's answer to our sufferings: *"Si comprehendis, non est Deus"* — "if you understand him, he is not God." Our protest is not meant to challenge God, or to suggest that error, weakness or indifference can be found in him. For the believer, it is impossible to imagine that God is powerless or that "perhaps he is asleep" (cf. 1 Kings 18:27). Instead, our crying out is, as it was for Jesus on the Cross, the deepest and most radical way of affirming our faith in his sovereign power. Even in their bewilderment and failure to understand the world around them, Christians continue to believe in the "goodness and loving kindness of God" (Titus 3:4). Immersed like everyone else in the dramatic complexity of historical events, they remain unshakably certain that God is our Father and loves us, even when his silence remains incomprehensible. (*Deus Caritas Est*, 38)

The Ethical Challenge

According to Pope Benedict, "the command of love of neighbor is inscribed by the Creator in man's very nature"; and Christians engaged in charitable work — and, by implication, all Christians — "need to be led to that encounter with God in Christ which awakens their love and opens their spirits to others. As a result, love of neighbor will no longer be for them a commandment imposed, so to speak, from without, but a consequence deriving from their faith, a faith which becomes active through love (cf. Gal. 5:6)" (*Deus Caritas Est*, 31). As "the typical biblical expression for the biblical notion of love," *agape* "expresses the experience of a love which involves a real discovery of the other, moving beyond the selfish character that prevailed earlier. Love now becomes concern and care for the other. No longer is it self-seeking, a sinking in the intoxication of happiness; instead it seeks the good of the beloved: it becomes renunciation and it is ready, and even willing, for sacrifice" (6). The divine love manifested and enacted in Jesus Christ is the inspiration and example: "The consciousness that, in Christ, God has given himself for us, even unto death, must inspire us to live no longer for ourselves but for him, and, with him, for others" (33). And again: "Faith, which sees the love of God revealed in the pierced heart of Jesus on the Cross, gives rise to love. . . . Love is possible, and we are able to practice it because we are created in the image of God. To experience love and in this way to cause the light of God to enter into the world — this is the invitation I would like to extend with the present Encyclical" (39).[28]

In the line of Joseph Ratzinger's sacramental faith and liturgical theology, the encyclical presents the Eucharist as paradigm and power for the exercise of love through death to self:

> Jesus gave [his] act of oblation an enduring presence through his institution of the Eucharist at the Last Supper. He anticipated his death and resurrection by giving his disciples, in the bread and wine, his very self, his body and blood as the new manna. . . . The Eucharist draws us into Jesus' act of self-oblation. More than just statically receiving the incarnate Logos, we enter into the very dynamic of his self-giving. (*Deus Caritas Est,* 13)

> [I]n sacramental communion I become one with the Lord, like all the other communicants. . . . Union with Christ is also union with all those to whom he gives himself. . . . Communion draws me out of myself towards him, and thus also towards unity with all Christians. We become "one body," completely joined in a single existence. Love of God and love of neighbor are now truly united: God incarnate draws us all to himself. . . . [T]here God's own *agape* comes to us bodily, in order to continue his work in us and through us. . . . Faith, worship and *ethos* are interwoven as a single reality which takes shape in our encounter with God's *agape.* (*Deus Caritas Est,* 14)

> The saints — consider the example of Blessed Teresa of Calcutta — constantly renewed their capacity for love of neighbor from their encounter

---

28. Joseph Ratzinger would likely endorse Eberhard Jüngel's definition of love as "die sich ereignende Einheit von Leben und Tod zugunsten des Lebens": "On the Cross of Jesus God defined himself as love," and so in turn love can be understood as "the occurrence of unity between life and death for the sake of life." See E. Jüngel, *Gott als Geheimnis der Welt* (Tübingen: Mohr-Siebeck, 1977), pp. 298, 434; cf. *God as the Mystery of the World,* trans. D. L. Guder (Grand Rapids: Eerdmans, 1983), pp. 220, 317. Agreement on this definition is probable despite Ratzinger's rejection (*Eschatologie,* pp. 68-70, 201; *Eschatology,* pp. 72-75, 266) of the Lutheran theologian's version of the theory of "total death" (i.e., with no intermediate state of "the soul" before the general resurrection), found in E. Jüngel, *Tod* (Stuttgart: Kreuz-Verlag, 1971).

with the Eucharistic Lord, and conversely this encounter acquired its realism and depth in their service to others. (*Deus Caritas Est,* 18)

In writing on "charity as a responsibility of the Church," Pope Benedict recalls that "Justin Martyr (c. 155), in speaking of the Christians' celebration of Sunday, also mentions their charitable activity, linked with the Eucharist as such. 'Those who are able make offerings in accordance with their means, each as he or she wishes; the Bishop in turn makes use of these to support orphans, widows, the sick and those who for other reasons find themselves in need, such as prisoners and foreigners' [*First Apology,* 67]" (*Deus Caritas Est,* 22). And of Lawrence the Roman deacon and martyr (d. 258) Pope Benedict says: "As the one responsible for the care of the poor in Rome, Lawrence had been given a period of time, after the capture of the Pope and of Lawrence's fellow deacons, to collect the treasures of the Church and hand them over to the civil authorities. He distributed to the poor whatever funds were available and then presented to the authorities the poor themselves as the real treasure of the Church" (*Deus Caritas Est,* 23). Martyrdom itself, of course, is the supreme instance of the triumph of life through death. In his *Eschatology,* Joseph Ratzinger had spoken of it as "a new assurance of life, and a new way of enduring death"; and that is a soteriological pattern that casts its light forward on the whole of Christian existence: "[T]hat justification is by faith and not by works means that justification happens through sharing in the death of Christ, that is, by walking in the way of martyrdom, the daily drama by which we prefer what is right and true to the claims of sheer existence, through the spirit of love which faith makes possible."[29]

The paradigm and power can be expounded through "the eucharistic words of Jesus," as in two other Munich sermons from 1978:

In these words Jesus transforms death into the spiritual act of affirmation, into the act of self-sharing love; into the act of adoration, which is offered to God, then from God is made available to men. . . . [T]he two together constitute this new event, in which the senselessness of death is given meaning; in which what is irrational is transformed and made rational and articulate; in which the destruction of love, which is what death means in itself, becomes in fact the means of verifying and estab-

29. *Eschatologie,* pp. 81, 87-89; *Eschatology,* pp. 90, 98-100.

lishing it, of its enduring constancy. If, then, we want to know how Jesus himself intended his death to be understood, how he accepted it, what it means, then we must reflect on these words; and, contrariwise, we must regard them as being constantly guaranteed by the pledge of the blood that was his witness.[30]

"This is my Body" means: This is my whole person, existent in bodily form. What the nature of this person is, however, we learn from what is said next: "which is given up for you." That means: This person is: existing-for-others. It is in its most intimate being a sharing with others. But that is why, since it is a matter of this person and because it is from its heart an opening up, a self-giving person, it can then be shared out.[31]

Reverting to the encyclical, we could therefore define the human love that corresponds to the divine love embodied in Christ as "being there for the other" (cf. *Deus Caritas Est,* 7). That would give us a view of true human existence as "Dasein für Andere."

The Quality of Culture

In the second half of *Deus Caritas Est,* Pope Benedict ventures more concretely into "the social context of the present day." Thus in paragraph 30(b), for instance: "For young people, this widespread involvement [in voluntary works of charity] constitutes a school of life which offers them a formation in solidarity and in readiness to offer others not simply material aid but their very selves. The anti-culture of death, which finds expression for example in drug use, is thus countered by an unselfish love which shows itself to be a culture of life by the very willingness to 'lose itself' (cf. Luke 17:33 et passim) for others."

The contrast between a "culture of life" and a "culture of death" runs as a leitmotif throughout John Paul II's 1995 encyclical on "The Gospel of Life" *(Evangelium Vitae),* issued while Cardinal Ratzinger was Prefect of

---

30. "God's Yes and His Love Are Maintained Even in Death," quoted from *God Is Near Us,* pp. 27-41, in particular pp. 29-30; *Gott ist uns nahe,* pp. 25-39, in particular p. 28.

31. "The Presence of the Lord in the Sacrament," quoted from *God Is Near Us,* pp. 74-93, in particular p. 79; *Gott ist uns nahe,* pp. 75-95, in particular p. 80.

the Congregation for the Doctrine of the Faith and the theological confidant of the Pope. Thus in paragraph 21 of *Evangelium Vitae:*

> In seeking the deepest roots of the struggle between the "culture of life" and the "culture of death," . . . we have to go to the heart of the tragedy being experienced by modern man: the eclipse of the sense of God and of man, typical of a social and cultural climate dominated by secularism, which, with its ubiquitous tentacles, succeeds at times in putting Christian communities themselves to the test. Those who allow themselves to be influenced by this climate easily fall into a sad vicious circle: when the sense of God is lost, there is also a tendency to lose the sense of man, of his dignity and his life; in turn, the systematic violation of the moral law, especially in the serious matter of respect for human life and its dignity, produces a kind of progressive darkening of the capacity to discern God's living and saving presence.

A "culture of death" can include a willful blindness to death itself. In his *Eschatology* Joseph Ratzinger analyzed the various ways — only superficially contradictory — in which contemporary North Atlantic society refuses to face the metaphysical questions posed by death.[32] On the one hand, death is "hidden away," both in medical and in funerary practice as well as in the loss of "the family home" as a "sheltering space which brings human beings together in birth and living, in sickness and dying."[33] On the other hand, there is "the materialistic trivialization of death": "On television, death is presented as a thrilling spectacle tailor-made for alleviating the general boredom of life." The price is high: "When human sickness and dying are reduced to the level of technological activity, so is man himself. . . . Repression and trivialization can only 'solve' the riddle by dissolving humanity itself." As a side-thought, Ratzinger mentions the "nihilist defiance of death": "Such an attitude is

---

32. For the phrases cited in this paragraph, see *Eschatologie,* pp. 66-68; *Eschatology,* pp. 69-72.

33. In this connection, one might think of Jessica Mitford's *The American Way of Death* (New York: Simon & Schuster, 1963) and *The American Way of Death Revisited* (New York: Knopf, 1998). She began: "O death, where is thy sting? O grave, where is thy victory? Where indeed. Many a badly stung survivor, faced with the aftermath of some relative's funeral, has ruefully concluded that the victory has been won hands down by a funeral establishment — in disastrously unequal battle" (p. 15/14).

for the chosen few who, refusing to play the game of hide-the-slipper with death, attempt to bear the meaningless by looking straight into its eyes."

This latter, more sophisticated attitude came increasingly to attract Ratzinger's philosophical and theological attention, whether in its starkest end-form as nihilism or in its ideological preparation by way of relativism. It shows itself "esthetically"; all that matters is "artistic competence": "There are no such things as good and bad books but only well-written or poorly written books, only well-produced or poorly produced films, and so on. The good and the moral no longer count, it seems, but only what one can do. . . . Whatever is feasible is permitted."[34] Even more drastically, technology is governed by "the desire to do and the actual doing of what it is possible to do"; but:

> We should see that human beings can never retreat into the mere realm of "art" or "skill." In everything that they do, they are themselves agents. Therefore they themselves, and creation with its boundary of good and evil, are always present as their moral standard *(Mass)*, and when they reject this standard they deceive themselves. They do not free themselves, but place themselves in opposition to the truth. And that means that they are destroying themselves and the world.[35]

Or again:

> The immense growth in man's mastery of the material world has left him blind to the questions of life's meaning that transcend the material world. We might almost call it a blindness of the spirit. The questions of how we ought to live, how we can overcome death, whether existence has a purpose and what it is — to all these questions there is no longer a common answer.[36]

In the document *Dominus Iesus* issued from the Congregation for the Doctrine of the Faith in 2000 over the name of Cardinal Ratzinger, the catalogue of "propositions of both a philosophical and theological nature

---

34. *Im Anfang schuf Gott*, pp. 52-53; *In the Beginning*, p. 68 (slightly altered).
35. *Im Anfang schuf Gott*, p. 54; *In the Beginning*, p. 69 (slightly altered).
36. *Der Geist der Liturgie*, p. 112; *The Spirit of the Liturgy*, pp. 130-31.

which hinder the understanding and acceptance of the revealed truth" is headed by "relativistic attitudes toward truth itself, according to which what is true for some would not be true for others."[37] By the time of his address to the College of Cardinals on the eve of his election as Pope, Joseph Ratzinger could speak of "la dittatura del relativismo."

"People today know of no standard [coming from the inner goodness of creation]," said Archbishop Ratzinger in his Munich catecheses of 1981; "to be sure, they do not want to know of any because they see standards as threats to their freedom." He pointed to the "aggressiveness" in society, which might also be labeled egotism.[38] There is, in fact, a sting in the tail of the hedonistic proverb, "Eat, drink, and be merry, for tomorrow you die." "Mit dem Tod ist alles aus," they say: "When you're dead, you're dead." Well, perhaps — unless the soul remains liable to judgment (cf. Luke 12:19-20; Matthew 10:28).

Solemnly put:

> The crisis of the Western world turns not least on a philosophy and program of education which try to redeem man by bypassing the cross. . . . The only sufficient answer to the question of man is a response which discharges the infinite claims of love. Only eternal life corresponds to the question raised by human living and dying on this earth.[39]

The Future and Final Prospect

In paragraph 31 (b) of *Deus Caritas Est,* Pope Benedict notes that "the modern age, particularly from the nineteenth century on, has been dominated by various versions of a philosophy of progress whose most radical form is Marxism." This amounts to "an inhuman philosophy": "People of the present are sacrificed to the *moloch* of the future — a future whose effective realization is at best doubtful." To the charge that Christian charity diverts attention from "the struggle for a better world," the Pope retorts that "one does not make the world more human by refusing to act humanely now. We contribute to a better world only by personally doing

---

37. *Dominus Iesus,* 4.
38. *Im Anfang schuf Gott,* pp. 49-50; *In the Beginning,* pp. 62-63.
39. *Eschatologie,* p. 91; *Eschatology,* p. 103.

good now, with full commitment and wherever we have the opportunity, independently of partisan strategies and programs."[40]

Already in his *Eschatology,* Ratzinger had pointed to the inadequacies — even the sheer falsity — of Marxism; and, as Prefect of the Congregation for the Doctrine of the Faith, it was for his correction of Marxist incidences in "theologies of liberation" that he most attracted journalistic attention. In introducing "the current state of the eschatology question," Professor Ratzinger characterized Marxism as an "anti-theistic messianism" — "demanding an unconditional commitment through its claim that here at last all reality has become scientifically knowable, the past, present and future of humankind receiving their exact interpretation." Yet "[t]he very attack on God and the historical religions fosters a religious pathos which attracts the often deracinated religious energies of numerous contemporary men and women to itself, as a magnet draws ore. This pathos also affects theology, which detects in it the opportunity to fill the eschatological message with a tangible, realistic content." True, "the question of the future and its relation to the present, and with that the whole theme of hope and its attendant 'praxis,' rightly belongs to the subject matter of eschatology" — but not divorced from "what is specific in the Christian view of the age-to-come and its presence here and now," which includes "the classical themes of the doctrine of the last things — heaven and hell, purgatory and judgment, death and the immortality of the soul."[41] To account for the historical development of those traditional doctrines and continu-

---

40. This refutation of Marxism — and indeed of other forms of utopianism — in favor of a much more modest view of the path towards God's goal for humanity was a constant theme of Lesslie Newbigin, British theologian and bishop in the Church of South India, beginning with his Bangalore lectures of 1941, "The Kingdom of God and the Idea of Progress." See Lesslie Newbigin, *Signs amid the Rubble: The Purposes of God in Human History,* ed. and intro. Geoffrey Wainwright (Grand Rapids: Eerdmans, 2003); and, for instance, *The Open Secret: An Introduction to the Theology of Mission,* rev. ed. (Grand Rapids: Eerdmans, 1995), pp. 102-20, where Newbigin writes that "[d]eath is the dark mystery that mocks any hope for a total liberation of humans in history" (p. 103).

41. *Eschatologie,* pp. 19-20; *Eschatology,* pp. 3-4. Elsewhere, Ratzinger formulates his critique of Marxism in terms of the rejection of creation: "Creation is the total contradiction of Marxism and the point at which Marxist 'redemption' shows itself to be damnation, resistance to the truth. The decisive option underlying all the thought of Karl Marx is ultimately a protest against the dependence that creation signifies: the hatred of life as we encounter it." See "The Consequences of Faith in Creation," in an appendix to *In the Beginning,* pp. 79-100, here p. 91.

ing theological reflection on them, Ratzinger emphasizes that "[t]he question of the meaning of one's own dying cannot be suppressed. To attempt to obliterate or to shelve the progressive deepening of that question in Christian reflection would not be a return to the source but a barbarianization that would quickly recoil on its perpetrators. We have only to look at the complete impotence of Marxist thought when it comes to the topic of death to see how little chance there is of sidestepping that particular question."[42] It may perhaps be observed that "liberation theologies" scarcely outlasted the end of "real-existing socialism" with the collapse of the Soviet empire.

It is the teaching of Pope Benedict in *Deus Caritas Est* that love looks to eternity. After the hint in paragraph 2 at that "love between man and woman, where body and soul are inseparably joined and human beings glimpse an apparently irresistible promise of happiness," we find this in paragraph 6:

> It is part of love's growth towards higher levels and inward purification that it now seeks to become definitive, . . . in the sense of being "for ever." Love embraces the whole of existence, including the dimension of time. It could hardly be otherwise, since its promise looks towards its definitive goal: love looks to the eternal.

In Ratzinger's *Eschatology* this was stated in more formal, "dogmatic" terms:

> In all human love there is an implicit appeal to eternity, even though love between two human beings can never satisfy that appeal. In Christ, God enters our search for love and its ultimate meaning, and does so in a human way. God's dialogue with us becomes truly human, since God conducts his part as a man. Conversely, the dialogue of human beings with each other now becomes a vehicle for the life everlasting, since in the communion of saints it is drawn up into the dialogue of the Trinity itself. This is why the communion of saints is the locus where eternity becomes accessible for us. Eternal life does not isolate a person, but leads him out of isolation into true unity with his brothers and sisters and the whole of God's creation.[43]

42. *Eschatologie*, p. 25; *Eschatology*, p. 12.
43. *Eschatologie*, p. 134; *Eschatology*, pp. 159-60.

The Munich catecheses of 1981 put the orientation towards the future and eternity in more pastoral terms, setting it also explicitly in relation to the initial question put by death concerning "origin and destination":

> Human beings are the creatures that can become one with Christ and thereby become one with God himself. Hence this orientation of the creation to Christ, of the first to the second Adam, signifies that human persons are beings en route, beings characterized by transition. They are not yet themselves; they must ultimately become themselves. Here in the midst of our thoughts on creation there suddenly appears the Easter mystery, the mystery of the grain of wheat that has died. Human beings must die with Christ like a grain of wheat in order truly to rise, to stand erect, to be themselves (cf. John 12:24). Human persons are not to be understood merely from the perspective of their past histories or from that isolated moment that we refer to as the present. They are oriented toward their future, and only it permits who they really are to appear completely (cf. 1 John 3:2). We must always see in other human beings persons with whom we shall one day share God's joy. We must look upon them as persons who are called, together with us, to be members of the Body of Christ, with whom we shall one day sit at the table of Abraham, Isaac, and Jacob, at the table of Jesus Christ himself, as their brothers and sisters, as the brothers and sisters of Christ, and as the children of God.[44]

As to "the content of eternal life, its *Was* as distinct from its *Dass*," the theologian Ratzinger says that divine revelation offers only "hints," and the tradition of faith is but "a helpful signpost for those in the here and now."[45] In his *Eschatology* he lights on Psalm 73 — "one of Augustine's favorites" — as "one of those texts where the Old Testament stretches forth to touch the New and most fully possesses its own deepest implications":

> Thou dost guide me with thy counsel,
>   and afterward thou wilt receive me to glory.
> Whom have I in heaven but thee?
>   And there is nothing upon earth that I desire besides thee.

---

44. *Im Anfang schuf Gott*, p. 41; *In the Beginning*, p. 49 (slightly altered).
45. *Eschatologie*, p. 135; *Eschatology*, p. 161.

My flesh and my heart may fail,
   but God is the strength of my heart and my portion for ever.[46]

Certainly, "[h]eaven must first and foremost be determined Christologically": "Jesus Christ, as God, is man, and makes space for human existence in the existence of God himself. One is in heaven when, and to the degree, that one is in Christ. . . . Heaven is thus primarily a personal reality, and one that remains forever shaped by its historical origin in the paschal mystery of death and resurrection." And Christology bears an ecclesiological aspect:

> If heaven depends on being in Christ, then it must involve a co-being with all those who, together, constitute the body of Christ. . . . It is the open society of the communion of saints, and in this way the fulfillment of all human communion. . . . It is because the Church knows this that there is such a thing as the Christian cult of the saints. That cult does not presuppose some mythical omniscience on the part of the saints, but simply the unruptured self-communion of the whole body of Christ — and the closeness of a love which knows no limit and is sure of attaining God in the neighbor, and the neighbor in God.[47]

So, then, we may take up again from Pope Benedict's encyclical the theme of the communion of the saints:

---

46. *Eschatologie*, pp. 80-81; *Eschatology*, pp. 88-90. Ratzinger's doctoral dissertation was devoted to Augustine: *Volk und Haus Gottes in Augustins Lehre von der Kirche* (Munich: Karl Zink Verlag, 1954). Almost inevitably, the young German theologian's work thus had an eschatological orientation built into it from the start: the *populus Dei* — the Church as the eucharistic body of Christ — appears in Augustine as the earthly "pilgrim colony" of the *civitas Dei;* and Ratzinger concludes with Augustine's vision of the endless Kingdom which has been the end of all our living (see pp. 324-28). In terms of the problem of sin and death, the concluding chapter of Augustine's *City of God* has this to say: "Because our nature, when it was free to sin, did sin, it took a greater grace to lead us to that larger liberty which frees us from the very power to sin. For just as the first immortality, which Adam lost by sinning, was a mere possibility of avoiding death but the last immortality will be the impossibility of dying, so the first free will was a mere possibility of avoiding sin but the last becomes an utter inability to sin"; sins will be forgotten, but not the love that redeemed them (*De civitate Dei* 22.30.3; *Patrologiae Cursus Completus, Series Latina*, 41:802).

47. *Eschatologie*, pp. 190-91; *Eschatology*, pp. 234-35.

The lives of the saints are not limited to their earthly biographies but also include their being and working in God after death. In the saints one thing becomes clear: those who draw near to God do not withdraw from men, but rather become truly close to them. (*Deus Caritas Est*, 42)

Joseph Ratzinger has written movingly of the singing of the Litany of the Saints by the entire congregation at his own priestly and episcopal ordinations:

The fact that the praying Church was calling upon all the saints, that the prayer of the Church really was enveloping and embracing me, was a wonderful consolation. In my incapacity, which had to be expressed in the bodily gesture of prostration, this prayer, this presence of all the saints, of the living and the dead, was a wonderful strength — it was the only thing that could, as it were, lift me up. Only the presence of the saints with me made possible the path that lay before me.[48]

And in terms of liturgical history, which has its own doctrinal and pastoral importance, Ratzinger wrote this in his *Eschatology:*

The immediate stuff of the prayer life of the Christian people in its corporate anxiety and hope is perhaps best grasped in the Litany of the Saints. By a development not all of whose phases are as yet clearly seen, this litany grew up by degrees from the Late Antique period onwards. It absorbed into itself all those concerns with which time harries us, while counterposing to them the pledge of hope through whose agency we may endure them. The first thing to strike us here is that the person who is thus set about by dangers in time and eternity finds a shelter in the communion of the saints. He gathers the redeemed of all ages around him and finds safety under their mantle. This signifies that the walls separating heaven and earth, and past, present and future, are now as glass. The Christian lives in the presence of the saints as his own proper ambience, and so lives "eschatologically."[49]

---

48. *Der Geist der Liturgie*, pp. 161-62; *The Spirit of the Liturgy*, p. 188.
49. *Eschatologie*, p. 23; *Eschatology*, pp. 8-9.

The Drawing of the Sting

We may end this exposition where we began, with death as what Joseph Ratzinger calls "the metaphysical thorn lodged in man's being." According to the Apostle Paul (and we have seen Ratzinger fully recognizing the point), the "metaphysischer Stachel" is sharpened by sin (1 Cor. 15:56; cf. Rom. 6:20-21, 23a).[50] But now, with the death and resurrection of Christ, "death is swallowed up in victory. O death, where is thy sting? O grave, where is thy victory?" (1 Cor. 15:55; cf. Rom. 6:22, 23b). And Joseph Ratzinger can write for us:

> The sting of death is extinguished in Christ, in whom the victory was gained through the plenary power of love unlimited. Death is vanquished where people die with Christ and into him. This is why the Christian attitude must be opposed to the modern wish for instantaneous death, a wish that would turn death into an extensionless moment and banish from life the claims of the metaphysical. Yet it is in the transforming acceptance of death, present time and again to us in this life, that we mature for the real, the eternal, life.[51]

As Christians, we may celebrate the paschal mystery. And Methodists in particular may join in with the words of Charles Wesley, "Love's redeeming work is done":

Lives again our glorious King;
Where, O death, is now thy sting?
Once he died our souls to save;
Where's thy victory, boasting grave?

Soar we now where Christ hath led,
Following our exalted Head;
Made like Him, like Him we rise;
Ours the cross, the grave, the skies:

50. The one German word "Stachel" covers both Ratzinger's metaphysical "thorn" and what the Apostle calls the "sting" of death.

51. *Eschatologie*, p. 87; *Eschatology*, pp. 97-98. "The sting is extinguished . . .": on this occasion, the word "sting" is actually an importation of the English translator, who is perhaps making a word-play; the German reads "Der Tod als Tod ist besiegt in Christus. . . ."

> King of glory! Soul of bliss!
> Everlasting life is this,
> Thee to know, Thy power to prove,
> Thus to sing, and thus to love: Alleluia!

"Saved in Hope"

Pope Benedict's second encyclical appeared on November 29, 2007, under the headline of a phrase from St. Paul's Letter to the Romans (8:24): *Spe Salvi,* "Saved in Hope." There the ultimate and unavoidable question posed by death for the meaning and conduct of life re-emerges at three (interconnected) levels: that of each and every human being, that of the social constitution of humankind, and that of the human race as a whole and its history.

As individuals, we appreciate and desire life, and yet we do not wish for its endless extension in our present state. "There is a contradiction in our attitude," says Pope Benedict, "which points to an inner contradiction in our very existence. On the one hand, we do not want to die; above all, those who love us do not want us to die. Yet on the other hand, neither do we want to continue living indefinitely, nor was the earth created with that in view" (*Spe Salvi,* 11). Thus a paradox marks our condition, certainly as sinners if not already as creatures. The Pope quotes an admittedly delicate passage from the funeral discourse of St. Ambrose for his deceased brother: "Death was not part of nature; it became part of nature. God did not decree death from the beginning; he prescribed it as a remedy. Human life, because of sin . . . began to experience the burden of wretchedness in unremitting labor and unbearable sorrow. There had to be a limit to its evils; death had to restore what life had forfeited. Without the assistance of grace, immortality is more of a burden than a blessing" (*Spe Salvi,* 10; citing Ambrose, *De excessu fratris sui Satyri,* II, 47, found in *Corpus Scriptorum Ecclesiasticorum Latinorum* 73, 274). Ambrose had already said: "Death is, then, no cause for mourning, for it is the cause of mankind's salvation." That, clearly, is a confession of the Christian faith and of the hope that is founded on Christ's death and resurrection. The "blessed life," "eternal life," says Benedict in dependence on St. Augustine and St. Paul, is something we can as yet know only in "a certain learned ignorance *(docta ignorantia)*":

To imagine ourselves outside the temporality that imprisons us and in some way to sense that eternity is not an unending succession of days in the calendar, but something more like the supreme moment of satisfaction, in which totality embraces us and we embrace totality — this we can only attempt. It would be like plunging into the ocean of infinite love, a moment in which time — the before and after — no longer exists. We can only attempt to grasp the idea that such a moment is life in the full sense, a plunging ever anew into the vastness of being, in which we are simply overwhelmed with joy. This is how Jesus expresses it in St. John's Gospel: "I will see you again and your hearts will rejoice, and no one will take your joy from you" (16:22). We must think along these lines if we want to understand the object of Christian hope, to understand what it is that our faith, our being with Christ, leads us to expect. (*Spe Salvi*, 12)

While salvation is a personal reality, begun now and perfected beyond death, it must not be conceived individualistically. Following Christ entails the giving of one's life for the sake of others, and that is the way of present and final salvation for all parties in the particular relationship. From his earliest theological days Joseph Ratzinger was inspired by St. Augustine, and it is the City of God according to that church father which stands behind what Pope Benedict says in his second encyclical also about the implications of life and death for social relations and for the entire human community and its history. Here come again into play what in my earlier exposition of Ratzinger's thought on life and death I called "the ethical challenge" and, more broadly, "the quality of culture." Invoking the "communal salvation" implied in the "city" of the Letter to the Hebrews (11:10, 16; 12:22; 13:14), Benedict notes that "sin is understood by the Fathers as the destruction of the unity of the human race, as fragmentation and division": "Hence 'redemption' appears as the re-establishment of unity, in which we come together once more in a union that begins to take shape in the world community of believers" (*Spe Salvi*, 14). St. Augustine, himself quoting St. Paul, is immediately quoted: "In order to be numbered among this people and to attain to everlasting life with God, 'the end of the commandment is charity that issues from a pure heart and a good conscience and sincere faith' (1 Tim. 1:5)." Pope Benedict concludes that "this real life, towards which we try to reach out again and again, is linked to a lived union with a 'people,' and for each individual it can only be attained with this 'we.' It presupposes that we escape from the prison of our 'I,' because only in the openness of this universal subject does our gaze open out to the source of joy, to love itself — to God" (*Spe Salvi*, 14; cf. 28-29, again with appeal to St. Augustine).

As to the future prospect for humanity and the world: "While this community-oriented vision of 'the blessed life' is certainly oriented beyond the present world, as such it also has to do with the building up of this world — in very different ways, according to the historical context and the possibilities offered or excluded thereby" (*Spe Salvi*, 15). In reference to humankind as a whole and its history, earthly hope is not wrong, but modesty befits it, even in what can be achieved through the inspiration of the Christian faith and the practice of Christian love, let alone through reliance on unaided reason and technical prowess (material and technical "progress" remains insignificant without moral, and indeed metaphysical, standards). As death brings the passing of the generations, inherited social structures — morally grounded — can help and guide, but each new generation has to engage in freedom with the challenges of its time (*Spe Salvi*, 22-27). For a pilgrim people on its way to the homeland, the "firm basis" of hope (so Benedict, in paragraphs 7-9 of *Spe Salvi*, interprets the *hypostasis/sub-stantia* of Hebrews 11:1) remains Jesus Christ himself, crucified and risen, in whom faith is placed.[52]

52. This chapter has also appeared as an article in *Nova et Vetera* 6, no. 3 (Summer 2008): 615-43.

5 Will the Ecclesiology of Cardinal Ratzinger Influence the Pontificate of Pope Benedict the XVI?

METROPOLITAN MAXIMOS OF PITTSBURGH

Introduction

The following article is a personal reflection on the ecclesiology of Cardinal Joseph Ratzinger regarding its impact on the pontificate of this great Bavarian Cardinal, now Pope Benedict XVI.

Everyone knows of the historical impasse not only of the reunification of the churches generated from the Reformation of the sixteenth century; but also of the impasse in the relationship between the Church of Rome and the Churches generated from the other four patriarchates in the East. This Pope may not like the title of Patriarch; however, not only was this one of the best titles of the Bishop of Rome during the united church in the first millennium, but it remains one of the best names of this same Church of Rome in the eyes of the Churches of the East to this day.

This brief paper will deal with some basic points: one, the problems between Eastern and Western Churches, as acknowledged by Cardinal Ratzinger; two, the special problems created by the *Letter to the Bishops of the (Roman) Catholic Church on Some Aspects of the Church Understood as Communion* and the Declaration *Dominus Iesus* from the Roman Congregation for the Doctrine of the Faith; three, the possible resolution of the ecclesiological problems between East and West, suggested by this same Cardinal; and, fourth and final, in discussing these problems, we will see how the ecclesiology of Cardinal Ratzinger, as expressed in some of his published statements, may influence the pontificate of this great Bavarian Pope and eventually lead to the rapprochement and full communion between these two sister churches, the Eastern Orthodox and the Roman Catholic Churches.

Basic Ecclesiological Problems, East and West

The main ecclesiological problems between East and West, which continue to exist, are the Roman primacy, or the primacy of Peter as the Western Church understands it, and the so-called "universal jurisdiction" or primacy, to be understood as "supremacy" of this same primate.

It seems that Cardinal Ratzinger does not understand this Petrine primacy any differently than the First Vatican and then the Second Vatican Councils *(Lumen Gentium)* understood it. Yes, he makes the statement that the Churches of the East cannot have an ecclesiology that is the same as that developed in the West at the nineteenth-century (Vatican I) and the twentieth-century (Vatican II) councils. However, it seems that he himself cannot have an ecclesiology different from these two councils. Not only is the primacy of Peter an exclusive primacy, having the Pope of Rome as the only beneficiary, and excluding the other primates from the same rights (according to Saint Cyprian of Carthage all the Bishops have a part of this primacy, together with all the other Bishops); but, he is the *only* primate, in spite of what the church had decided during the first millennium of its united life (the second Council of 381, the fourth of 451, and the eighth of 879-880). The united church of the first millennium recognized more than one primacy of Peter, that is, all the primacies in its life, and all the primacies of the local churches, and of the Bishops in their own Metropolises.

Second, Eastern and Western ecclesiologies differ in their understanding of so-called "universal ecclesiology," "universal church," and "universal jurisdiction." According to the best teaching and doctrine of the Eastern Orthodox Church, *none of these terms are acceptable;* they are false names (misnomers). "Universal ecclesiology" presupposes an *addition of local churches* to make this "universal church" and its related ecclesiology. The Church of Christ, the Church of the Creed, "One, Holy, Catholic and Apostolic," is fully present in the one local church, presided over by the Bishop, as the representative of Christ, Peter, and the other Apostles. There is no such a thing as a "universal church," which would be the result of an addition of many local churches or ecclesiastical provinces. As one of the main Orthodox theologians in the West would have said it, "one and one and one in ecclesiology will only make one" (Father Nicholas Afanasieff), as "one and one and one" in God will also make "one," without that "one" meaning "many gods."

Finally, if there is not a "universal church" and not a "universal ecclesiology," there is also no room for a "universal jurisdiction," as the Western theologians following the definitions of the two Vatican councils have invented it. A "universal jurisdiction" presupposes a "universal church," the addition of all local churches, and, by the same token, the destruction of all these local churches. This is not the ecclesiology of Saint Paul and the Holy Scripture; it is not the ecclesiology initiated by Christ and the Christian faith; it is not the ecclesiology of the Church Fathers, East *and* West; it is not the ecclesiology of the united church, the church of the first Christian millennium, or the church before the year A.D. 1204.[1]

These are the basic differences between Eastern and Western teachings in ecclesiological matters, which have to be reconciled before we may enter into a real rapprochement between East and West, and before we may begin thinking of healing the schism and re-establishing communion between East and West.

The Letter to the Roman Catholic Bishops on Communion, and the Declaration *Dominus Iesus*

At the conclusion of the previous, and the beginning of the present millennium, two important documents were published by the Roman Congregation for the Doctrine of the Faith (the previous "Holy Inquisition"), under the figured leadership of Cardinal Joseph Ratzinger: the first was a Letter to the Roman Catholic Bishops, regarding "Some Aspects of the Church Understood as Communion," and the second, a Declaration named *Dominus Iesus*. Both of these documents, under the leadership of Cardinal Ratzinger, are of great value for the developments in the Cardinal's mind of the "case" of the Eastern Orthodox Churches.

---

1. This is the date of the Fourth Crusade, and its result — the duplication of jurisdictions, with the Western prelates doubling the Episcopal sees in the Churches of the East. Also, note that this date is the most commonly held among prevalent Church historians as the date of the schism between Eastern and Western Churches.

The Letter to the Roman Catholic Bishops on Communion

In nineteen articles, the Congregation dealt with important aspects of the Church as Communion *(Koinonia)*.[2] The sub-titles are: The Church, Mystery of Communion; Universal Church and Particular Churches; Communion of the Churches, Eucharist and Episcopate; Unity and Diversity in Ecclesial Communion; and Ecclesial Communion and Ecumenism.

The Congregation dealt with the topic of Communion, rightly stating that this Communion is at the heart of the Church's self-understanding as church. In the section "Universal Church and Particular Churches," the *Theologoumenon* of the "universal church" as "pre-existing" the particular church has been presented and utilized. My personal opinion agrees with that of Cardinal Walter Kasper, according to whom the so-called "universal church" at least co-exists with the "particular churches," which, celebrating the Eucharist under the authority of their Bishops, not only "subsist in," but *are* the "universal church" of Christ, One, Holy, Catholic, and Apostolic according to the Creed of Nicea/Constantinople. In the section on Eucharist and Episcopacy, we strongly disagree with the statement of the "primacy of Peter" supposedly being the primacy of Rome, as if Peter had only one successor, the Bishop of Rome. Church history tells us something very different, for there were many successors of Peter in many Apostolic Sees, including for example Saint Cyprian of Carthage. Every Bishop is a successor of Peter. It is obvious that the ecumenical section of the letter is the most problematic: not only is the Western opinion according to which the Pope is the only successor of Peter emphasized, but also, those who consider this statement mistaken are referred to as "wounded brothers"! It is the understanding of the Orthodox Church that the contrary is correct: that is, those who consider the Bishop of Rome as the only successor of Peter are the "wounded brothers"; moreover, those who identify the "universal church" with the Church of Rome are afflicted with the same disease of arrogance, and are fatally wounded.

This remark makes my reaction clear with regard to the statement on Eastern Orthodox Churches. The Roman theologians say that these Churches, in spite of rightly deserving the title of "particular churches" as a result of their Apostolic Succession and their One Eucharist of Christ, are

2. Congregation for the Doctrine of the Faith, *Letter to the Bishops of the Catholic Church on Some Aspects of the Church Understood as Communion.* Rome, May 28, 1992.

"wounded brothers" because they refuse to accept the Roman primacy, especially as it developed in the nineteenth and twentieth centuries. Cardinal Ratzinger himself rightly refused to accept this misstatement, as we will see later. It is our persuasion that, not only do the Orthodox Churches, as does the Roman Catholic Church, "subsist in" the One, Holy, Catholic, and Apostolic Church of the Creed; but we Orthodox also believe that "they (we) are" that One, Holy, Catholic, and Apostolic Church of the common Ecumenical Creed, that of Nicea/Constantinople.

The Declaration Dominus Iesus

The Declaration *Dominus Iesus* of the same Roman Congregation for the Doctrine of the Faith, presided over by the same Cardinal Ratzinger, is a statement addressed to everyone who is interested in the Roman Catholic teaching regarding "the unicity and salvific universality of Jesus Christ and the Church."[3]

In its twenty-three articles, this text is both a Roman and a Christian statement regarding the definitiveness and universality of salvation in Christ and his One Holy Church, Catholic and Apostolic.

In the introduction, one is impressed by the quotation of the Christian Creed of Nicea/Constantinople, without the addition of the *Filioque*. Without realizing it, the Congregation preceded the work of the Orthodox–Roman Catholic Theological Consultation in the U.S.A., which suggests to the Roman Church the elimination of the *Filioque* from today's Roman Creed.

The first section deals with the fullness and definitiveness of the revelation of Jesus Christ, as a response to those who try to diminish the completeness and definiteness of the revelation of God in his Christ. The next section deals with the cooperation of the Incarnate *Logos* of God and God's Holy Spirit in the work of salvation, indicating that there is only one "economy" (dispensation) of both the Word of God and his Holy Spirit. Characteristically, the text indicates that the incarnation is a Trinitarian event, and that the Holy Spirit, abundantly bestowed by the Son of God who became flesh, is "the animator of all" (cf. John 3:34). In the next sec-

---

3. Congregation for the Doctrine of the Faith, *Declaration "Dominus Iesus" on the Unicity and Salvific Universality of Jesus Christ and the Church.* Rome, August 6, 2000.

tion, "Unicity and Universality of the Salvific Mystery of Jesus Christ," a comparison is made between Christ's work and the work of pseudo-saviors of other religions. The work of Christ suffices when it comes to the universality of its consequences. The following section deals with the unicity and the unity of the Church of Christ, indicating that there is one Body and One Bride of Christ, but, at the same time, indicating that those who do not believe in the Roman understanding of Saint Peter's primacy, according to which only the Pope has the privilege of being the successor of Saint Peter, are "wounded brothers." We have already spoken of the fallacy of this statement, and suggested that the contrary is true. Indeed, it is the statement of the Declaration that is the fallacy — historically, ontologically, and theologically — that the Pope of Rome is the only successor of Peter's primacy, the term *primacy* to be understood as supremacy.

It is to be noticed that in this section, the language has been reduced, with regard to the Orthodox Churches. There is a hint regarding their having been "separated" from the Roman Catholic Church, without also referring to the possibility of the opposite, which is equally plausible. Also, there is a misleading statement according to which the other churches derive their legitimacy from the "fullness of grace and truth entrusted to the [Roman] Catholic Church," with no indication that the same is true of the Orthodox Churches, which were also being entrusted with this same fullness of grace and truth.

In answer to the question as to why the language of the Declaration tends to devalue the Orthodox Churches, and eventually other Christians, it may be that the president of the Pontifical Council for Promoting Christian Unity (Cardinal Walter Kasper) was also a member of the Roman Catholic Congregation for the Doctrine of the Faith, as stated in the text of the Response to the Objections Against this Declaration by the Commission for the Doctrine of the Faith.

The next section deals with the Church as being simultaneously the kingdom of God and the kingdom of Christ. The final section is dedicated to the Church and the other religions in relation to salvation, proposing — and rightly so — that the only Savior is the Lord and Savior Jesus Christ, and the only Ark of Salvation is the Holy Church of Christ. The other religions may have "seeds" of salvation, which are only good if they lead to Christ the Savior and His Holy Church.

Statements like this last one induced people to oppose this Declaration, and, by mistake, Cardinal Ratzinger, who correctly stated that he was only the chairperson of the Congregation and, moreover, only one of its members. In an article in *The Ecumenist*,[4] the editor, Professor Gregory Baum, a Roman Catholic theologian, is very critical of Cardinal Ratzinger, lamenting his severe way of dealing with theologians who favor a positive look at non-Christian religions. He says: "The Declaration offers a harsh criticism of Catholic theologians who try to deal with religious pluralism in a manner that seems to relativize the uniqueness and universality of God's self-revelation in Jesus Christ." In his article, he criticizes the Cardinal for his fear of other theologians and other religions, for fear of pluralism and relativism when it comes to revelation in Christ and salvation in him, the only and unique Savior according to Christianity. Professor Baum criticizes the Declaration, and, consequently, Cardinal Ratzinger, for rendering impossible true dialogue among religions, for prompting a colonial missionary activity among non-European people, for persecution by Roman Catholics of other religious faithful, for not exemplifying the love of Christ, and for not allowing a dialogue of truth to be instituted between Christians and other religions.

The Letter to the Roman Catholic Bishops on Communion and the Declaration *Dominus Iesus* are important declarations of the Christian faith from a Roman Catholic point of view. We cannot expect the authors not to be Roman Catholics, that is, not to advance the Roman teachings regarding papal primacy. We cannot condemn Cardinal Ratzinger for being the only author of these documents, and we understand the possible progress and growth in his thought as a Christian and as a theologian. Indeed, he has progressed in his theological teachings and statements, and his leadership has given us a fine Christian example to follow during these recent days, as we will see later.

Possible Resolution of Conflicting Eastern and Western Ecclesiologies Suggested by Cardinal Ratzinger

There is no doubt that the two basic ecclesiologies underlying the positions of East and West regarding the Church are in direct conflict. We can attest to this in the conflict between the ecclesiologies of Cardinal Walter

4. Gregory Baum, "The Theology of Cardinal Ratzinger: A Response to *Dominus Iesus*," *The Ecumenist* 4 (Fall 2000).

Kasper and Cardinal Joseph Ratzinger. For Cardinal Walter Kasper, now president of the Pontifical Council for Promoting Christian Unity, and Cardinal Joseph Ratzinger, now Pope Benedict XVI, the two ecclesiologies — one of the so-called "universal church" (Ratzinger) and one of the so-called "local church" (Kasper) — are in contradiction, in spite of an attempt by Cardinal Walter Kasper to harmonize the two by considering a common foundation for both in a simultaneous "pre-existence." This pre-existence allows both ecclesiologies to co-exist, without the one annihilating the other.[5]

The latter is the case of the Eastern Orthodox understanding of "Eucharistic ecclesiology" that does not allow the existence of the so-called "universal ecclesiology." The scriptural and historical foundation of Eucharistic ecclesiology is destroyed by the "universal ecclesiology" of Cardinal Joseph Ratzinger. Cardinal Walter Kasper is defending the foundation of his ecclesiology of the local church, both in the Holy Scripture and the (historical) Apostolic Tradition, a foundation that Cardinal Joseph Ratzinger accuses of being "Protestant," without realizing that it is as "Orthodox" as it is "Protestant."

Cardinal Ratzinger considers the Greek word *ecclesia* of the New Testament to mean the "universal church," without realizing that such a church does not actually exist in Holy Scripture, or even in the Apostolic and the common tradition of the Fathers in both Churches, East and West. This is the foundation of the two ecclesiologies, Eastern (ecclesiology of the local church), and Western, a later development in ecclesiology, especially in the nineteenth and twentieth centuries, the so-called "universal ecclesiology."

However, the same Cardinal Ratzinger had always taken a position according to which Rome had no control over the Eastern Churches. Her authority was a "moral authority." Cardinal Walter Kasper says: "In sum, the ecclesiology of the first millennium excluded a one-sided emphasis on the local churches as well as a one-sided emphasis on the universal church." He then quotes Cardinal Ratzinger as saying: "In 1976, in a lecture in Graz, Austria, Cardinal Ratzinger stated: 'What was possible in the Church for a thousand years cannot be impossible today. In other words, Rome must

---

5. Cardinal Walter Kasper, "On the Church," *America, The National Catholic Weekly,* April 23, 2001; Philip Blosser, "The Kasper-Ratzinger Debate and the State of the Church," *The New Oxford Review,* April 1992, pp. 18-25.

not demand from the East more recognition of the doctrine of primacy than was known and practiced in the first millennium.' This so-called 'Ratzinger's proposition' was well received; it had wide echo and has become the major theme of several ecumenical dialogues."[6]

Also, in an earlier text,[7] Cardinal Ratzinger expresses the same original and truly unique statement which resolves the ecclesiological problems of East and West. He states that the two Churches had a shared, but also diversified ecclesiology for so long, namely, during the years of the so-called "undivided church," or the church of the "first millennium." This means that the church may "return" to the years of its unity, and that the Western Church cannot impose its own ecclesiological developments of the nineteenth and twentieth centuries upon the Churches of the East. Characteristically, the Cardinal is remembered as saying that the "Church of the West cannot shovel down the throat of the Eastern Church its own recent developments in ecclesiology." Very precisely, the Church of the West (Roman Catholic) cannot impose the development of its understanding of the "primacy of Peter" upon the Church of the East, which has its own understandings of this primacy. This would have resolved the problem of misunderstandings between the two Churches, and achieved full unity in full communion between the two Churches, an aim that allegedly this Pope has identified as one of the main goals of his pontificate.

Cardinal Joseph Ratzinger stated: "Certainly, no one who claims allegiance to the Catholic Theology can simply declare the doctrine of primacy null and void, especially not if he seeks to understand the objections and evaluates with an open mind the relative weight of what can be determined historically. Nor is it possible, on the other hand, for him to regard as the only possible form and, consequently, as binding on all Christians, the form this primacy has taken in the nineteenth and twentieth centuries."[8]

The Cardinal provides an example of a way to work out of this "historical impasse," the example of Pope Paul VI: "The symbolic gestures of Pope Paul VI and, in particular, his kneeling before the representative of the Ecumenical Patriarch were an attempt to express precisely this and, by such signs, to point the way out of the historical impasse. Although it is

6. Kasper, "On the Church."
7. Cardinal Joseph Ratzinger, *Principles of Catholic Theology: Building Stones for Fundamental Theology* (Fort Collins, CO: Ignatius Press, 1987), pp. 193-203.
8. *Principles*, pp. 193-203.

not given us to halt the flight of history, to change the course of centuries, we may say, nevertheless, that what was possible for a thousand years is not impossible for Christians today." He gives a fine example of comparison between peoples of the past and peoples of the present: "After all, Cardinal Humbert of Silva Candida, in the same bull in which he excommunicated the Patriarch Michael Cerularius and thus inaugurated the schism between East and West, designated the Emperor and people of Constantinople as 'very Christian and orthodox' although their concept of the Roman primacy was certainly far less different than that of Cerularius than from that, let us say, of the First Vatican Council."[9]

Following this, the Cardinal issues a lengthy statement on what Rome can expect from the Church of the East regarding the "primacy" of Rome. The unity of the Church, East and West, should be based on what this unity was during the first millennium of our Christian era. In other words, Rome must not require more from the East with respect to the doctrine of primacy than had been formulated and was lived in the first millennium. When the Patriarch Athenagoras, on July 25, 1967, on the occasion of the Pope's visit to Phanar, designated him as the successor of St. Peter, as the most esteemed among us, as one also [who] presides in charity, this great Church leader was expressing the essential content of the doctrine of primacy as it was known in the first millennium. Rome need not ask for more. Reunion could take place in this context if, on the one hand, the East would cease to oppose as heretical the developments that took place in the West in the second millennium and would accept the Catholic Church as legitimate and orthodox in the form she had acquired in the course of that development, while, on the other hand, the West would recognize the Church of the East as orthodox and legitimate in the form she has always had.[10]

This is a courageous statement towards resolving the long and separate ecclesiological developments in the Churches of both East and West, and a way out of the impasse in which each finds itself — an impasse that does not allow them to come closer or to settle their differences and achieve full communion again.

There is no doubt that the two Churches have had different developments in terms of ecclesiology. The West developed the doctrine of Petrine

9. *Principles,* pp. 193-203.
10. *Principles,* pp. 193-203.

primacy in such a way that the Church of the East can neither comprehend nor accept. In the meantime, the Eastern Church had its own developments in terms of its own primacies, which multiplied according to the needs of its communities. There is no doubt that an impasse is created in terms of these two mutually exclusive ecclesiologies. However, Cardinal Ratzinger recognizes the developments of both Churches as legitimate and orthodox, and suggests a justifiable way of resolving them, by each Church acknowledging the legitimacy of the other and considering it a sister Christian Church with which they can re-enter into full and complete communion as it existed during the first millennium of our Christian era.

In other words, Cardinal Ratzinger proposes a solution to the serious division between the main Christian Churches, East and West, without damaging the ecclesiological developments in each of them, and without being prejudiced as to who is right and who is wrong. We can wish that his suggestion will be taken seriously by each, and, thus, the two major Christian Churches, East and West, finally re-uniting according to the will of the Master, who wants his disciples "to be one" (John 17:21). Should this come to pass, Cardinal Ratzinger, now Pope Benedict XVI, will not only be a great Pope, certainly not a "transition Pope" as some people wanted him to be, but one of the greatest Popes in Christian history, the one who finally achieved making a reality of the desire of Christ himself, "that they may all be one" (John 17:21).

Will the Ecclesiology of Cardinal Ratzinger Influence the Pontificate of Pope Benedict XVI?

Many people, interested in the well-being of Christianity, and, more generally, in the well-being of truth versus falsehood, true religion versus a pluralism of religions and a plurality of ways of seeking salvation, are very much interested in a sign of change with regard to what has been established. They are interested in seeking salvation through the only Savior and through the only way to salvation, which is that of the Christian Church.

These people are very much interested in the former Cardinal Joseph Ratzinger, now Pope Benedict XVI, and the possibility of his delivering on his promise that he would see Eastern Orthodoxy and Roman Catholicism becoming one again before the end of his pontificate. I too am very much interested in this possibility and this promise.

In 2006, the Pope visited Constantinople and his Brother in Christ and in Episcopacy, Patriarch Bartholomew of Constantinople. The Patriarch invited the Pope to come to the Phanar for the feast of Saint Andrew, patron saint and founder of the Church of Constantinople. The Pope decided to go to Turkey, in spite of the threats against his life by a group of Muslim fanatics. The Pope not only delivered, but made a significant visit. He participated in the services at the Saint George Cathedral, and he recited the "Our Father" in Greek. At the end of the service, together with the Patriarch he climbed onto the second floor of the Patriarchal Palace, and together with the Patriarch he blessed the crowds in the front yard of Saint George. It was an excellent sign of true brotherhood in Christ, and support of Patriarch Bartholomew and the sister Church of Constantinople, New Rome, by the Bishop of Ancient Rome. The visit will never be forgotten by all of its witnesses.

I was able to follow the visit by way of the news media. The Americans who did so will never forget it. Congratulations to both of our Church leaders for a superb sign of brotherhood, the way our forebears expected it to happen during the first millennium of our Christian era. In spite of opposition from fanatical people in both the East and the West, the efforts of bringing East and West closer together will continue on both sides, insofar as we have enlightened leaders such as Pope Benedict XVI of Rome and Bartholomew of Constantinople.

The feast of Saint Andrew in 2007 was equally impressive. I had the privilege of being present as I was a member of the Holy and Great Synod of the Phanar, representing the Greek Orthodox Archdiocese of America for one year (my term ended in March 2008). I took part in the Patriarchal and Synodal Divine Liturgy at the Saint George Cathedral on November 30th, the feast of Saint Andrew. Cardinal Walter Kasper, accompanied by a very distinguished group of prelates representing Ancient Rome, attended the Divine Liturgy. At the end, he responded to the Patriarch's welcome with a special message he had brought from Pope Benedict XVI. Also, the Cardinal brought a signed copy of the recent papal encyclical, *Spe Salvi*.

The Patriarch himself made the following statement:

Your Eminence, Cardinal Walter Kasper, and beloved brothers in Christ comprising the Delegation of the Church of Rome,
It is with particular joy that we welcome you today at the historical Center of Orthodoxy, on the occasion of our celebration of the joyous feast of the Ecumenical Throne. Your presence here both strengthens

and seals the bonds of love and trust between our Churches, bonds which have been cultivated in recent decades and which have been especially established by the visit here last year of His Holiness, our most beloved Brother in Christ, Pope Benedict XVI of Rome, and his fervent participation in the Feast of the Throne of the Ecumenical Patriarchate.

We are particularly moved today because, this year, we enjoy the distinct blessing and spiritual pleasure of honoring the founder and patron of the Church of Constantinople, the glorious and first-called among the Apostles, Andrew, whose sacred relics were generously and graciously permitted by the love of His Holiness to be donated to us during our recent visit to Naples, being returned from Amalfi to the Throne of the Patriarchate in order to remain here for the sanctification of our faithful and as a sign of communion with the Apostle, whom we commemorate today, as well as of fraternal unity of Christians throughout the world.

It is with fond memories that we recall our recent meeting with His Holiness in Naples, together with our constructive and brotherly conversation there. This encounter contributed further to the cultivation of an atmosphere of friendship and cooperation of our two Churches, strengthening yet further the relations among us. We always believe that the peaceful coexistence of Christians, in a spirit of unity and concord, must constitute the fundamental concern of us all.

This is precisely what we confirmed and cosigned jointly with His Holiness in the joint Declaration during his visit here last year, urging "that we share the same emotions and the same intentions of brotherhood, cooperation and communion in love and truth" (*Common Declaration* of Pope Benedict XVI and Patriarch Bartholomew).

In an age when, as we once again jointly emphasized last year, we observe "the rise of secularism and relativism, or even nihilism, especially in the western world" *(Common Declaration),* we must derive inspiration from the example of the Apostle Andrew, who "endured many trials in every land and spoke of numerous difficulties" (see the *Life of St. Andrew,* according to the *Synaxaristes* of Constantinople), "and yet remained upstanding through the strength of Christ and for the sake of the faithful."

Therefore, the feast of this Apostle provides the appropriate occasion for us to pray together more intently for the restoration of unity within the Christian world. The fracture of this unity has been the cause of so much trouble in humanity, while its consequences have proved tragic. The philosophy of the Enlightenment in the West and the French Revolution sparked a truly cultural revolution aimed at replacing the previous Christian tradition of the Western world with a new, non-Christian, concept of man and society. This revolution gave rise in many ways to the practical materialism of contemporary societies but also to diverse forms of militant atheism and totalitarianism that, over the last two centuries, have unfortunately claimed the lives of millions of innocent victims. Those who remained faithful to the Christian values were led to this new cultural environment by means of various processes to the loss also of the concept of mystery in God and of His living worship, which is genuinely preserved in the East, as well as to the reduction of religious life to a humanistic ethic by means of the relativization of doctrinal formulations.

Today, then, it is our obligation more than ever to reclaim the Christian roots of Europe and the spiritual, sacramental and doctrinal unity that it enjoyed prior to the Schism of our two Churches. The re-evangelization of our peoples is "today, more so than ever before, timely and necessary, even within traditional Christian lands," as we admitted and confessed in common here exactly one year ago.

Thus, we believe that Western and Eastern Europe must cease regarding themselves as foreign to one another. Contrast among Christians of the Latin tradition and the Orthodox faith may be rendered most productive for both sides. The feast of the Apostle Andrew, whom we commemorate and celebrate today, constitutes a vocation for all Christians of the world to return to the fullness, youthfulness and purity of the Christian tradition of the early Church. The example bequeathed to us by the Apostle Andrew, who remained faithful to His teacher throughout even the most grueling circumstances, preferring the Cross of Christ in place of any other compromise, invites us to an uncompromising resistance before the destructive consequences of the consumer culture today, before the increasing relativization of our doctrine and faith, before "the diverse forms of exploitation of the poor, migrants, women and children," as we declared again last year, as well as to "joint action to preserve a respect for human rights in every human being created in the image and likeness of God." The First-Called among the Apostles, Andrew, could have modified the demands of his preaching in order to yield and avoid a horrible death, threatened at the time by the

Governor of Patras. Yet he preferred the eternal glory of the Lord instead of any fleeting compromise, "considering the abuse that he suffered for Christ to be greater wealth" (Heb. 11:26). It is he who today calls all Christians, and especially ecclesiastical leaders and shepherds, "to choose rather to share ill-treatment with the people of God than to enjoy the fleeting pleasures of sin" (Heb. 11:26).

Today's celebration is an invitation extended to both our Churches to the unity of the Cross. Just as our Lord Jesus Christ stretched out His arms upon the Cross, uniting all that was formerly divided, so also His Apostle, in imitation of the Master, stretched out his arms, gathering us all today and calling us to stretch out our arms upon the Cross spiritually in order to achieve the unity that we desire.

Elder Rome has the foremost St. Peter as its Apostle and Patron. New Rome, Constantinople, has the brother of St. Peter, the first-called of the Apostles, Andrew. Both invite us to the fraternal unity that they shared with each other and that can only be acquired when the Cross becomes our point of reference and experience of approach.

Let us, therefore, beseech these two brothers and great Apostles that they may grant peace to the world and lead everyone to unity, in accordance with the particularly timely *troparion* today of Saint Symeon Metaphrastes, Archbishop of Thessalonika:

You, Andrew, were first-called of the Apostles;
Peter was supremely honored among the Apostles.
Both of you endured the Cross of Christ,
Proving imitators of Your Lord and Master,
And one in mind and soul. Therefore, with Him,
As brothers, grant peace to us. Amen.[11]

On November 30, 2007, after the concelebrated Divine Liturgy at Saint George's Cathedral, Cardinal Walter Kasper, President of the Pontifical Council for Promoting Christian Unity, after he presented the Patriarch with a signed copy of the recent papal encyclical *Spe Salvi,* read the following message on behalf of Pope Benedict XVI:

11. *Ecumenical Patriarch Delivers Greetings to Vatican Delegation on Feast of Saint Andrew the Apostle.* Order of Saint Andrew the Apostle, Archons of the Ecumenical Patriarchate. http://archons.org/news/detail.asp?id=192.

To His Holiness Bartholomaios I, Archbishop of Constantinople, Ecumenical Patriarch,

The feast of Saint Andrew the Apostle, brother of Peter and Patron of the Ecumenical Patriarchate, gives me the opportunity to convey to Your Holiness my prayerful good wishes for an abundance of spiritual gifts and divine blessings.

Rejoice in the Lord, always; again I will say, Rejoice! (Phil. 4:4)

These words of Saint Paul inspire us to share our joy on this happy occasion. The feast of Saint Andrew, like that of Saints Peter and Paul, has enabled us each year to express our common apostolic faith, our union in prayer and our joint commitment to reinforce the communion between us. A delegation from the Holy See, led by my venerable brother Cardinal Walter Kasper, President of the Pontifical Council for Promoting Christian Unity, will attend the solemn Divine Liturgy presided over by Your Holiness together with members of the Holy Synod. In my heart I vividly recall my personal participation last year in the celebration of this feast at the Ecumenical Patriarchate and I remember with deep gratitude the warm welcome extended to me on that occasion. That encounter, the presence of my delegate this year at the Phanar, as well as the visit from a delegation of the See of Constantinople for the feast of Saints Peter and Paul in Rome, all represent authentic signs of the commitment of our Churches to an ever deeper communion, strengthened through cordial personal relations, prayer and the dialogue of charity and truth.

This year we thank God in particular for the meeting of the Joint Commission which took place in Ravenna, a city whose monuments speak eloquently of the ancient Byzantine heritage handed down from the undivided Church of the first millennium. May the splendour of those mosaics inspire all the members of the Joint Commission to pursue their important task with renewed determination, in fidelity to the Gospel and to Tradition, ever alert to the promptings of the Holy Spirit in the Church today.

While the meeting in Ravenna was not without its difficulties, I pray earnestly that these may soon be clarified and resolved, so that there may be full participation in the Eleventh Plenary Session and in subsequent initiatives aimed at continuing the theological dialogue in mutual charity and understanding. Indeed, our work toward unity is according to the will of Christ our Lord. In these early years of the third millennium, our efforts are all the more urgent because of the many challenges facing all Christians, to which we need to respond with a united voice and with conviction.

I therefore wish to assure you once more of the Catholic Church's commitment to nurture fraternal ecclesial relations and to persevere in our theological dialogue in order to draw closer to full communion, as stated in our Common Declaration issued last year at the conclusion of my visit to Your Holiness.

Once again we take our inspiration from Saint Paul's words to the Christians of Philippi, with which he urges them to seek perfection through the imitation of Christ, and reminds them to hold true to what we have attained (Phil. 3:16).

With these sentiments of fraternal affection in the Lord, I embrace Your Holiness and all the members of the Holy Synod. I greet also the Orthodox faithful, praying that the peace and the grace of the Lord may be with you all.

From the Vatican, 23 November 2007
Benedictus PP. XVI.[12]

Both of these recent statements are a renewal of the commitment of both Church leaders to continue the dialogue of charity and truth. Both of them recognize the difficulties they have to face courageously, with the hope that the difficulties will vanish in due time. However, both Church leaders are very much aware of the human imperfections and shortcomings that do not allow us to advance as much as we would like. I do remember Patriarch Athenagoras of blessed memory, who answered thus the question: What separates East and West? The response was: "Nine centuries of separation!" We can be as optimistic as the late Patriarch, and pray to the Lord to make what is impossible for men, possible for him. Meanwhile, we have important statements in our recent past, due to eminent Church leaders that the Lord has sent to his Church. We have seen them in the preceding pages. We can hope for the best.

To the question — how will the theology of Cardinal Joseph Ratzinger

---

12. *Pope Benedict XVI Sends Greetings to Ecumenical Patriarch on the Feast of Saint Andrew the Apostle.* Order of Saint Andrew the Apostle, Archons of the Ecumenical Patriarchate. http://archons.org/news/detail.asp?id=193.

influence his pontificate? — the answer is a very positive one, judging by his actions and by his very Christian and Apostolic words. The unity between Eastern and Western Christianity may soon become a reality — if not during the lifetime of those of us now living, at least in a few more decades of Christian life and mission — if the two Churches, Eastern and Western, continue to press towards this goal.

6 Of Like Passion:
A Pentecostal Appreciation
of Benedict XVI

CHERYL BRIDGES JOHNS

Things are not always the way they appear, and people are not always the way they are caricatured. Many Protestants have embraced an image of Joseph Cardinal Ratzinger, now Benedict XVI, as an ultraconservative who, as the author of *Dominus Iesus,* sought to withdraw from many of the ecumenical strides of post–Vatican II Roman Catholicism. Pentecostals, fearful of a retreat to the days when "sectarian" defined their identity in the eyes of the Roman Catholic hierarchy, and not knowing the new pontiff, were cautious of Ratzinger's election. In spite of over thirty years of international dialogue between Roman Catholics and Pentecostals, there are many places in the world where relations between the two groups are tenuous at best. And while strides have been made toward mutual understanding and common witness, there are still polemics on both sides.

Pentecostals, too, have been caricatured. We are viewed as proselytizers, "rapacious wolves" who steal sheep from other Christian traditions, and as zealous but lacking in theological depth. For this reason, Cardinal Kasper's appeal for Catholics to engage in a "self-critical inquiry" regarding Pentecostals has been welcomed as an open and honest move toward true mutual engagement.

As is often the case, caricatures have some element of truth, but are often deeply flawed. As Prefect of the Congregation for the Doctrine of the Faith, Cardinal Ratzinger was zealous in reeling in those he considered to be teaching contrary to the truth. The silencing of liberation theologian Leonardo Boff is but one example of Ratzinger's exercise of Magisterium power. For the sake of "truth" over "praxis," the Prefect was willing to make himself a lightning rod of controversy and criticism.

As a Pentecostal theologian and ecumenist I have come to believe that while Benedict XVI seeks to conserve doctrine and to make clear the ecumenical boundaries, he is not of the temperament to stir up religious wars or to denigrate other Christians. In fact, in reading a small portion of his many writings and lectures, I have discovered a person who is driven by a vision of love. Benedict is indeed first and foremost a scholar with a keen mind and a penchant for preciseness. This often masks the deep passion that fuels his vocation as a scholar, prefect, and now Bishop of Rome.

It was no accident, therefore, that for his first papal encyclical, Benedict chose to write on love. *Deus Caritas Est* reveals that Benedict's passion is a cord woven together with three strands: love for Christ, love for Christ's church, and love for the truth of the gospel. These three loves flow together as a unified passion that, while on one hand is non-negotiable and tight in its logic, on the other hand is open to dialogue, not only with other Christians, but with those who claim no faith. Like Benedict XIV (1740-1758), himself an intellectual who offered himself in dialogue with Voltaire, so too Benedict XVI seeks to engage others in reasoned conversation.

Such willingness to dialogue is vitally important, especially within the landscape of today's religious landscape. Sociologists of religion point out that the face of world Christianity is rapidly changing. It is no longer a religion found predominantly in the Western world; instead, the axis of Christianity has shifted to the global south. Here the two dominant Christian groups are Roman Catholics and Pentecostals. Indeed, Christianity of the twenty-first century looks very different from that of a century ago. The typical Christian today is non-white, young, poor, and female. She most likely lives not in Geneva or Rome but in a mega-city found within the majority world. Her Christianity looks very different from her North American counterparts, and her questions are posed from the position of one who looks to Christ as her only hope.

In many ways Christianity's two largest bodies are intersecting more than ever. In places such as Africa, Roman Catholicism is "pentecostalized," with emphasis on miracles, visions, and dreams. Charismatic movements within Roman Catholicism are growing at a steady rate. In Europe and in the United States Pentecostals are finding a home in the ancient creeds and liturgies of the church. However, it must be admitted that on the whole there is much work to be done toward mutual understanding and joint evangelization. There is a pressing need to do this work. Europe is ever more secular and needs to be re-evangelized, and in countries such as Brazil, more people are choosing alternatives — not only to Roman Catholicism, but to Christianity.

Several years ago the Roman Catholic–Pentecostal International Dialogue was held at a Protestant retreat center in Europe that had originally been a monastery and church founded by Cistercian missionaries. The dialogue meeting occurred at the same time that another group was exploring pre-Christian spirituality. At times I would catch glimpses of their gatherings, and I was fascinated by their attempts to find spirituality in neo-pagan rituals. During the course of the week I often thought about how ironic is was that while we were debating the great gulf between Pentecostals and Roman Catholics, next door to us were people who had abandoned Christianity altogether. Another irony was how our task was becoming similar to that of the Cistercian missionaries who first sought to evangelize Europe.

Today, more than ever, Roman Catholics and Pentecostals face a huge challenge of "Handing On the Faith in an Age of Disbelief."[1] It is important, therefore, that we at least acknowledge our like passion: passion for Christ, passion for the church, and passion for the truth of the gospel that brings good news to a hurting world.

Passion for Christ

Benedict's theology is explicitly christocentric. It was no accident that he chose as his theme for the papal visit to the United States "Christ Our Hope." Benedict's vision of Christ extends as far as the cosmos, but it draws near and penetrates deep within the human heart in Eucharistic union. At the heart of creation is the eternal *Logos* who fills the universe with his power and presence. "Life is not a simple product of laws and the randomness of matter," observes Benedict, "but within everything and at the same time above everything, there is a personal will, there is a Spirit who in Jesus has revealed himself as Love."[2]

The *Logos* is both the philosophical and Eucharistic center of Bene-

---

1. See Joseph Cardinal Ratzinger, with Archbishop Dermot J. Ryan, Godfried Cardinal Danneels, and Franciszek Cardinal Macharski, *Handing on the Faith in an Age of Disbelief* (San Francisco: Ignatius Press, 2006).

2. *Spe Salvi*, 5.

dict's theology. At this center, reason and love are joined in a unified passion. In Christ, the eternal wisdom, there is grounding for all human wisdom. Thus, "Christianity has understood itself to be the religion of the *Logos,* to be a religion in keeping with reason."[3] Moreover, in Christ, the *Logos* becomes "food for us — as love," Benedict observes. Furthermore, he notes that in the Eucharist, "more than just statically receiving the incarnate *Logos,* we enter into the very dynamic of his self-giving."[4] Herein there is union with God, the creator of the universe who through the self-giving of Jesus' body and blood joins himself to humanity.

The goal of the Christian faith, therefore, is not merely justification. It is union with God through Jesus. It involves a "sacramental mysticism" wherein there is oneness, a "sharing in Jesus' self gift, sharing in his body and blood."[5] This union produces not only the fruit of love, it provides a grounding for knowledge and ethics. Christ, the *Logos,* holds together the tension between reason and love, the universal and the personal, philosophy and theology, the church and the world.

Pentecostals share Benedict's passion for Christ. They would concur that at the heart of the Christian faith is the living Jesus who has made God's love known to humanity. What many people do not realize is that throughout its short history, and especially in its early period, Pentecostalism was decidedly christocentric rather than pneumatocentric. Many preached what is known as the fivefold gospel: Jesus as Savior, Sanctifier, Baptizer, Healer, and Coming King. Christ's presence and power is thus the focal point of Pentecostal worship and life.

While many Pentecostals would agree with Benedict that union with Christ is realized concretely, they would not conceive of this union as being centered on the Eucharist alone as the *communio portal.* Rather, they would envision union and communion with Christ as pneumatically constituted and found wherever faith is being manifest.

Knowledge of Christ, for Pentecostals, also involves a "sacramental mysticism," and the goal of relationship with Christ is seen as union and communion rather than merely forensic justification. For Pentecostals, "sacramental mysticism" is created by the presence of the Holy Spirit, who

3. Joseph Ratzinger, *Christianity and the Crisis of Cultures* (San Francisco: Ignatius Press, 2006), p. 47.

4. *Deus Caritas Est,* 13.

5. *Deus Caritas Est,* 13.

brings the presence of Christ into human history. Congregational worship thus becomes "thin space" wherein Christ comes directly to the believers, bringing salvation, healing, and his baptism of fire. Sacramental mysticism is achieved by the power of the Holy Spirit to the degree that even the most common space becomes sacred. Common people are sanctified, common tongues become tongues of fire, and Christ is made known in the preached word and in glossolalia.

What Pentecostal sacramentalism misses is how to integrate the Eucharistic presence into this dynamic. While Pentecostals show respect and reverence for what is often called "communion," they fail to appreciate how Eucharistic power and presence are a vital aspect of Christian worship. Some Pentecostal theologians are calling for Pentecostals to appropriate the power of the Eucharist as the focal point of their worship. Pentecostal theologian Simon Chan wants Pentecostals to locate the *repeatable* events of the Spirit's in-filling in the Eucharist. He observes that as the Holy Spirit is evoked during the *epiclesis,* Pentecostals could envision Holy Communion as an opportunity for a "powerful manifestation of God."[6]

Trinitarian Oneness

In regards to the nature of the Trinity, Benedict again places love as the central point of theological reflection. The triune God, "Love itself — the uncreated, eternal God — must therefore be in the highest degree a mystery — 'the' *mysterium* itself."[7] This triune God exists in "pure relation, pure unity," and Christ's prayer for his disciples is for that unity and relation to be extended to believers. Just as Christ "is a completely open being, a being 'from' and 'towards,' that nowhere clings to itself and nowhere stands on its own," so too "being a Christian means being like the Son, becoming a son; that is, not standing on one's own and in oneself, but living completely open in the 'from' and 'towards.'"[8] Therefore, being with Christ would mean that a Christian would "want to hold on to nothing of its own indi-

6. Simon Chan, *Pentecostal Theology and the Christian Spiritual Tradition* (Sheffield, UK: Sheffield Academic Press, 1993), p. 94.

7. Joseph Ratzinger, *Introduction to Christianity* (New York: Herder & Herder, 1970), p. 114.

8. Ratzinger, *Introduction to Christianity,* p. 134.

viduality (cf. — also Phil. 2.6f.)."[9] For Benedict "it is the nature of the Trinitarian personality to be pure relation and so the most absolute unity."[10]

The stress on the unity of the triune God over against diversity, and the oneness of Christ with the Father stand as the linchpin for Benedict's vision of the Christian life. As Miroslav Volf points out in his critique of Ratzinger, "*all* the crucial elements in his ecclesiology and entire theology are rooted in the doctrine of the Trinity."[11] It is important to note the emphasis that Benedict places on the self-emptying of Christ, who is being "from" and "towards," who nowhere clings to himself and nowhere stands on his own. This Christ serves as the fountain for all who belong to him in their own self-emptying and being towards others. The "I" of the Christian is dissolved into the unity of the body of Christ just as the "I" of Christ is dissolved into the unity of the triune life. Furthermore, the "I" is freely given towards others and not reserved for itself. Thus, the Christian life is one of unity and self-emptying service.

In an age when individuality is stressed over community, diversity over unity, and self-fulfillment over self-emptying, Benedict's passion for oneness is an important corrective. The Pentecostal tradition has been victim to the hyper-individualization and privatization of the faith. It has often preached a gospel that stresses the personal benefits of salvation to the exclusion of the power of the gospel to draw persons into the triune life and into a life characterized by self-emptying for the sake of others. On the other hand, many Pentecostals would concur with Volf's assessment that Ratzinger's vision of the triune life overemphasizes the one substance of the Trinity at the expense of the three relations. Furthermore, Pentecostals would make pneumatology more prominent than does Benedict, especially in regards to how the triune life intersects with human life. The life of God, while self-emptying into Jesus of Nazareth, also extends to humanity in the person and presence of the Holy Spirit. This embrace creates a unity, but it also empowers the "I" to be a subject and to act as agent of God in the world. The empowered "I" can know God, speak for God, and be a vessel of miracles, continuing the work of Jesus on the earth. This empowerment is a critical element of Pentecostal soteriology.

9. Ratzinger, *Introduction to Christianity*, p. 135.
10. Ratzinger, *Introduction to Christianity*, p. 135.
11. Miroslav Volf, *After Our Likeness: The Church as the Image of the Trinity* (Grand Rapids: Eerdmans, 1998), p. 67.

Passion for the Church: Christ's Body

For Benedict, the heart of God is poured out in love through the incarnate Christ, and the heart of Christ is poured out in love through his body, the church. The church is the presence of Christ in such a way that it embodies the mystery of the divine life. The church is not merely a vehicle for the presence of Christ; it is in sacramental mysticism the real body of Christ.

Inasmuch as the goal of sacramental mysticism is "union with God through sharing in Jesus' self gift, sharing in his body and blood,"[12] it follows to reason that "union with Christ is also union with all to whom he gives himself . . . we become 'one body,' completely joined in a single existence."[13]

For Benedict the church is a collective subject whose *communio* supersedes any personal communion with God. The individual becomes part of the one believing subject and receives from this subject a "guarantee" of the divine presence. This "guarantee" comes from the sacramental communality of the mediation of faith as it exists in both the local and universal expressions under the ministry of the bishops. "When I say, 'I believe,'" notes Benedict, "then this means precisely that I am going beyond the limits of my private subjectivity as to enter into the collective subject of the Church and, in her, to enter into the knowledge that transcends the ages and the limits of time."[14]

Because the church is the "guarantee" of the presence of God, the believer is first and foremost called on "to receive" that which is mysteriously held in the arms of mother church. The act of faith, therefore, is the act of receiving. To believe as a Christian "means in fact entrusting oneself to the meaning which bears up me and the world."[15] Furthermore, "it means affirming that the meaning which we do not make but can only receive is already granted to us, so that we have only to take it and entrust ourselves to it."[16]

The believer, as one who receives, is thus seen as an object of God's grace, a grace channeled through the church. The human as subject or maker in the world and over the world is eclipsed by the human who first

12. *Deus Caritas Est*, 13.
13. *Deus Caritas Est*, 13.
14. Ratzinger et al., *Handing on the Faith*, p. 25.
15. *Deus Caritas Est*, 13.
16. *Deus Caritas Est*, 13.

is object — the receiver. Although Benedict makes it clear that the entire worshiping community is the subject of the liturgical event inasmuch as it makes Christ, *the* subject of the church, present, there is still a sense that the subject is one who "receives" over "making." In addition, because there is the one subject of the *communio sanctorum* of all places and all times, individual communities should not fashion their own liturgy, but should mirror that which is found in the church as a whole.[17] For it is this whole that "guarantees and demonstrates that something more and greater is taking place here . . . than human beings could ever do on their own; as such, it expresses the objective empowerment for joy and participation in the cosmic drama of Christ's resurrection, with which the status of the liturgy stands or falls."[18]

This "primacy of reception" is especially problematic for Pentecostals on several fronts. Pentecostals would acknowledge with most Protestants that salvation is by faith and to be received, not earned (we are to be objects of grace). However, there is inherent within the Pentecostal movement a strong sense that the church as pneumatically constituted offers through the *charismata* not necessarily a democratization of the church, but certainly an empowerment of people to be subjects who make as well as receive.

Pentecostals would conceive of the Holy Spirit as creating the church and sustaining its life in Christ. Therefore, ecclesiology is to be understood in light of pneumatology and not vice versa. The real presence of Christ in Eucharistic celebration, in the preached word, and in the other liturgical events of the church is guaranteed by the Holy Spirit. Likewise, it is the Holy Spirit who as the author of Scripture makes Scripture a living witness to the revelation of God. It is the Holy Spirit, distributing gifts within the church, who makes human vessels sacred instruments of grace. In this sense, the receiving and the making are twin moments. The Holy Spirit thus does more than "animate" the sacramental actions of the church (as if the Spirit is somehow obligated to be present because the institution has been established). Rather, as Volf points out, the institutional church is a "product" of the Spirit, thereby giving the Spirit the role of key director in *an open ecclesial process.* Therefore, "the pluriform ecclesial ministries actually derive from the sovereign Holy Spirit present both in individuals

17. "Liturgie und Kirchenmusik," *Internationale Katholische Zeitschrift "Communio"* 15 (1986): 249.
18. Ratzinger, *Das Fest des Glaubens,* 60, quoted in Volf, *After Our Likeness,* p. 64.

and in the congregation as a whole as the first-fruits of the eschatological reign of peace."[19]

In areas of great oppression and human suffering, the empowerment of persons as subjects through an open ecclesial process is a critical element of Pentecostalism's rapid growth. In many places Pentecostalism has taken the "church from below" identity in place of liberation theology. During the 1980s Cardinal Ratzinger's ongoing critical engagement with liberation theologians centered on his fears of Marxist ideology, with its materialistic dialectic replacing Christian truth. As early as *Introduction to Christianity* he is critical of the "historicization" of God, wherein meaning is "no longer simply the creator of history, instead, history becomes the creator of meaning and the latter becomes its creation."[20] Along with this criticism is his fear that liberation theology's emphasis on historical action toward the liberation from oppressive structures would ultimately strip Christianity of its eschatological vision. Human forms of utopia are unable to deliver from the "radical slavery of sin," something that can only be done by the "gifts of grace." Ratzinger pointed out that, in the long run, those who champion freedom create their own forms of totalitarianism.

His passion for the church also fueled Ratzinger's criticisms of liberation theology. For him, *the truth about the church* was in danger of being lost to social visions of the church's role. Defending his intervention and silencing of liberation theologians such as Leonardo Boff, Ratzinger observes: "It is in the name of the truth about man, created in the image of God, that the Church has intervened. Her hierarchical constitution is said to be opposed to equality, her Magisterium to be opposed to freedom of thought. It is true that there have been errors of judgment and serious omissions for which Christians have been responsible in the course of the centuries."[21] However, Ratzinger goes on the defensive: "but these objections disregard the true nature of things. The diversity of charisms in the people of God, which are charisms of service, is not opposed to the equal dignity of persons and to their common vocation of holiness."[22] In other words, for Ratzinger the Magisterium of the church is God's gift for correction and guidance over against historical movements that while having

---

19. Volf, *After Our Likeness*, p. 243.
20. Ratzinger, *Introduction to Christianity*, p. 120.
21. "Instruction on Christian Freedom and Liberation," 20.
22. "Instruction on Christian Freedom and Liberation," 20.

good intentions, seek to draw the church into human utopias. Therefore, the church from below becomes a church lost in history and at the mercy of class struggles and agendas. Hence, the dualism necessary for the church to be separate from the world goes missing and the church loses its eschatological vision.

Boff's insistence that it is ultimately the life of the Spirit in the church that is the last word for correction and guidance was a direct challenge to the hierarchical structures of Roman Catholicism. These structures, for Ratzinger, are not optional models of church; rather they reflect the Divine image and the life of Christ in the world.

Ratzinger not only disagreed with liberation theologians regarding the nature of the mission of the church in society; he expressed strong concerns over the epistemology of praxis. For him, the emphasis on praxis represented a "*partisan* consciousness" that called into question the concept of truth itself. This is because "the fundamental structure of history is characterized by *class-struggle*."[23] In this situation "the truth is a truth of class: there is no truth but the truth in the struggle of the revolutionary class."[24]

Moreover, for Ratzinger, when praxis is placed over truth, method is viewed as superior to content and anthropology stands above theology. With this "radical anthropocentrism" the center of gravity shifts to a primacy of experience as the "measure for one's understanding of the faith heritage."[25]

Pentecostalism suffers criticism from liberation theology precisely because of its eschatological vision that insists on the need for God to intervene in human history as the Subject who moves in history and the Subject over history. What appears to the critics as an "opiate" and an "escapist" form of Christianity is in actuality quite the opposite. Instead of escaping from the world, Pentecostal churches offer a means whereby the chaos, oppression, and evil found in the world can be taken into the sacred circle and tamed.[26]

Richard Shaull, one of the grandfathers of liberation theology and an architect of the base communities in Brazil during the 1960s, devoted the

23. "Instruction on 'Theology of Liberation,'" VIII.5.
24. "Instruction on 'Theology of Liberation,'" VIII.5.
25. Ratzinger et al., *Handing on the Faith*, p. 16.
26. Harvey Cox, *Fire from Heaven: The Rise of Pentecostal Spirituality and the Reshaping of Religion in the Twenty-First Century* (Reading, MA: Addison-Wesley, 1995), p. 120.

last years of his life to researching Pentecostalism. He was fascinated by the exodus of the poor from base communities to Pentecostal churches. What he found surprised him and caused him to reconsider his own presuppositions. According to Shaull, the key distinctive of Pentecostalism is its ability to offer "the reconstruction of life in the power of the Spirit."[27] In his research among Brazilian Pentecostals, Richard Shaull found that people living in desperate situations were less inclined than previous generations to turn to or trust in ideologies or political movements for their liberation. After years of disappointments, many have come to the conclusion that "they cannot count on any merely human movement to rescue them; their only hope lies in a Power beyond themselves."[28] Traditional Roman Catholicism failed to offer this power, as did the base communities.

From his research Shaull concluded that Pentecostalism offered "something I and my communities of faith did not have and thus could not offer."[29] He notes, "God is experienced intimately and intensely as broken lives are reorganized, as those considered 'worthless' and 'insignificant' discover their worth before God, and as those who thought they could do nothing to change their situation or the world are empowered to act."[30] Furthermore, "this reality is communicated, not by a rational word or doctrinal exposition, but by a ritual of praise and worship."[31]

This open ecclesial process has the ability to offer a unique dialectic of receiving and making. Persons whose lives are trapped in a vicious circle of oppression, violence, and addictions receive the grace of God as objects. However, they are further empowered through the Spirit-led and infused liturgy to act and to speak as subjects, not only in the worshiping community through the distribution of gifts, but in daily life as agents of God in the world. This is a conscientization initiated and maintained by a transforming encounter with God, "which prefigures the corresponding historical action."[32] Eschatological conscientization keeps what Ratzinger was insistent on, namely, the otherness of God and the kingdom of God over

27. Richard Shaull and Waldo Cesar, *Pentecostalism and the Future of the Christian Churches* (Grand Rapids: Eerdmans, 2000).

28. Shaull, *Pentecostalism and the Future of the Christian Churches*, p. 117.

29. Shaull, *Pentecostalism and the Future of the Christian Churches*, p. 118.

30. Shaull, *Pentecostalism and the Future of the Christian Churches*, p. 146.

31. Shaull, *Pentecostalism and the Future of the Christian Churches*, p. 146.

32. Cheryl Bridges Johns, *Pentecostal Formation: A Pedagogy Among the Oppressed* (Sheffield, UK: Sheffield Academic Press, 1993), p. 65.

against human history. This eschatological vision does not remove one from human history; rather it re-figures historical action into a discerning vocation of leading a Spirit-filled life.

For many women, especially in countries in Latin America, the empowerment of the Spirit to be a historical subject is a critical element in their move from Roman Catholicism to Pentecostalism. For them, it is not enough "to receive"; they desired to "make" history and to be agents on both the ordained and lay level. They reject the image of woman as patient in the face of enduring hardship. They do not see that it is their unique role to mirror Mary as she is portrayed by Benedict with "her dispositions of listening, welcoming, humility, faithfulness, praise and waiting."[33] They would question how women are to particularly mirror the church's role of "receiving" as the Bride of Christ. Instead, they are empowered not only to image the Bride of Christ (as are all Christians); they are to image Christ in the world. These strong women wear "spirited vestments" that give them an ontological identity as priests and prophets. They are thus free to act, to lead as pastors and bishops, and to engage in spiritual warfare.

In the majority world, faith communities are often the vital centers of believers' lives. These outposts of the kingdom offer a *communio sancto* over against a profane and often violent world. Corporate worship is practiced daily, and the communion of saints supersedes all other relationships. "Brothers" and "sisters" in the Christian family define identity. The corporate identity and the oneness between Christ and the church are fueled by a passion for the kingdom.

In North America, however, the Pentecostal tradition is in danger of individualization and the loss of the true communion. An open ecclesial process married to a culture of narcissism has reaped bitter fruit of hyperindividualism, departure from Scripture and tradition, and the collapse of the Christian faith into extreme patriotism. Here the passion of Benedict for the oneness of the church and its timeless organic unity with Christ is an important corrective.

In light of this lack of ecclesial identity among Pentecostals, Simon Chan calls for adoption of an "ecclesial pneumatology" rather than an "individual pneumatology." Here the primary focus of the work of the Spirit is not in the individual Christian but in the church. For Chan, "to be bap-

33. "Letter to the Bishops of the Catholic Church on the Collaboration of Men and Women in the Church and in the World," 16.

tized into Christ is to be incorporated into a Spirit-filled, Spirit-empowered entity."[34] A "pneumatic ecclesiology" would merge a "church from below," that empowers people as historical agents, with a "church from above," that would stress the sacramental mystery of the entity as a whole.

At his episcopal ordination as Archbishop of Munich on the Vigil of Pentecost, May 28, 1977, Ratzinger expressed his passion for the church: "All of us long for a pentecostal church in which the Spirit rules, and not the letter; a church in which understanding breaks down the fences we erect against each other. We are impatient with a church that seems so unpentecostal, so unspiritual, so narrow and fearful." Pentecostals would join in like passion for such a church.

A Passion for Truth

It is Benedict's love for truth that receives much of his energy and time, and it is this passion, above all else, that has generated the most controversy. For him, the church must take a stand for truth over against an ever-encroaching relativism. Speaking out of his disappointment regarding the preamble to the European Constitution, Benedict criticizes the "relativism, which is the starting point of this whole process." Relativism blindly "becomes dogmatism that believes itself in possession of the definitive knowledge of human reason."[35] For Benedict, Europe's disregard of its foundation in Christian truth has created a culture that "in a manner hitherto unknown to mankind, excludes God from public awareness."[36] The result of the banishment of God to the realm of subjective choices is a "purely functional rationality that has shaken the moral consciousness in a way completely unknown to the cultures that existed previously."[37] In this context the concept of truth vanishes and nothing is seen as good or evil in itself.

For Benedict it is the *Logos* which serves as the source of truth. "Christianity," observes Benedict, "must always remember that it is the religion of the *Logos*. It is faith in the '*Creator Spiritus*,' in the Creator Spirit from

---

34. Chan, *Pentecostal Theology*, p. 99.
35. Ratzinger, *Christianity and the Crisis of Cultures*, p. 45.
36. Ratzinger, *Christianity and the Crisis of Cultures*, p. 30.
37. Ratzinger, *Christianity and the Crisis of Cultures*, p. 30.

which proceeds everything that exists."[38] This is precisely Christianity's philosophical strength. Truth is thus grounded in a timeless and transcendent source that stands over against relativism.

Because truth is grounded in the eternal *Logos* to which the church is mysteriously and sacramentally joined, it is the church's vocation to be the witness to and faithful protector of truth. She does this both internally through catechesis, and externally by proclaiming the gospel and by contributing "to the purification of reason and to the reawakening of those moral forces without which just structures are neither established nor prove effective in the long run."[39]

While affirming that religion must continually be purified by reason, Ratzinger pointed out that "reason too, must be warned to keep within its proper limits, and it must learn a willingness to listen to the great traditions of mankind."[40] Hence, there is to be a dialectical relationship between religion and secular philosophy. In 2004 in his dialogue with Ratzinger regarding the "Pre-political Moral Foundations of a Free State," Jürgen Habermas noted that "the expectation that there will be continuing disagreement between faith and knowledge deserves to be called 'rational' only when secular knowledge, too, grants that religious convictions have an epistemological status that is not purely and simply irrational."[41] In this dialogue Ratzinger, while acknowledging the often destructive force of religion in the world, called the reliability of reason into question. It is human reason, he pointed out, that created the atomic bomb and it is human ingenuity that has made human genetics a matter of selection.

Pentecostals would affirm that reason should be purified. The human mind, while serving as the guiding agent in historical action, is under the effect of sin. Critical reasoning, however astute, is subject to the will to power and self-interest over against the good of humankind. The power of sin can make the irrational appear rational and can justify evil. Ratzinger has called this the "pathologies of reason."[42]

38. "Christian Morality," in *The Essential Pope Benedict XVI*, edited by John Thornton and Susan Varenne (San Francisco: Harper, 2007), p. 334.

39. *Deus Caritas Est*, 29.

40. Ratzinger et al., *Handing on the Faith*, p. 77.

41. "Letter to the Bishops of the Catholic Church on the Collaboration of Men and Women in the Church and the World," 16.

42. Jürgen Habermas and Joseph Ratzinger, *The Dialectics of Secularization* (Freiburg im Breisgau: Herder, 2005), p. 77.

For Pentecostals reason must be purified by the critical agency of the Holy Spirit. In fact, the deconstruction of human reason and language is required. The criticism of the Holy Spirit pushes deep into the human psyche, exposing the epiphanies of darkness that surround the fabric of human existence. Such criticism calls for the emergence of a "new subject" whose mind is participatory with the mind of the Spirit. Discernment becomes a critical epistemological mode that, while employing human reason, submits it to an ever more critical agency. In this sense, glossolalia signifies the limits of human discourse and reason. It symbolizes the reversing of Babel into a new order of creation. The mind is renewed and becomes a "participatory mind" purified of its self-willed agendas and its darkened understanding, and thus able to express itself in all forms of human knowledge.

There is currently a great deal of speculation regarding the demise of what has been called "the Protestant era." This epoch, following the Reformation and the Enlightenment, brought to humanity the gifts of liberation from "ecclesiastical servitude" and the democratization of political life in both the religious and secular spheres. But it has also been an era that has witnessed the rise of a secularity devoid of any religious underpinnings. It has been during this era that nature has been stripped of its sacramental status and human life has become a commodity. In light of this dilemma, one he was already beginning to observe in 1948, Paul Tillich called for a dialectical relation between the secular world and the "Gestalt of grace."[43] While he hoped for a continuation of the Protestant era, he tempered it with a call for a renewed sense of "theonomy." His meaning of the word conveyed the creation of "a culture in which the ultimate meaning of existence shines through all finite forms of thought and action; the culture is transparent, and its creations are vessels of a spiritual content."[44]

In many ways the Pentecostal movement signals an end to the Protestant era. It points toward a re-enchanting not only of Christianity, but of the natural world. In light of this, perhaps Pentecostals and Catholics together can offer a new theonomy that fills the spiritual void left behind by secularization. Together we can move forward toward a vision of life as sacred, one in which it is possible for humanity to live as "inspired flesh," holy unto the Lord. With the Eucharist as the symbol of "divinized flesh," we could together offer hope for a world collapsing into itself in despair.

43. Paul Tillich, *The Protestant Era* (Chicago: University of Chicago Press, 1948), p. 207.
44. Tillich, *The Protestant Era,* p. xvi.

Finally, it is impossible to speak about the nature of truth without addressing the role of Scripture as a primary normative agent in knowing the one who is "the way, and the truth, and the life" (John 14:6). Pentecostals are closer to Benedict's understanding of the organic unity of the Bible and the church than most Protestants. Both Pentecostals and Benedict see the Bible as part of a larger, "perpetually inexhaustible process of revelation." However, Benedict would give the "copyright of the Bible" to the church because the Bible is "part of a living organism, through which it came into being in the first place."[45] Pentecostals would counter that the Holy Spirit retains the copyright, all the while making present the Word within the church. The church would therefore be a steward of the Word.

It is also important for Pentecostals to see a close connection between Spirit and Word. The fusion of Spirit-Word makes Scripture alive and present, transcending time and space. It convicts of truth. Steven Land points out that for Pentecostals the relationship between Spirit and Word "is based on that of the Spirit to Christ. Even as the Spirit formed Christ in Mary, so the Spirit uses Scripture to form Christ in believers and vice versa."[46]

Furthermore, for Pentecostals the Spirit's work is not limited to illuminating the Scriptures (as is the case in much of Evangelicalism). The Word exists dynamically within the church. Often, however, Spirit-Word becomes highly individualized and free from the judgment of the church. In light of this, Chan observes that the dynamic presence of the Word means "that connection between Christ the Truth, the Head of the Church, and the tradition of the church is far more profound than is usually acknowledged in Protestantism."[47] He calls for a more adequate approach that locates the Spirit-Word within the ecclesial community and the Eucharistic event in order "to avoid illuminism and retain the dynamism of the Word."[48] Furthermore, according to Chan, "only within their ecclesial location can Spirit and Word retain their dynamism and continuity. Christ as the truth in the church is realized in the Eucharist where he is sacramentally present. Christ the truth is made present in the church by the action of the Spirit in the preaching of the Word and in the sacrament."[49]

45. Ratzinger et al., *Handing on the Faith*, p. 31.
46. Steven J. Land, *Pentecostal Spirituality: A Passion for the Kingdom* (Sheffield, UK: Sheffield Academic Press, 1993), pp. 100-101.
47. Chan, *Pentecostal Theology*, p. 106.
48. Chan, *Pentecostal Theology*, p. 107.
49. Chan, *Pentecostal Theology*, p. 107.

Toward a Viable Future

Decades ago Princeton Theological Seminary's President John Mackay, reflecting on the future of Christianity, made a startling statement: "The Christian future may lie with a reformed Catholicism and a mature Pentecostalism."[50] In 1969 few believed his futuristic projection. Now in 2009, while there may be debate as to how much Roman Catholicism has reformed and Pentecostalism has matured, there is little debate as to where the future of Christianity is headed. With a joint passion for Christ, the church, and the gospel, those who have been "erstwhile enemies" may yet learn to truly love each other and offer hope for a hurting world. Then, together, we can say with Pope Benedict, "Christ *our* hope."

50. John Alexander Mackay, *Christian Reality and Appearance* (Richmond, VA: John Knox Press, 1969), pp. 88-89.

7 The Professor, the Prefect, and the Pope: Joseph Ratzinger — A Reformed Appreciation

JOSEPH D. SMALL

Reformed churches, like their Lutheran and Anglican counterparts, have roots in the anti-Catholic polemic of the sixteenth century. In our time, however, both formal condemnations and habitual prejudices have been replaced, for the most part, by openness and appreciation. Recently, Presbyterian and Reformed churches in North America have taken official actions to affirm that anti-Catholic language in their Reformation-era confessions of faith do not apply to the contemporary Catholic Church. Yet, unlike Lutherans, Anglicans, and their descendants, nearly all Reformed churches have remained unalterably opposed to episcopal ordering of the church. Sixteenth-century rhetoric, reinforced by events in Scotland and the Netherlands, and solidified by the minority experience of Reformed communities in Europe and Latin America, have produced continuing suspicion of bishops generally, Catholic episcopacy specifically, and popes most pointedly.

From time to time, anti-episcopal instincts intensify doctrinal differences, bringing to the surface residual Reformed resistance to Catholic thought and life. This was evident in an incident surrounding celebrations of the Holy Year 2000. The Vatican invited the World Alliance of Reformed Churches to be part of an ecumenical committee on the Jubilee, and WARC accepted, appointing as its representative a minister of the Waldensian Church. When it was learned that Pope John Paul II would grant indulgences to Holy Year pilgrims, WARC withdrew from the ecumenical committee and, alone among the world communions, refused to participate in the ceremonial opening of the Holy Door which marked the commencement of the Jubilee Year.

Reformed wariness about episcopal authority and the power of the papacy grew deeper when Joseph Cardinal Ratzinger became Pope Benedict XVI. Long in the public eye, as a theologian at Tübingen and Regensburg, as archbishop in Munich, and, most notably, as prefect of the Congregation for the Doctrine of the Faith, Joseph Ratzinger began his pontificate as a "known commodity." Unlike most popes before him, Benedict XVI was familiar in Protestant as well as Catholic circles before his elevation. His reputation preceded him, and even now, he remains "Ratzinger" to many. Assessment of this known commodity was mixed at best. Sometimes denigrated as "God's Rottweiler," critics conceded that although Joseph Ratzinger was evidently brilliant, he was seen as using his finely honed theological mind in the service of conservative, authoritarian, even repressive Vatican policies. In some circles, the pontificate of Benedict XVI was greeted with apprehension.

Lacking the public charm and charisma of John Paul II, the more distant Benedict XVI was characterized by some as a cold, determined proponent of centralized Vatican hegemony. The Reformed were not alone in ruing Cardinal Ratzinger's inquiry of Hans Küng, Leonardo Boff, Charles Curran, and other prominent Catholic theologians. Protestant progressives bemoaned his opposition to liberation theologies, theologies of religious pluralism, feminism, and other liberal movements. Additionally, as the recognized author of the infamous *Dominus Iesus*, the new pope was assumed to represent a withdrawal from the ecumenical generosity of *Ut Unum Sint*. All of this seemed to confirm innate Reformed distrust of Catholic faith and order.

Yet "all of this" is little more than a political cartoon, a caricature in service of simplified, often uninformed opinion. Benedict XVI began his pontificate as the author of a large body of theological writing that does not lend itself to easy classification, and certainly not to hasty dismissal. Reformed Christians can benefit from careful attention to the Ratzinger corpus, for theological issues that are at the core of his concern are issues that have always been central to the Reformed tradition. Many of the questions that engaged Joseph Ratzinger as professor and as prefect are questions that occupied John Calvin and continue to concern Calvin's heirs. Ratzinger's answers are not always congenial to Reformed faith and life, but even his different conclusions may sharpen Reformed questions and enrich Reformed resolutions.

Scholars who are thoroughly familiar with the thought of Joseph

Ratzinger observe that he has been remarkably consistent in his views, at least since the supposed "conservative turn" in the late 1960s. Nevertheless, it is risky to trace straight lines from professor to prefect to pope. Professors, even professors of Catholic theology, speak and write from a far more personal social location than heads of Vatican congregations and commissions. The constraints on prefects are different from the momentous responsibilities of popes. The professor who wrote *Introduction to Christianity*, the prefect who was responsible for *Dominus Iesus* and *Letter to the Bishops of the Catholic Church on Certain Aspects of the Church as Communion*, and the pope who delivered *Deus Caritas Est* are the same man, yet one whose intellectual work has taken place in different settings and has had different purposes. A professor's books and a prefect's clarifications do not predetermine a pope's encyclicals. Even so, the concerns of a lifetime have not undergone wide swings; consistent themes have been both deepened and focused through immersion in a remarkable ecclesial life.

Truth and the Church

Controversy

Controversy is a common thread woven throughout the career of Professor Ratzinger, the vocation of the cardinal prefect of the Congregation for the Doctrine of the Faith, and the pontificate of Benedict XVI. His prominence throughout the Protestant as well as the Catholic world has often taken the form of notoriety, as his statements and writings have elicited disagreement and even outrage. This has not escaped his attention, of course. He is well aware that some look upon him as "the inquisitor" or "the enforcer." With more than a touch of annoyance, Cardinal Ratzinger noted in 2002 that ". . . it seems nowadays to have become a veritable duty, for theologians who have any self-confidence, to deliver a negative judgment upon documents issued by the Congregation for the Doctrine of the Faith."[1] Controversy has resulted from genuine theological differences, of course, but it is also a consequence of the enduring spirit of the professor

---

1. Joseph Cardinal Ratzinger, "The Ecclesiology of the Constitution *Lumen Gentium*," in *Pilgrim Fellowship of Faith: The Church as Communion* (San Francisco: Ignatius Press, 2005), p. 133.

in the words of the bishop, cardinal, and prefect. "Professor Ratzinger" is a man of evident erudition, but one whose thinking typically reflects an inclination toward academic disputation and sharp debate that virtually invites continuing argument. A scholarly turn of mind that seems always to have opponents in view produces writing that is inherently polemical.

For decades, Joseph Ratzinger has contended with others over the correct interpretation of Vatican II. Thus, the controversy surrounding him has been due, in part, to his position with the Congregation for the Doctrine of the Faith, which afforded him heightened capacity to make his interpretation of the council prevail. But, additionally, he has attracted antagonism and opposition because of his characteristically piercing critique of those with whom he disagrees. The rhetoric of Cardinal Ratzinger is often cutting and dismissive:

> That all-too-guileless progressivism of the first postconciliar years, which happily proclaimed its solidarity with everything modern, with everything that promised progress, and strove with the self-conscious zeal of a model schoolboy to prove the compatibility of what is Christian with all that is modern, to demonstrate the loyalty of Christians to the trends of contemporary life — that progressivism has today come under suspicion of being merely the apotheosis of the late capitalistic bourgeoisie, on which, instead of attacking it critically, it sheds a kind of religious glow.[2]

It is understandable that those on the receiving end of such withering derision would level their own return fire. It is also understandable that those who agree with the cardinal's thought would relish his tone. Thus the controversy moves beyond intellectual disagreement into wider, more public ecclesial arenas.

Ecclesial Truth

The contentious tone of Cardinal Ratzinger's writing is not simply the consequence of an academician's penchant for debate, however. It also re-

---

2. Joseph Ratzinger, *Principles of Catholic Theology: Building Stones for a Fundamental Theology* (San Francisco: Ignatius Press, 1987), p. 56.

flects a churchman's deep passion for the truth of the gospel and its vital importance for the life of the faithful. In a wide-ranging 1984 interview with Vittorio Messori, Cardinal Ratzinger made clear the connection between truth and the well-being of believers: "One should not forget that for the Church faith is a 'common good,' a wealth that belongs to everybody, beginning with the poor who are least protected from distortions. Consequently, the Church sees in the defense of right belief also a social work for the benefit of all believers."[3] Truth matters to the faith and faithfulness of ordinary Christians — to their prayers, their service, and the shape of their lives. The cardinal's commitment to truth is not only the conceptual dedication of a scholar, but also the passionate responsibility of a pastor.

For Joseph Ratzinger, truth is knowable and error is real. Truth and error are not academic categories, but vital distinctions that affect the lives of persons, the life of the Christian community, and the life of entire societies. That is precisely why the theological rights of the church community trump the rights of the individual theologian. In the Messori interview, Cardinal Ratzinger went on to say, "Broad circles in theology seem to have forgotten that the subject who pursues theology is not the individual scholar but the Catholic community as a whole, the entire Church."[4] Because theological work is an ecclesial service before it is private inquiry, the personal work of the individual theologian must always proceed from the church and be directed to the church. Theology, then, "turns to something we ourselves have not devised. . . . The path of theology is indicated by the saying, 'Credo ut intelligam': I accept what is given in advance, in order to find, starting from this and in this, the path to the right way of living, to the right way of understanding myself."[5]

The question of truth goes deeper than the vocation of the theologian; truth is the vocation of the church. This church vocation must be lived fully, for "If the question of truth is no longer being considered, then what religion essentially is, is no longer distinguishable from what it is not; faith is no longer differentiated from superstition, experience from illusion."[6]

3. Joseph Ratzinger, with Vittorio Messori, *The Ratzinger Report* (San Francisco: Ignatius Press, 1985), p. 25.

4. Ratzinger, *The Ratzinger Report*, p. 71.

5. Ratzinger, "What in Fact Is Theology?" in *Pilgrim Fellowship of Faith*, p. 31.

6. Ratzinger, "Presentation of the Declaration *Dominus Iesus*," in *Pilgrim Fellowship of Faith*, p. 213.

The necessity of a community of truth is most apparent — and most vital — in baptism and its necessary complement, the catechumenate. Baptism and the catechumenate are dramatic confirmation of the fact that persons do not and cannot confer faith upon themselves. The decision of faith "is not an isolated and autonomous decision of the subject, but is essentially a reception: a sharing in the already existing decision of the believing community. . . . One is incorporated, as it were, into the already existing decision of the Church. One's own decision is an accepting of and a letting oneself be accepted into the decision that has already been made."[7] Christian truth is not an elusive phantom to be sought by isolated individuals, but an antecedent reality that is given to individuals by the believing community that has itself received truth as gift from the Lord.

Emphasis upon truth, and upon the ecclesial character of truth, is incompatible with Western culture's strange ambivalence about truth. On the one hand contemporary culture takes it for granted that there are indisputable truths, knowable by use of the scientific method. Yet our culture also supposes that there are things about which there is no truth. Most dramatically, the culture assumes that there is no true social or moral order — or that there are many different but equally true social and moral orders. Whatever "truths" exist appear to be little more than relative, personal points of view. No one perspective is true while others are false, and so virtually every perspective must be tolerated. All are true in their own way, and so all must be accorded equal space in the marketplace of ideas. Cardinal Ratzinger has understood that in this cultural context, "insisting that there is a universal, binding, and valid truth in history, which became flesh in Jesus Christ and is handed on through the faith of the Church, is regarded as a kind of fundamentalism, as an attack upon the modern spirit, and as a threat to tolerance and freedom."[8]

Can the truth about God be known? Can truth claims about God be tolerated in pluralistic societies? As professor and prefect, and now as pope, Joseph Ratzinger has contended against the diminution of confidence in the revealed truth of Christian faith, and the correlative "belief" that renouncing claims to truth in the Christian faith is a condition for the end of religious violence and the advent of universal peace. His well-known concern for the future of Europe grows from his recognition that

7. Ratzinger, *Principles of Catholic Theology*, p. 37.
8. Ratzinger, "Presentation of the Declaration *Dominus Iesus*," p. 211.

"Atheism is beginning to be the fundamental public dogma and faith is tolerated as a private opinion, which means that ultimately its essence is not tolerated."[9] In the face of a pervasive belief that Christian truth claims are a social problem, Ratzinger makes the audacious assertion that only the public acknowledgment of God provides a foundation for ethics and law that can overcome the real social dangers: resurgent nationalism and world revolution!

Truth for Cardinal Ratzinger is never a socially disembodied conception. Rather, truth is integral to the actual life of the church. His understanding of truth's deeply ecclesial character, embedded in the lived experience of faith, accounts for his persistent focus on baptism and the catechumenate. Truth is not simply a matter of doctrine set forth in abstraction from the believing community; truth resides at the heart of faith — both the faith of the individual and the faith of the church. Moreover, the truth of faith is not static, but reaches out to the world. This conviction is most often set forth in the context of Christian faith's missional essence, grounded in the intrinsically evangelistic character of the believing community. Consistently, Ratzinger emphasizes the *missional* necessity of truth.

Truth's missional character is grounded in the recognition that Christian faith has always been intended as proclamation. Ratzinger points to the foundational text, "God is our Savior, who desires everyone to be saved and to come to the knowledge of the truth" (1 Tim. 2:4). The church's proclamation of God's intention declares God's love and seeks to draw men and women into love's communion with God and with others. Proclamation of the love of God is more than a generalized assurance of divine favor, however; it is the announcement of love in the form of the cross. "If God so loves us," says Ratzinger, "then we are loved in truth. Then love is truth, and truth is love. Then life is worth living. This is *evangelium*."[10] The reality of God's love for humankind is known only when faith's love does not disregard faith's truth: "The faith that reaches out to the other reaches out of necessity to his questioning as well, to his need for truth; it enters into this need, shares in it, for it is only by sharing in the question that word becomes answer."[11]

---

9. Joseph Ratzinger, "Europe: A Heritage with Obligations for Christians," in *Church, Ecumenism and Politics* (New York: Crossroad, 1988), p. 234.

10. Ratzinger, *Principles of Catholic Theology*, p. 81.

11. Ratzinger, *Principles of Catholic Theology*, p. 337.

Conversion to the truth of the gospel does not normally begin with a person's agreement with doctrine or commitment to a program, but with an attraction to the character of the Christian community's life, directly fostered by personal relationships with Christians. Coming to faith, then, proceeds through the Church and is realized in "sharing in faith with the church as the new and greater 'I.' The 'I' of 'I believe' is not my old 'I' shut in on itself; it is the 'I' of the *anima ecclesiastica*, that means the 'I' of the human being in whom the entire community of the Church expresses itself, with which he lives, which lives in him and which he lives."[12] Faith overcomes solitude as it confers community, an enduring community that encompasses time as well as space. The individual believer is not alone, but is welcomed into a concrete local community. This community of faith is not limited to the local church, however. The believer is also welcomed into a broader and deeper community "because he knows, too, that he has behind him the great community of those who, in every age, have traveled the way he is traveling and have become his brothers and sisters."[13] The communion of saints proceeds to and from the local church, spanning time as well as space.

For all of this, conversion to faith is not simply incorporation into the Christian community, even the communion of saints, for it also involves "a purposeful turning to the truth that the community has received and that is its distinctive characteristic."[14] The Christian community is a communion in truth. Just as faith itself is a gift of the community of faith, so too, the content of faith is a gift of the church. Throughout his writings, Joseph Ratzinger has stressed that Christian faith is not something we create for ourselves, but rather something we receive as a reality that is antecedent to us. As early as *Introduction to Christianity* he stated the theme that has endured over the decades: to believe as a Christian "means affirming that the meaning we do not make but can only receive is already granted to us. . . . Christian belief is the option for the view that the receiving precedes the making."[15]

We receive the faith of the church through the classic *symbola* of the ecumenical creeds. The baptismal *symbolum*, present to us in the Apostles'

12. Ratzinger, "Luther and the Unity of the Churches," in *Church, Ecumenism and Politics*, p. 127.

13. Ratzinger, *Principles of Catholic Theology*, p. 83.

14. Ratzinger, *Principles of Catholic Theology*, p. 128.

15. Joseph Ratzinger, *Introduction to Christianity* (San Francisco: Ignatius Press, 1969), p. 73.

Creed, both reflects and preserves "an independent linguistic subject that is united by the common basic experience of faith and is thus possessed of a common understanding."[16] Because the baptismal *symbolum* presupposes the catechumenate, it is less an objectification of doctrine than "the expression of a personal decision (made by a whole community) for a way that is attainable only by means of such a decision."[17] While the language of the Apostles' Creed is both informative and performative, the emphasis is on its performative function. It is the expression of a process of decision that is both the climax and commencement of the way of the catechumenate.

The conciliar *symbolum,* the Nicene-Constantinopolitan Creed, serves as a clarification for the whole church, "a regulation of the proper understanding of the baptismal decision — explanations that are indispensable for proclaiming it but not of themselves a necessary content of such proclamation."[18] Because it was formulated on the episcopal level, in council, Nicea is an instrument of unity for the whole church. The conciliar *symbolum* is not itself a baptismal creed, but it remains grounded in the faith inaugurated in baptism, and leads baptismal faith further on the way of reflection, providing "basic reference points" for a deepened understanding of the faith.

So, in Christian belief, "the receiving precedes the making," but "the making" is not irrelevant to "the receiving." A proper understanding of the baptismal decision, together with the necessary proclamation of that decision, accounts for Ratzinger's emphasis on the catechumenate as a necessary element of the church's missional life. The turning from (renunciations and exorcism) and the turning toward *(regula)* that is at Baptism's core must be preceded or followed by sustained attention to the truth of faith — catechesis. The way of the catechumenate is not merely a process of intellectual instruction, of course, but rather a process of conversion in which the whole person is incorporated into the body of Christ. "Faith is located in the act of conversion," says Ratzinger. "It is not a recitation of doctrines, an acceptance of theories about things which in themselves one knows nothing and therefore asserts something all the louder; it is an all-encompassing movement of human existence."[19] Nevertheless, the way of catechesis is the way of the gospel's truth that leads to new life: "One be-

---

16. Ratzinger, *Principles of Catholic Theology,* p. 125.
17. Ratzinger, *Principles of Catholic Theology,* p. 124.
18. Ratzinger, *Principles of Catholic Theology,* p. 126.
19. Ratzinger, *Introduction to Christianity,* p. 88.

comes oneself by becoming a confession of faith, an open Yes, when one is received into the community of the faithful, when one is incorporated into the community of the faithful, when one is immersed in and allows oneself to be immersed in it."[20]

Challenges to Reformed Faith and Life

Contemporary Reformed Christians are likely to recoil at Cardinal Ratzinger's assertion that the church possesses the truth of the gospel into which persons are received. Yet John Calvin, forebear of the Reformed tradition, famously followed Cyprian in understanding the church — the visible, actual church — as mother: "There is no way to enter into life unless this mother conceive us in her womb, give us birth, nourish us at her breast, and lastly, unless she keep us under her care and guidance. . . . Our weakness does not allow us to be dismissed from her school until we have been pupils all our lives."[21] Calvin's use of this rich image was more than a nod in the direction of a Church Father. While he did not hold that God's power is bound to the use of the outward means of the church, he was convinced that normally, God uses the ordinary means of the church's proclamation and teaching to make the shape of the gospel known. For Calvin, the consequences of disregarding the church's teaching of Christian faith are dire, leading directly to infidelity to the gospel:

> Many are led either by pride, dislike, or rivalry to the conviction that they can profit enough from private reading and meditation; hence they despise public assemblies and deem preaching superfluous. But, since they do their utmost to sever or break the sacred bond of unity, no one escapes the just penalty of this unholy separation without bewitching himself with pestilent errors and foulest delusions.[22]

Like Cardinal Ratzinger, Calvin did not imagine that the church's teaching authority derives from its own insight or wisdom. He would have

---

20. Ratzinger, *Principles of Catholic Theology,* p. 111.

21. John Calvin, *Institutes of the Christian Religion,* ed. John T. McNeill, trans. Ford Lewis Battles (Philadelphia: Westminster Press, 1960), 4.1.4, p. 1016.

22. Calvin, *Institutes,* 4.1.5, p. 1018.

approved of Ratzinger's ready acknowledgment that "the Church knows and confesses, in the act of receiving [the faith], that she does not act in her own right as a separate and independent subject but in the name of the Father, Son and Holy Spirit; that her act of receiving is, in its turn, contained in the act by which she, too, is received and lets herself be received."[23] Calvin would also agree with Ratzinger's conviction that the unity of the church comes from communion with the apostles, that is, with "persistent remaining in the teaching of the apostles. Unity thus has a content that is expressed in teaching."[24] Yet neither Ratzinger nor Calvin finds contemporary Reformed approval for their conviction that the faith of the church is prior to the faith of the individual and shapes individual fidelity to the gospel, and that the unity of the church is unity in the apostolic faith.

Calvin attempted a difficult balancing act. In his view, the church of God exists "wherever we see the Word of God purely preached and heard, and the sacraments administered according to Christ's institution."[25] This church is "the faithful keeper of God's truth," and so "no one is permitted to spurn its authority, flout its warnings, resist its counsels, or make light of its chastisements — much less to desert it and break unity."[26] But where is this church of pure proclamation and faithful sacramental practice? Calvin himself followed his bold definition with numerous qualifications that were intended to recognize the reality of fault in the church's life while preserving its authority in matters of faith. On the one hand, Calvin takes the Creed to profess that we "believe the church" (not *in* the church), and so the church is understood not as faith's object, but rather faith's preserver and transmitter. Christian faith is sharing in the faith of the whole church. And yet, on the other hand, the faith of the whole church is subject to evaluation and can be found wanting. Whose evaluation? What criteria?

The Protestant answer to those questions has always been "the word of God." The motto of the Reformed tradition — *ecclesia reformata semper reformanda secundum verbum Dei,* "the church reformed always to be reformed according to the word of God" — expresses the enduring belief that God judges and reforms the church, and that Scripture is the criterion of reformation. Yet Protestants have easily transmuted *sola scriptura* into

23. Ratzinger, *Principles of Catholic Theology,* pp. 111f.
24. Ratzinger, "Communion," in *Pilgrim Fellowship of Faith,* p. 64.
25. Calvin, *Institutes,* 4.1.9, p. 1023.
26. Calvin, *Institutes,* 4.1.10, p. 1024.

"scripture in isolation," especially from the "control" of the church. In the Messori interview, Cardinal Ratzinger commented tellingly on the separation of church and Scripture, saying that "the Bible without the Church is no longer the powerfully effective Word of God, but an assemblage of various historical sources, a collection of heterogeneous books from which one tries to draw, from the perspective of the present moment, whatever one considers useful." To this uncomfortably accurate description of the way too many Protestants use the Bible, the Cardinal adds a vivid coda: "An exegesis in which the Bible no longer lives and is understood within the living organism of the Church becomes archaeology: the dead bury their dead."[27]

As exclusive reliance on the "historical-critical" method wanes, Protestant scholarship and Protestant churches must re-think the relationship between church and Scripture. The church cannot live without Scripture; Scripture cannot live without the church. If Scripture only breathes within the church, how is Scripture's critical voice heard above "the noise of solemn assemblies"? At least part of the answer lies in the exercise of the church's teaching office. It is the teaching office of the church that bears responsibility for the preservation and transmission of faith's truth. Although this is differently understood by Catholic and Reformed, their insights can be complementary, enriching both.

Calvin placed great weight on the role of the church's pastors, not because he had confidence in their personal capacity for fidelity, but because he believed them to be the God-given bond of unity: "One is appointed pastor to teach the rest, and those bidden to be pupils receive the common teaching from one mouth. For if anyone were sufficient to himself and needed no one else's help (such is the pride of human nature) each man would despise the rest and be despised by them."[28] But what happens — as it does too often today — when pastors are the ones who feel self-sufficient, and do not think they are bidden to be pupils who receive teaching from the mouth of the church? When biblical and confessional authority erodes, Reformed church structures are no longer able to receive, preserve, and pass on the truth of the church's faith.

In an uncharacteristically personal aside at the conclusion of a subtle treatment of tradition and apostolic succession, Cardinal Ratzinger voiced a lament that many Protestants could echo:

27. *The Ratzinger Report*, p. 75.
28. Calvin, *Institutes*, 4.3.1, p. 1054.

Today, many Christians, myself included, experience a quiet uneasiness about attending divine services in a strange church; they are appalled at the thought of the half-understood theories, the amazing and tasteless personal opinions of this or that priest they will have to endure during the homily — to say nothing of the personal liturgical inventions to which they will be subjected. No one goes to church to hear someone else's personal opinions. I am simply not interested in what fantasies this or that individual priest may have spun for himself regarding questions of Christian faith. . . . When I go to church, it is not to find there my own or anyone else's innovations but what we have all received as the faith of the Church — the faith that spans the centuries and can support us all.[29]

The difficulty is not confined to any one ecclesial tradition. What is true, to one degree or another, in all churches is certainly true within churches of the Reformed tradition: fidelity to the gospel is in continual danger of succumbing to forms of "I Determine What God Is,"[30] coupled with individualistic (idiosyncratic?) readings of the Bible, selective attention (inattention?) to the confessions, benign neglect (willful disregard?) of the church's polity, and isolation (alienation?) from colleagues in ministry. In North America, all of this occurs within the pervasive reality of the church's cultural disestablishment, minimizing its capacity to speak convincingly to an uninterested public.

The all-too-common reality of idiosyncratic proclamation points to the necessity of a vital teaching office within the church. Reformed churches have always conceived the teaching office functioning within conciliar structures. The church's councils — local sessions/consistories, regional presbyteries/classes, national general assemblies/general synods — are composed of pastors (teaching elders) and ruling (canon) elders. The Presbyterian Church (U.S.A.) charges these councils with responsibility to "frame symbols of faith, bear testimony against error in doctrine and immorality in life, resolve questions of doctrine and of discipline, give counsel in matters of conscience, and decide issues properly brought before them."[31] Yet it must be acknowledged that organizational and legisla-

29. Ratzinger, *Principles of Catholic Theology*, p. 283.
30. Ingolf Dalferth, "I Determine What God Is!" *Theology Today* 57, no. 1 (April 2000).
31. Presbyterian Church (U.S.A.), *Book of Order* (Louisville: Office of the General Assembly, 2005), G-9.0101b.

tive functions have combined with pervasive diversity in faith and life to overwhelm the capacity of councils to articulate and transmit "the doctrine of the faith."

There is no ready solution to the problems of the Reformed (and other Protestant) "teaching office." It may be at this point that the theological work of Professor/Cardinal Ratzinger can most helpfully shape the pontificate of Benedict XVI. Popes are called to be teachers of the faith. In the Catholic view, the Roman primacy is a function of the acknowledgment of Rome as the criterion of right apostolic faith. Benedict's lifelong passion for the truth of the faith presents the possibility of a de facto papal teaching office for the *whole* church. Protestants generally, and the Reformed in particular, have often focused their gaze on the failings of popes and continuing doctrinal disputes. Yet we may acknowledge, along with Cardinal Ratzinger, that "with the same realism with which we declare today the sins of the popes . . . we must also acknowledge that Peter has repeatedly stood as the rock against ideologies, against the dissolution of the word into the plausibilities of a given time, against subjection to the powers of this world."[32]

Teachers are not supreme authorities, whose dicta are to be received passively. The papal teaching office is not accorded unquestioned acceptance even in the Catholic Church. Yet it is a fact that Christians from all ecclesial traditions pay attention to popes when they speak and write. Reformed Christians tacitly acknowledge a measure of papal authority, even when we disagree with aspects of papal theological and moral teaching. (As a friend of mine said to me upon her return to the Catholic Church, "At least there's something there to disagree with.") Benedict's evident faith and keen theological mind present the possibility of genuine engagement, throughout the churches, with the questions of faith's truth that have occupied him for decades.

Cardinal Ratzinger once expressed a hope for the papal ministry that Benedict XVI has the possibility of fulfilling:

> Even when the claims of his office are disputed the pope remains a point of personal reference in the world's sight for the responsibility he bears and expresses for the word of faith, and thus a challenge perceived by everyone and affecting everyone to seek greater loyalty to this word, as

32. Joseph Ratzinger, *Called to Communion: Understanding the Church Today* (San Francisco: Ignatius Press, 1996), p. 73f.

well as a challenge to struggle for unity and to be responsible for the lack of unity. In this sense even in division the papacy has a function of establishing unity, and ultimately no-one can imagine the historical drama of Christendom without this function.[33]

The churches today, especially the churches of the West, experience a certain crisis of confidence in the universal truth of the gospel. The challenges of religious pluralism, social secularization, and the "postmodern" impulse combine to place churches in a defensive posture that relies on communication technique, market-driven programming, and the downplaying of Christian distinctives in order to achieve institutional success. Benedict's work has prepared him to engage all Christian churches in a deep exploration of faith's truth, and the means of proclaiming that truth to the world as well as embedding that truth in the life of the Christian community.

The Church as Communion

Ecclesiology and Reformation

What do we mean when we speak the word "church"? Because the nature of the church is a central issue in the reception, preservation, and transmission of Christian truth, ecclesiology has been a point of friction between Reformed and Catholic from the beginning. While Reformation judgment was leveled against church abuses, current critique focuses on church structure. Underlying both is a deep difference in understanding the essential nature and meaning of the church. Cardinal Ratzinger has readily acknowledged that "the difference in the ways in which Church is understood . . . has proved to be an insuperable barrier."[34]

Calvin's concern was reform of the church, not its division. His remarkable reply to Cardinal Sadolet makes it clear that his primary objection was to perceived theological, liturgical, and ecclesial departures from the faith and order of the ancient church. In response to Sadolet's accusation of schism, Calvin asserted that the state of the Catholic Church at the

33. Ratzinger, "The Papal Primacy and the Unity of the People of God," in *Church, Ecumenism and Politics*, pp. 44f.
34. *The Ratzinger Report*, p. 160.

opening of the sixteenth century was the impetus to its reformation, not its division: "the light of divine truth had been extinguished, the Word of God buried, the virtue of Christ left in profound oblivion, and the pastoral office subverted. . . . Do those who contend against such evils declare war against the Church? Do they not rather assist her in extreme distress?"[35] But the intention of Calvin, Luther, and other early reformers was not fulfilled. Schism was the result, setting off a process of ecclesial fragmentation and proliferation.

Nearly five centuries have passed, and thoughtful observers agree that while theological, liturgical, and ecclesiastical deficiencies and abuses may have characterized the Catholic Church in the sixteenth century, the Catholic Church of the twenty-first century cannot be accused of egregious departures from foundational Christian truth. Clear differences between Catholic and Protestant remain, of course, especially on matters of ecclesiology. The past five centuries have seen the widening of the ecclesiological gulf between Catholic and Reformed, so that talk about the nature of the church is conducted now in two different languages, neither of which is easily translated into the other.

Ecclesiology is at the heart of Joseph Ratzinger's theology, not because he has an unnatural attraction to institutions or a penchant for power, but because he is ceaselessly concerned with the truth of Christian faith. Faith's truth is not doctrine distant from life, not even, in the first instance, "the doctrine of the faith," but rather the living truth of the church's faith lived out in the lives of believers. Thus, "In both her sacramental life and in her proclamation of the Word, the Church constitutes a distinctive subject whose memory preserves the seemingly past word and action of Jesus as a present reality."[36] Pilate's infamous question — what is truth? — finds its answer in Jesus Christ, who is himself the way, the truth, and the life for the world. But it is the church that is the means by which Christ makes himself present, and so Ratzinger can even say, "The Church is not an idea but a body, and the scandal of the incarnation, over which so many of Jesus' contemporaries came to grief, is continued in the infuriating aspects of the Church."[37]

35. John Calvin, "Reply to Sadolet," in *Calvin: Theological Treatises*, ed. J. K. S. Reid (Philadelphia: Westminster Press, 1954), p. 241.

36. Ratzinger, *Called to Communion*, p. 19.

37. Ratzinger, "The Ecclesiology of the Second Vatican Council," in *Church, Ecumenism and Politics*, p. 6.

The Body of Christ

The ground of Cardinal Ratzinger's ecclesiology is Christological and Trinitarian. "Ecclesiology appears as dependent upon Christology, as belonging to it," he says. "Yet because no one can talk correctly about Christ, the Son, without also straightaway talking about the Father, and because no one can talk about the Father and the Son without listening to the Holy Spirit, then the Christological aspect of ecclesiology is necessarily extended into a Trinitarian ecclesiology."[38] The Christological and Trinitarian core of his understanding of the church is not simply a theological assertion, but one that focuses, in the first instance, on the presence of Christ in the lives of believers. Christ does not live in the recesses of the church's memory, nor does he preside over the church in remote splendor. Christ's presence is living and active. The living Lord of the church is not confined to history, for he is always a dynamic actuality in the present and the future. The implications are twofold: the church has no existence apart from the presence of Christ, and Christ's presence is not dependent upon the church. Because the church is nothing less than Christ's body, Christ continuously originates the church and sustains the church. "The Church is the presence of Christ," says Ratzinger, "the fact that we are contemporaneous with him, that he is contemporaneous with us." The presence of Christ in the church is not, primarily, presence in the institution, however, but in the lives of believers. Ratzinger repeatedly makes the point that "The source of [the Church's] life is the fact that Christ is present in people's hearts: it is from there that he shapes the Church, and not the other way round."[39]

Because Christ is the center of the church, the church's life is characterized by two dynamic elements. First, separated people are drawn together by moving toward God. Second, the dynamic of the unification between God and people, and the unification among people, finds its point of convergence in Jesus Christ. The dual reality of people drawn together, in Christ, is *visible* in the Eucharist. Throughout his extensive writing on Eucharist, Cardinal Ratzinger stresses that "Eucharist, seen as the permanent origin and center of the Church, joins all of the 'many,' who are now

38. Ratzinger, "The Ecclesiology of the Constitution *Lumen Gentium*," in *Pilgrim Fellowship of Faith*, p. 140.
39. Ratzinger, "The Ecclesiology of the Second Vatican Council," p. 4.

made a people, to the one Lord and to his one and only Body."[40] The church-forming nature of Eucharist is far more than a pale reflection of conceptual unity, as in the annual "World Communion Sunday" celebrated in many Reformed churches. Ratzinger insists that Eucharist really does make the church, not by virtue of the Church's initiative, but by the real presence of Christ who continues to call and gather a people. "The content of the Eucharist, what happens in it, is the uniting of Christians," says Ratzinger, "bringing them from their state of separation into the unity of the one Bread and the one Body. Eucharist is thus understood entirely in a dynamic ecclesiological perspective. It is the living process through which, time and again, the Church's activity of becoming the Church takes place."[41]

Among Reformed Christians, Calvin's rich theology of the Lord's Supper must always contend with Zwingli's mere memorialism. Even within Reformed churches that incorporate Calvin's rather than Zwingli's sacramental theology, the notion that the Eucharist "makes" the church seems odd. It also seems presumptuous when coupled with claims that true Eucharist is linked to a particular understanding of apostolic succession and thus confined to the Catholic and Orthodox Churches. Tragically, Eucharist remains the most visible instance of the church's disunity, not only between Catholic and Protestant churches, but also among Protestant churches. Overcoming this great divide is unlikely as long as "ministry" is seen as the problem to be solved. Yet, if these matters can be bracketed, the church-forming character of Eucharist might be recovered in Reformed circles. The pontificate of Benedict XVI can enhance the life of all "ecclesial communities" if it reflects Cardinal Ratzinger's rich understanding of the inherent relationship of the church as body of Christ and the Eucharist as body of Christ. "You are the body of Christ" is more than a Pauline trope, "This is my body" is more than a memorable simile, and the connection between the two is more than linguistic.

Cardinal Ratzinger has accentuated an understanding of the church as Eucharistic communion. This emphasis has clear ecclesiastical as well as ecclesiological implications, of course, but divisive institutional realities are not foundational. Benedict XVI can provide a profound ecumenical

40. Ratzinger, *Called to Communion*, p. 29.

41. Joseph Ratzinger, *God Is Near Us: The Eucharist, the Heart of Life* (San Francisco: Ignatius Press, 2003), pp. 114f.

service through the compelling teaching of Cardinal Ratzinger — now addressed to the whole Christian community — that "The content of the Eucharist, what happens in it, is the uniting of Christians, bringing them from their state of separation into the unity of the one Bread and the one Body." The Cardinal's conclusion is that "the Church is not just a people: out of the many peoples of which she consists there is arising *one* people, through the *one* table that the Lord has spread for us all. The Church is, so to speak, a network of Eucharistic fellowships, and she is united, ever and again, through the *one* Body we all receive."[42] In Ratzinger's view, these words are descriptive of the Catholic Church, but, as such, they are normative for "ecclesial communities" as well. Papal teaching that is invitational — not as a call to return to the Catholic Church, but rather as an encouragement to explore the fullness of Eucharistic ecclesiology — can benefit all, with especially salutary implications for Reformed churches.

Reformed churches are notorious for their tendency toward schism. Of the great ecclesial movements emerging from the sixteenth-century Reformation and its aftermath — Catholic, Lutheran, Anabaptist, Anglican, Methodist, and Reformed — it is the Reformed family of churches that has multiplied by a continual process of division born of disagreement, controversy, and separation. Division and schism are not unknown in other ecclesial families, of course, but the scale is smaller and the pace slower. For Reformed Christians, schism is not the last resort, but often the first instinct. A question posed by Catholic Eucharistic ecclesiology, then, and particularly by Benedict's Eucharistic emphases, is whether Reformed sacramental minimalism, especially neglect of the Eucharist, is a significant, largely unrecognized element in the endemic splintering of Reformed churches.

In spite of Calvin's identification of faithful churches by the dual marks of Word and sacraments, Reformed churches tend to be churches of the Word alone. The Reformed tradition exalts preaching and takes pride in theological precision, but even with the recent increase from quarterly to monthly Communion, it remains a tradition that marginalizes sacramental life. The consequence is that churches of the Word alone too easily become churches of words alone . . . and words are what we fight about and fight with. Reformed unity is often restricted to doctrinal accord, thus paving the way for doctrinal disagreements to produce ecclesial disunity.

42. Ratzinger, *God Is Near Us: The Eucharist, the Heart of Life*, pp. 114f.

Recovery of the church's sacramental heart does not mean abandonment of "the pure ministry of the Word," but rather renewed appropriation of the inseparable connection between the Word made flesh and the body of Christ. If Word and sacrament are the heart of the church's true and faithful life, neglect of one leads inexorably to deformation of the other, for when either Word or sacrament exists alone, it soon becomes a parody of itself. Reformed Christians have always been quick to point out that sacraments can become prey to superstitious excess in churches where preaching and teaching are minimized. But Reformed Christians are less aware of how easily preaching and teaching can deteriorate into institutional marketing or human potential promotion in churches that magnify the word while marginalizing Baptism and Eucharist.

Calvin placed Word and sacrament together at the core of the church's true life because he took it as "a settled principle that the sacraments have the same office as the Word of God: to offer and set forth Christ to us, and in him the treasures of heavenly grace."[43] Sixteenth-century Reformation disputes — between reformers and the Catholic Church and among the reformers — centered on the presence of Christ in the Eucharist. The categories in which these debates occurred no longer name the real issue before us all: the real, bodily presence of the risen Christ in Eucharist and in the church formed by Eucharist. Benedict XVI's potential contribution to this matter can be sensed in a 1978 essay, "The Presence of the Lord in the Sacrament." The essay is, on the one hand, a clear and moving account of the real presence of Jesus Christ in the Eucharist as "a power that catches us up and works to draw us within itself," transforming us into the very body of Christ.[44] The essay is also an intra-Catholic argument about the proprieties of liturgical reform and innovation. Reformed Christians will be uninterested in the latter, but could be enriched by clear teaching of the former.

Reformed churches — so committed to engaging social realities in order to "transform culture" — can also be enriched by the insight that Eucharist is a primary source of the church's mission. The cardinal has emphasized that the church's apostolicity is experienced as the church receives the source of its life through the apostolic tradition, which, in turn, sends the church out to and for the world. It is Eucharist that shapes

43. Calvin, *Institutes*, 4.14.17, p. 1292.
44. Ratzinger, *God Is Near Us: The Eucharist, the Heart of Life*, pp. 74-93 and esp. p. 77.

the church's mission by drawing it back to Christ. In his characteristically acerbic style, Ratzinger says that, "In order for mission to be more than propaganda for certain ideas or trying to win people over for a given community — in order for it to come from God and lead to God, it must spring from a more profound source than that which gives rise to resource planning and operational strategies. It must spring from a source both deeper and higher than advertising and persuasion."[45] Eucharist is "the deeper source" that grounds the church's mission in Christ, and thus draws the church's actions into the *missio dei.*

Cardinal Ratzinger is clear that as the church is drawn into the Eucharist, becoming a Eucharist, it is freed from the moralism of its activity, and freed for witness to Christ and service in Christ. Eucharist does not form the church for its own sake, then, but for the sake of God's mission, by which he draws all people to himself and unites them in the very body of Christ. The question of the origin and shape of the church's mission is one that confronts all churches, especially in Europe and North America. The danger confronting the churches is that recognition of the end of the Constantinian era, the disestablishment of the church, and the advent of "post-Christian" Europe (and North America?) will simply lead to a set of organizational initiatives and institutional programs designed to create a "missional" church. A church that is the subject of its own constructive activities inevitably becomes self-promoting, and thus an offense to the gospel. The church cannot be allowed to imagine that its mission is shaped by its own actions. Ratzinger reminds all Christians that

> The Church is there so that God, the living God, may be made known — so that man may learn to live with God, live in his sight and in fellowship with him. The Church is there to prevent the advance of hell upon earth and to make the earth fit to live in through the light of God. On the basis of God's presence, and only through him, it is humanized.[46]

Benedict XVI's pastoral service to all the churches of the West will be significant if he achieves an appropriate balance between identifying causes of "the advance of hell upon earth," and the shape of "making the

45. Ratzinger, "Eucharist and Mission," in *Pilgrim Fellowship of Faith,* p. 121.
46. Ratzinger, "The Church on the Threshold of the Third Millennium," in *Pilgrim Fellowship of Faith,* p. 286.

earth fit to live in through the light of God." Cultural critique is necessary in a time when Western Christians simply assume the givenness, and even the goodness, of "the way things are." It is not surprising that Cardinal Ratzinger has declared consistently that "Among the most urgent tasks facing Christians is that of regaining the capacity of nonconformism, i.e., the capacity to oppose many developments of the surrounding culture."[47] But preoccupation with the culture's ills can be perceived as little more than conservative nostalgia, a call for return to the past, and thus unrelated to hopes for the future and faithfulness in the present. The more important issue is "making the earth fit to live in through the light of God." This is a matter of thinking as well as doing. Pope Benedict can lead all churches in the effort "to revive the argument about the rationality of belief or unbelief," for he understands that "The struggle for the new presence of the rationality of faith is . . . an urgent task for the Church in our century."[48] The task is not that of the Catholic Church alone, for alone, the Catholic Church cannot accomplish it. All Christian churches have common cause in bearing rational witness to the presence of God in the midst of human history. It is the experiential knowledge of God's presence rather than fixation on the advance of hell that makes "nonconformism" possible.

Universal Church and Local Church

The question remains: What is this "church" that Cardinal Ratzinger writes about so perceptively? Vatican II opened a rich conversation, within the Catholic Church and beyond it, on the nature, purpose, and mission of the church. As professor, cardinal, and prefect, Joseph Ratzinger has been a central participant in the discussion. Tracing all lines of the ecclesiological dialogue occasioned by *Lumen Gentium* is too complex a task for this essay, but the heart of the matter may be seen in the distinction between local church and universal church, and in the shape of the relationship between the two.

Eucharist makes the church; the church is Eucharist. Cardinal Ratzinger repeatedly makes the point that the church came into being when Jesus gave bread and wine, body and blood, and said, "Do this in re-

---

47. *The Ratzinger Report*, p. 115.
48. Ratzinger, "The Church on the Threshold of the New Millennium," p. 291.

membrance of me," for the church is the response to this commission. Because Eucharist is the act of a real community of believers, the Eucharistic nature of the church points first of all to the local gathering: "Eucharist is celebrated in a concrete place together with the men who live in it. It is here that the event of gathering begins."[49] Thus, the church's origin and basis in Eucharist is the source of its nature as *communion* — communion with the one triune God through communion with Christ, and communion among those who share in the body of Christ, becoming the body of Christ.

Although the church as *communio,* made concrete in Eucharist, points first to the local Eucharistic community in Ratzinger's view, it is not confined to the local church. The multitude of Eucharistic celebrations "cannot stand side by side as autonomous, mutually independent entities" and so the Church "cannot become a static juxtaposition of essentially self-sufficient local Churches."[50] There is *one* Christ and so there is *one* body of Christ and so there is *one* holy catholic apostolic church. The church's unity and catholicity are guaranteed in the communion of local churches with their bishop, the communion among bishops, and the communion of bishops with the pope. Thus, *church* signifies "not only the cultic gathering but also the local community, the Church in a larger geographical area and, finally, the one Church of Jesus Christ herself. There is a continuous transition from one meaning to another, because all of them hang on the Christological center that is made concrete in the gathering of believers for the Lord's Supper."[51]

It would be possible to conceive of this communion as building the one church from the bottom up. Cardinal Ratzinger has contended vigorously against this view, in both its Orthodox and Protestant forms, through communications from the Congregation for the Doctrine of the Faith as well as in numerous essays and addresses. He has emphasized repeatedly that communion among local churches derives from their communion with the one body of Christ, the universal church. The order — universal church, local Church — is made clear in the Congregation for the Doctrine of the Faith's *Letter to the Bishops of the Catholic Church on Some Aspects of the Church Understood as Communion.* "Aspects of the Church" attempts to draw to-

49. Ratzinger, *Called to Communion,* p. 77.
50. Ratzinger, *Called to Communion,* pp. 29 and 85.
51. Ratzinger, *Called to Communion,* p. 32.

gether Vatican II's multivalent uses of the term "universal Church" by stressing one aspect of the council's teaching: "the universal Church cannot be conceived as the sum of particular Churches, or as a federation of particular Churches, but, in its essential mystery, it is a reality ontologically and temporally prior to every individual particular Church."[52] In a vivid image, *Aspects of the Church* states that the universal church is the mother of local churches, not their product.

Aspects of the Church, offered as an authoritative exposition of the Second Vatican Council's teaching, bears the marks of the cardinal prefect's effort to advance the view that the council's communion, collegiality, and people of God references are to be understood in relation to unity, hierarchy, and body of Christ. The ontological priority of the universal church is at the center of an ongoing discussion that did not end with "Aspects of the Church." Most notably, the discussion was heard in a public exchange of articles between Cardinals Kasper and Ratzinger, prompting the prefect to write, "This ontological precedence of the Church as a whole, of the one Church and the one body, of the one bride, over the empirical and concrete realizations in the various individual parts of the Church seems to me so obvious that I find it difficult to understand the objections raised against it."[53]

The Reformed tradition, together with other Protestant traditions, contains a particular version of this issue in the invisible-visible church distinction. Although the priority of the invisible church is implicit, the notion of invisible church generally serves as a way of distinguishing the flawed church we can see from the one holy catholic and apostolic church that is spiritual and hidden in the purposes of God. In its popularized versions, the invisible church is the true church while the visible church is the flawed church, true church only to the extent that it conforms its faith and life to the invisible church. The result is a denigration of all institutional embodiments of the visible church, together with a view of their dispensability, that often results in justification for the multiplication of separated local churches.

Cardinal Ratzinger's understanding of universal church and local church emphasizes their coherence, not their distinction. His emphasis is

---

52. Congregation for the Doctrine of the Faith, *Letter to the Bishops of the Catholic Church on Some Aspects of the Church Understood as Communion*, 9.

53. Ratzinger, "Ecclesiology of the Constitution *Lumen Gentium*," pp. 134f.

on the *visibility* of the ontologically prior universal church in the life of the local church. "The Church of Christ is not hidden behind the multitude of human constructions, intangible and unattainable; she exists in reality as a corporal Church that shows her identity in the Creed, in the sacraments, and in the apostolic succession."[54] This visibility of the one and catholic church is captured in *Lumen Gentium*'s well-known formulation: the one holy catholic apostolic church *"substitit in Ecclesia catholica."* Ratzinger accentuates the way in which the *substitit* formulation counters all "ecclesiological relativism" by proclaiming that there is a church of Jesus Christ in the world. "The Council is trying to tell us that the Church of Jesus Christ may be encountered in this world as a concrete agent in the Catholic Church."[55]

Reformed churches, together with virtually all Protestant churches, reject the position of Vatican II and its vigorous championing by Joseph Ratzinger. Reformed churches have reacted with aggrieved anger whenever they are relegated to the status of "ecclesial communities," particularly when this lesser status is coupled with assertions that the one holy catholic apostolic church subsists in the Catholic Church alone. Thus, *Dominus Iesus* was greeted with dismay when it declared that "the ecclesial communities which have not preserved the valid Episcopate and the genuine and integral substance of the Eucharistic mystery, are not Churches in the proper sense."[56] The recent deliverance from the Congregation, "Responses to Some Questions Regarding Certain Aspects of the Doctrine of the Church," occasioned a heated rejoinder from the World Alliance of Reformed Churches when it reiterated the Catholic position that the universal church subsists in it alone and that the ecclesial communities born out of the sixteenth-century Reformation are not churches in the proper sense. Both documents' acknowledgment that "elements of sanctification and truth" are present in ecclesial communities has not been sufficient to overcome Reformed dismay at Catholic Church claims that in it alone are found all the elements of church that Christ instituted.

Reformed ecclesiology embodies an understanding of the church as communion that bears a certain conceptual resemblance to the Catholic view, but that places the dynamics of communion in councils rather than

54. Ratzinger, "Ecclesiology of the Constitution *Lumen Gentium*," pp. 146f.
55. Ratzinger, "Ecclesiology of the Constitution *Lumen Gentium*," p. 149.
56. Congregation for the Doctrine of the Faith, *Dominus Iesus*, 17.

the episcopacy. In the Reformed view, the church is the body of Christ, in communion with Christ who alone is head of the church. A local church (congregation) is gathered in communion by Word and sacraments, served and led by the pastor and elders together in council (session, consistory). Congregations are in communion with one another as pastors and representative elders gather in regional councils (presbyteries, classes). Regional councils are in communion with one another in national councils (general assembly, general synod). Reformed churches are quick to assert the advantages of conciliar over episcopal systems, but less aware of their inherent dangers. Among the dangers of Reformed communion ecclesiology is the obvious tendency for communion to be confined within political boundaries. The absence of a global structure of communion is due, in part, to the "invisibility" of the "universal" church, and thus to the natural limitations of "bottom-up" fellowship. An ancillary danger results from the tendency of trans-congregational communion to be reduced to practical legislative relationships, effectively confining communion in Word and sacraments to congregational life.

Reformed churches will not abandon conciliarity, of course, but could benefit from considering Cardinal Ratzinger's caution, hearing in it a challenge to the Reformed tendency to conceive the church as the object of our action.

> [N]obody can turn himself or herself into the Church. A group cannot simply come together, read the New Testament, and say: "We are now the Church, because the Lord is present wherever two or three are gathered in his name." An essential element of the Church is that of receiving, just as faith comes from hearing and is not the product of one's own decisions or reflections. For faith is the encounter with what I cannot think up myself or bring about by my own efforts but must come to encounter me. . . . The Church is not something that one can make but only something one can receive, and indeed receive it from where it already is and where it really is: from the sacramental community of his body that progresses through history.[57]

---

57. Ratzinger, "The Ecclesiology of the Second Vatican Council," p. 10.

The Ecumenical Situation

Apprehension about the pontificate of Benedict XVI intensifies when the matter at hand is the current ecumenical situation and the future path of ecumenism. Among Reformed Christians there is a sense that the openness of *Ut Unum Sint* is only grudgingly acknowledged. It has not gone unnoticed that the widespread appreciation of the Lutheran-Catholic *Joint Declaration on the Doctrine of Justification* was accompanied by observations from Cardinal Ratzinger that seemed almost churlish. After remarking that the problem with *JDDJ* is that "hardly anyone knows anything about the issue with which it is concerned," Ratzinger went on to criticize ecumenical engagements that concentrate on the issue of Eucharistic fellowship. If ecumenical agreement "appears to reduce our entire consciousness of the faith to the celebration of communion . . . we must be fearful also that the Eucharist itself . . . has atrophied into a kind of communal act of socialization. . . . What counts is simply the ritual representation of unity."[58]

The language is biting, and the sentiment may lack a measure of generosity, but Reformed churches may be able to appreciate Ratzinger's point as a useful caution against ecumenical engagement that elides issues of truth in order to achieve a certain level of "agreement." He has noted that "the experiences of so-called consensus ecumenism have shown how difficult it is to do justice to the demands of truth. . . . So it is that people are often inclined to invert the relationship between consensus and truth."[59] He is equally critical of ecumenism that gives action primacy over truth. Once again it is abiding concern for the truth of the faith that leads him to cut against the grain. Much intra-Protestant ecumenism may focus too narrowly on Eucharistic sharing, settle too readily on consensus in theological commonplace, and assume too quickly that common mission activity represents genuine unity. Exercise of the papal teaching office in a manner that helps to refocus the ecumenical movement on the truth of the gospel can reinvigorate it by clarifying and refining its aims.

Critique of Ratzinger's ecumenical "hard line," noticeable in earlier writing and in the recently approved "Responses to Some Questions Re-

58. Joseph Ratzinger, "The Augsburg Concord on Justification: How Far Does It Take Us?" in *International Journal for the Study of the Christian Church* 2, no. 1 (2000).

59. Ratzinger, "On the Ecumenical Situation," in *Pilgrim Fellowship of Faith*, p. 260.

garding Certain Aspects of the Doctrine on the Church," should take note of a recent statement adopted by the Ninth Assembly of the World Council of Churches. "Called to Be the One Church" is a statement on ecclesiology that bears significance for the future of ecumenism. It concedes that "churches have not always acknowledged their *mutual responsibility* to one another, and have not always recognized the need to give account to one another of their faith, life, and witness, as well as to articulate the factors that keep them apart." The statement calls for the churches "to engage in the hard task of giving a candid account of the relation of their own faith and order to the faith and order of other churches. Each church is asked to articulate the judgments that shape, and even qualify, its relationship to the others. The honest sharing of commonalities, divergences, and differences will help all churches to pursue the things that make for peace and build up the common life."[60] The World Council of Churches and Benedict XVI seem to share the conviction that the ecumenical task of the churches is better served by candor than by courteous avoidance of deep difference. Ecumenical honesty is sometimes painful, but it is only through open acknowledgment of deeply held convictions that genuine dialogue can occur. Premature pressure for thin agreement leads, at best, to peaceful coexistence, not to unity. It may be that Benedict's open statements and the WCC's new position provide grounds for a different kind of ecumenical engagement.

In the view of Cardinal Ratzinger, ecumenism begins with the acknowledgment that God has revealed himself and his purpose for humankind: "God has spoken — if we think we know better, then we get lost in the darkness of our own opinion; we lose unity instead of moving toward it."[61] Therefore, truth must remain constitutive, but since revelation is not perfectly appropriated, the assertion of its priority is not the end of the matter. If truth is the heart of the matter, ecumenical dialogue can be genuine. Ratzinger has set forth marks of a more "relaxed" ecumenical search that must accompany the necessary search for complete unity that continues to investigate obstacles to unity and develop models of unity. "This kind of [relaxed] unity," he says, "for whose continuing growth we can and must exert ourselves without putting ourselves under the all too human

60. World Council of Churches, Ninth Assembly (2006), "Called to Be the One Church," Document PRC 01.1, paragraphs V.12 & V.13.

61. Ratzinger, "On the Ecumenical Situation," p. 264.

Joseph D. Small

pressure of having to succeed by reaching our goal, has a variety of approaches and therefore demands a variety of effort."[62]

This more relaxed ecumenism begins with discovering, discerning, and acknowledging evidence of the kinds of unity that already exist, such as joint reading of the Bible as the word of God, confession of the Nicene and Apostles' Creeds, Trinity, Christology, baptism and the forgiveness of sins, prayer, and the essential ethical instruction of the Decalogue, as well as areas of common ethical action. This catalogue of existing unity is significant, and so should be "put to work," deepening and broadening it at all levels (ministers, theologians, lay people) and embodying it in joint action.

A second aspect of ecumenical engagement that does not press toward premature agreement is "not to want to force anything on the other that still threatens him or her in his or her Christian identity."[63] This means, for example, that Catholics should not try to pressure Protestants on recognition of the papacy and a certain understanding of apostolic succession. Protestants, in turn, should not press the issue of intercommunion on the basis of their understanding of the Lord's Supper. "This kind of respect for what constitutes for both sides the 'must' of the division does not delay unity," the cardinal writes, "it is a fundamental pre-condition for it."[64]

Ratzinger ends his essay, "The Progress of Ecumenism," with the suspicion that not everyone will be pleased with his concept. The Reformed family of churches should be pleased, however. Commitment to the truth of the faith, honest acknowledgment of divergences, generous recognition of the real instances of unity in faith and life among us, and respect for the Christian integrity of the other have been hallmarks of the Reformed tradition from Calvin to the present. Furthermore, neither Reformed churches nor Cardinal Ratzinger confuses more "relaxed" ecumenical engagement with dilatory ecumenical endeavor. The effort is real because the reality of division is an offense to the gospel. At their best, contemporary Reformed Christians echo John Calvin's words in a letter to Archbishop Cranmer: "This other thing is to be ranked among the chief evils of our time, viz., that the churches are so divided, that human fellowship is scarcely now in any repute among us, far less that Christian intercourse

62. Ratzinger, "The Progress of Ecumenism," in *Church, Ecumenism and Politics*, p. 140.
63. Ratzinger, "The Progress of Ecumenism," p. 141.
64. Ratzinger, "The Progress of Ecumenism," p. 141.

which all make profession of, but few sincerely practice. . . . Thus it is that the members of the Church being severed, the body lies bleeding."[65]

At his best, Joseph Ratzinger has combined unstinting passion for the truth of the faith with openness to the presence of faith's truths in other churches and ecclesial communities. The contribution of Benedict XVI to deeper appropriation of Christian truth throughout the worldwide Christian community, and to fuller expressions of Christian unity, will depend on the way this balance is maintained and expressed. The churches need truth more than bourgeois toleration, and the Bishop of Rome is uniquely placed to engender deep ecumenical engagement in "the doctrine of the faith."

65. Calvin, "Letter to Archbishop Thomas Cranmer," in *Selected Works of John Calvin, Tracts and Letters*, ed. Henry Beveridge and Jules Bonnet (Grand Rapids: Baker Book House, 1954), vol. 5, part 2, p. 345.

8 Benedict XVI: Apostle of the "Pierced Heart of Jesus"

SARA BUTLER, M.S.B.T.

What can we expect of Pope Benedict, given his personal experience and his career as a theologian? We can expect to hear more of what we find in his first encyclical, *Deus Caritas Est.* It is traditional, after all, for a newly elected Pope to use a first encyclical to announce his priorities. It was not surprising that he should propose anew the central truth that God is love. The encyclical features biblical passages and themes that appear repeatedly in his writings on Christology. One can assume that these texts are among his favorites, that he prays with them, and that he wants to share them with us. They culminate in a single exhortation, the invitation to gaze upon "the pierced heart of Jesus on the Cross."[1] Clearly, as a pastor, Pope Benedict XVI has a burning desire to bring the Catholic faithful to a devotional knowledge and love of Jesus Christ as their Savior. This love must be the source of the good works by which we serve our neighbor and bring God's saving message to the world.

It is not unexpected that the theologian who wrote *Behold the Pierced One*[2] many years ago should write the encyclical *Deus Caritas Est.* For decades, Joseph Ratzinger has been calling our attention to the mystery of God's love, revealed in the pierced heart of the Redeemer. That he should spend "every free moment" since his election as Pope working on a two-volume *Jesus of Nazareth*[3] shows us his urgent preoccupation: that it is

---

1. *Deus Caritas Est,* §39. *Acta Apostolicae Sedis (A.A.S.)* 98 (2006): 217-52.

2. Joseph Cardinal Ratzinger, *Behold the Pierced One: An Approach to a Spiritual Christology,* trans. Graham Harrison (San Francisco: Ignatius Press, 1986.) German original: *Schauen auf den Durchbohrten* (Einsiedeln: Johannes Verlag, 1984).

3. Joseph Ratzinger, Pope Benedict XVI, *Jesus of Nazareth: From the Baptism in the Jordan to the Transfiguration,* trans. Adrian J. Walker (New York: Doubleday, 2007), p. xxi.

necessary to proclaim the gospel anew to generations who seem not to know that Jesus Christ — "the same, yesterday, today, and forever" (Heb. 13:8) — has set his heart on us and invites us to enter a living relationship with him, here and now. Those who have some acquaintance with his theological corpus are probably aware that his favorite devotional image or icon is the pierced side — or, more frequently, the pierced *heart* — of Christ Crucified. Benedict XVI insistently invites believers to follow the lead of John the evangelist to "gaze upon him whom they have pierced" (John 19:37, citing Zech. 12:10).

There is no doubt that this is a central theme in Benedict's Christology and in his personal prayer life.[4] Why would he so regularly recommend Jesus the Savior to our gaze according to this motif, unless he himself found it life-giving? If this is in fact a favorite theme, we may suppose that he will continue to bring it to our attention during his pontificate. From his conviction that faith can flourish only when it is personally appropriated through prayer and devotion, Pope Benedict urges us to look upon Christ and see in his open, broken heart the revelation of the Father's love and the fountain of salvation from which the Holy Spirit streams forth. He begs us to drink from this divine wellspring and let ourselves be transformed by God's abundant love. The Pope repeatedly presses this point home by appealing to biblical texts and motifs that play a large part in Pope Pius XII's encyclical on devotion to the Sacred Heart of Jesus, *Haurietis Aquas* (1956).[5]

On May 15, 2006, the fiftieth anniversary of *Haurietis Aquas,* Pope Benedict wrote to Father Peter-Hans Kolvenbach, the Superior General of the Jesuits, summing up that encyclical's teaching and remarking on the "irreplaceable importance" of devotion to the Heart of Christ.[6] In a few short pages, he recalled the mystery of God's love revealed in Christ crucified, a love that awaits our response. Appealing to the "biblical icon"

---

4. For confirmation, see Réal Tremblay, "Regarder le Christ transpercé, lieu d'émergence de la vie et de l'amour: Indications pour une morale fondamentale," *Studia Moralia* 45 (2007): 73-82, and Mark D. Kirby, "The Sacred Heart of Jesus in the Theology of Benedict XVI," *L'Osservatore Romano* (25 May 2005): 10 in the Weekly Edition in English, available at http://www.ewtn.com/library/Theology/heartb16.htm.

5. *Acta Apostolicae Sedis (A.A.S.)* 48 (1956): 309-53.

6. "Papal Letter on 50th Anniversary of 'Haurietis Aquas," accessed from http://www.zenit.org on 11/20/2007. A.A.S. 98 (2006): 458-62. The Jesuits were entrusted with the responsibility of spreading this devotion.

promoted by *Haurietis Aquas,* Pope Benedict wrote, "it is only possible to be a Christian by fixing our gaze on the Cross of our Redeemer, 'on him whom they have pierced' (Jn 19:37; cf. Zech 12:10)." We must encounter the Person of Christ in order "to know and to believe in the love God has for us" (1 John 4:16). Devotion to Jesus' pierced heart, he claimed, is "as old as Christianity itself." Those who practice it learn to confess with Thomas, who probed Jesus' wounded side with his hand, "My Lord and my God!" (John 20:28). They come to know God's love and to experience it personally, welcoming it and consecrating themselves to it. By fixing their gaze on the One who "took our infirmities and bore our diseases" (Matt. 8:17, citing Isa. 53:4), and on the blood and water streaming from his open heart, they are able to "become for others a source from which 'rivers of living water' flow (John 7:38)." Benedict concluded: "The adoration of God's love, whose historical and devotional expression is found in the symbol of the 'pierced heart,' remains indispensable for a living relationship with God." At four points in the course of this short letter, the Pope cited his own first encyclical, and so signaled the connection between *Haurietis Aquas* and *Deus Caritas Est.*

There is reason to believe that Benedict XVI is moved not only by the desire to promote a devotion that is especially meaningful to him but also by the need to remedy an increasingly grave state of affairs, namely, the decline of "devotion" to Christ. In some parts of the Catholic world, people have lost the sense that it is possible to encounter the Lord personally in prayer. Certain practices and devotions that gave life to the personal piety of past generations have been discouraged and then abandoned; they must be revived and given new expression. All are called to know Christ and to experience his intimate friendship; it is this experience of "being loved" that gives rise to a response of love. But is it really possible, today, to know Jesus Christ?[7] The Pope understands this existential question, and puts all his energy into providing an answer.

Here we shall examine two of Ratzinger's seminal essays from the early 1980s, "The Mystery of Easter" and "Taking Bearings in Christology." In these essays he already expressed his concern that the loss of devotion to Christ betokens a serious crisis of faith and a dangerous deviation from the only sure path to an intimate relationship with him. Following that we

---

7. His colleague, Hans Urs von Balthasar, called attention to this in *Does Jesus Know Us? Do We Know Him?* trans. Graham Harrison (San Francisco: Ignatius Press, 1983).

shall consider more recent evidence for our supposition that the proclamation of the love of God displayed in the pierced heart of the crucified Christ, a proclamation that has distinguished Ratzinger's contributions as a theologian, will continue to be one of his highest priorities.

Confronting a Crisis in Faith and Devotion

Between 1978 and 1982 Joseph Ratzinger became quite involved with efforts to address a surprising decline in the once immensely popular devotion to the Sacred Heart. While on a trip to Ecuador in 1978, some members of the Latin American branch of the International Institute of the Sacred Heart of Jesus presented him with a proposal that prompted him to enlist the help of several German theologians. In 1980, as Cardinal Archbishop of Munich and Freising, he acted as the patron of a symposium held in anticipation of the twenty-fifth anniversary of the encyclical, *Haurietis Aquas*. The goal of the theologians who participated was to articulate "the unity of Christology and the devotion to Christ, with special reference to the cult of the Heart of Jesus."[8] Ratzinger did not contribute a paper of his own, but he surely must have had a hand in selecting both the topics and the presenters.[9] The very high-quality contributions to this undertaking addressed themes that continue to be central to his own theological work. The symposium papers themselves regularly refer to a prior collection of papers published twenty years earlier under the title *Cor Salvatoris*.[10] It is easy to discover the contributions that these two collections, and the encyclical itself, have made to Ratzinger's Christology and to his abiding interest in the role "devotion" plays in sustaining and nourishing Christian faith.[11]

8. *Faith in Christ and the Worship of Christ*, ed. Leo Scheffczyk, trans. Graham Harrison (San Francisco: Ignatius Press, 1986), p. 11. German original, *Christusglaube und Christusverehrung: Neue Zugänge zur Christusfrömmigkeit* (Aschaffenburg: Paul Pattloch Verlag, 1982).

9. The contributors were Hans Urs von Balthasar, Joachim Becker, Josef Heer, Felix Heinzer, Leo Elders, Walter Baier, Anton Mattes, Johann Auer, Norbert Hoffmann, and Leo Scheffczyk. This volume remains an extremely valuable source for the study of this topic.

10. Joseph Ratzinger, *Heart of the Saviour*, ed. Josef Stierli, trans. Paul Andrews (New York: Herder & Herder, 1957). This earlier volume contains lectures originally given in 1951 that helped prepare the way, theologically, for *Haurietis Aquas*.

11. Leo Scheffczyk's essay "Devotion to Christ as a Way of Experiencing Him," in *Faith*

In 1984 Ratzinger published *Behold the Pierced One (Schauen auf den Durchbohrten)*, a collection of Christological essays and reflections. This small volume includes the two essays we shall examine, "The Mystery of Easter: Substance and Foundation of Devotion to the Sacred Heart," and "Taking Bearings in Christology." In the preface, Ratzinger explains their origin. The first was addressed to a Congress on the Sacred Heart of Jesus held in Toulouse in 1981. While preparing it he felt the impetus to consider Christology "from the aspect of its spiritual appropriation." That same year, taking the occasion of the 1300th anniversary of the Third Council of Constantinople (681) to research its achievements, he discovered that this council was also concerned to develop a "spiritual Christology," and that its work sheds significant light on the formulations of the Council of Chalcedon (451). Ratzinger incorporated this concern and his recent research into "Taking Bearings in Christology," presented the following year (1982) in Rio de Janeiro at a congress on Christology organized by CELAM, the Conference of Latin American Bishops.

These two essays provide a useful introduction to Ratzinger's abiding concern. "The Mystery of Easter" proposes devotion to Christ's pierced heart as the necessary counterpart to the objective spirituality of the liturgical movement. Here we find key biblical texts that support this devotion. "Taking Bearings" argues that the quest for the "historical Jesus" is incomplete without the knowledge that comes through faith and contemplation. We cannot come to faith in Jesus as the Christ by means of historical-critical scholarship; we truly know and understand him only by participating in his prayer, that is, by acts of self-surrender and love. In these essays, then, we find intimations of themes that continue to be prominent in his thought.

Before we consider Ratzinger's response to these difficulties, however, let us briefly glance at a 1978 sermon, "The Wellspring of Life, from the Side of the Lord, Opened in Loving Sacrifice,"[12] in which he ponders the evangelist's purpose in supplying an account of the piercing of Jesus' side. According to John's Gospel, the crucifixion coincides with the sacrifice of the lambs in the Temple for the Passover (John 19:14). This detail points to

---

in *Christ and the Worship of Christ* (pp. 207-13), is especially valuable. Scheffczyk defines "devotion" as "a form of worship of God in which the powers of the soul deliberately focus on some particular mystery" (p. 212).

12. See Joseph Cardinal Ratzinger, *God Is Near Us*, ed. Stephan Otto Horn and Vinzenz Pfnür and trans. Henry Taylor (San Francisco: Ignatius Press, 2003), pp. 42-55. In this sermon, Ratzinger stresses the sacrificial nature of the Eucharist.

Jesus' identity as the true Paschal lamb. Then, at the Cross, two prophecies are fulfilled. The first again reveals Jesus as the Passover lamb. The fact that the soldiers do not break the dead Jesus' legs fulfills a ritual instruction for the preparation of the Passover victim: "Not a bone of him shall be broken" (John 19:36, citing Exod. 12:46). (Ratzinger comments that this brings full circle the theme introduced in John 1:29: "Behold the Lamb of God, who takes away the sin of the world!") Second, to ensure that Jesus was dead, one of the soldiers took a lance and pierced his side, and at once blood and water came out (John 19:34). According to the evangelist, this fulfilled the prophecy of Zechariah that says, "They shall look on him whom they have pierced" (John 19:37, citing Zech. 12:10).[13] Looking ahead to the Book of Revelation (1:7), Ratzinger directs attention to the relation between the prophecy of Zechariah, fulfilled on the Cross, and the Day of Judgment, "on which the one who was pierced will rise over the world as its judgment and its life."[14] Ratzinger focuses attention on the prophet's admonition to believers and links the key biblical texts associated with devotion to the Sacred Heart to an explanation of the Eucharist as a sacrifice.[15] In this sermon, we can already glimpse the outline of his message.

The Crisis in Devotion to the Sacred Heart of Jesus

The first paper to be examined here is "The Mystery of Easter: Substance and Foundation of Devotion to the Sacred Heart."[16] It was given to commemorate the twenty-fifth anniversary of *Haurietis Aquas.* In it Ratzinger notes that an unanticipated consequence of the liturgical movement has been the displacement and even the abandonment of certain devotions

13. The Greek word for "side" is the word usually translated as "rib" in the account of the creation of Eve. By means of this detail the evangelist depicts Jesus as the "New Adam" in the "sleep" of death, from whose side — "opened up in loving sacrifice" — issues "the beginning of a new humanity," and "a spring of water that brings to fruition the whole of history." Ratzinger, *God Is Near Us,* pp. 42-43.

14. Ratzinger, *God Is Near Us,* p. 55. Ratzinger calls attention to the flow of blood and water from the Savior's side — symbols of the sacraments, Eucharist and Baptism, as the source of the new community, the Church.

15. We shall not attempt to pursue this rich theme, so important to Ratzinger's overall contribution; we use it only to supply an example of his homiletic use of certain biblical texts.

16. Ratzinger, *Behold the Pierced One,* pp. 47-69. We shall cite pages from this essay within the text.

that had sustained the piety of generations of Catholics. The liturgical movement sought to restore to the faithful the possibility of full, conscious, and active participation in the public worship of the Church. It sought to provide the faithful with a solid biblical piety, nourished by a communal celebration of Word and sacrament executed in the sober and classical style of the Roman rite in the patristic era. As lay people assumed their proper roles in the Church's Sunday worship, however, many abandoned the devotions that had previously sustained them. As the objective value of liturgical worship was promoted, these devotions were sometimes disparaged for fostering a "Jesus and me" spirituality. In many places, public devotion to the Sacred Heart of Jesus, with its hymns, litanies, formulas of personal consecration, First Fridays, holy hours, indulgenced prayers, badges, and confraternities, simply died out.

"The Mystery of Easter" notes that the spirituality recommended by the liturgical movement required the subordination of the emotional, subjective forms of nineteenth-century piety to the more sober and objective liturgical forms.[17] Many regarded the prayers, hymns, and pictorial representations associated with devotion to the Sacred Heart of Jesus as sentimental and extravagant. Theologians charged that the actual object of the devotion was unclear: Christ's bodily heart? His love? His physical heart as a symbol of his love? They questioned what it meant to exhort worshipers to "console" the Savior as if he were still sorrowing and suffering (even in a "self-pitying" way, on account of unrequited love) and could be comforted by their sympathy.[18] The advocates of liturgical renewal were pressing for forms that were more clearly shaped by biblical and classical patristic theological themes.

In response, Ratzinger argues that the encyclical of Pius XII had answered these contemporary objections in terms that already anticipated the conciliar reforms.[19] If the teaching of *Haurietis Aquas* has been dis-

---

17. See his similar observations on Marian piety: "On the Position of Mariology and Marian Spirituality within the Totality of Faith and Theology," in *The Church and Women: A Compendium,* ed. Helmut Moll (San Francisco: Ignatius Press, 1988), pp. 67-71.

18. In this devotion, the faithful are invited to "console" our Lord in his Agony in the Garden, making reparation by their love for the rejection he suffered from sinners. Karl Rahner asked whether this was only pious "make-believe" and attempted to provide a solid theological foundation for it. See "Some Theses on the Theology of the Devotion," in *Heart of the Saviour,* pp. 131-55, at 150-54.

19. *Haurietis Aquas,* which marked the 100th anniversary of the extension of the Feast of the Most Sacred Heart of Jesus to the universal Church, acknowledged these concerns

missed, he suggests, it is due to a mentality that regards everything prior to the council as invalidated by it. He makes the case for a hermeneutic of continuity, recapitulating and developing some important themes from the encyclical. In his defense of this devotion as central to Christian spirituality, we discover the biblical passages and themes that continue to find a place in his theology.

A Biblical Icon: The "Pierced Heart" of Jesus

According to *Haurietis Aquas,* devotion to the Sacred Heart of Jesus belongs to biblical revelation and is central to Christian piety. Even if centuries passed before it took its present shape, this devotion was not unknown in the early Church. It did not originate with private revelations to St. Margaret Mary Alacoque in seventeenth-century France, nor with the thirteenth-century German mystics.[20] Rather, it has its source in the Gospel of St. John, as read and interpreted by the Fathers and theologians of the Church.[21] The biblical icon of this devotion is the "pierced side" of the Redeemer (John 19:34) from which springs the fountain of "living water" he promised to those who believe in him (John 7:37-39). The encyclical, which opens with a verse from the prophet Isaiah (12:3), "You will draw water with joy, out of the Savior's fountain," identifies the Redeemer's wounded heart as the living sign and symbol of his love.[22] What is said of Jesus' "pierced side" came to be said of his "heart" as the devotion matured and spread to the whole Church.[23] In making this connection, *Haurietis Aquas* proposed a new rationale for the devotion; it set forth a biblical and patristic foundation that provided a new icon, the pierced heart of the Savior.[24] By tracing devotion to the Sacred Heart of Jesus to its biblical roots,

---

(§§10-13). See Richard Gutzweiler, "The Objections," in *Heart of the Saviour,* pp. 1-14, for a fuller description of these objections. Ratzinger says Pope Pius XII set out to overcome "the dangerous dualism between liturgical spirituality and nineteenth-century devotion" (p. 49).

20. *Haurietis Aquas,* §§96-97; §21. For more on this, see the essays by Walter Baier and Johann Auer in *Faith in Christ and the Worship of Christ,* pp. 81-117.

21. *Haurietis Aquas,* §§90; 45-51, 77.

22. *Haurietis Aquas,* §4, citing Zechariah 13:1.

23. *Haurietis Aquas,* §§77-78.

24. Perhaps this was referred to as a new "icon" to meet objections lodged against the devotional image associated with the private revelations granted to St. Margaret Mary.

Sara Butler, M.S.B.T.

Pope Pius XII hoped to revitalize it as a privileged means of urging the faithful to greater love of God and neighbor.

In "The Mystery of Easter," Ratzinger recalls that it was the research of Hugo Rahner, S.J., that secured the biblical foundation for this devotion.[25] In his study of patristic symbols of the Church, Rahner discovered that certain Fathers of the Church, in commenting on the piercing of the Savior's side with a lance (John 19:34), understood this incident to fulfill Jesus' own promise that "fountains of living water" would spring from his heart (John 7:37-39).[26] The tradition of patristic exegesis from Asia Minor that favored this interpretation punctuated John 7:37-39 in such a way as to indicate that Jesus presented *himself* — rather than the one who believes in him — as the source of the "living water."[27] According to this "Ephesian" interpretation, John 7:37-39 reads: "On the last and great day of the feast, Jesus stood and cried, saying:

If any man thirst, let him come to me,
And let him drink, who believes in me.
As the Scripture says:
Fountains of living water
Shall flow from his bosom [*koilia*].[28]

The more familiar, "Alexandrian" interpretation, suggested by a different punctuation, reads:

If any man thirst, let him come to me and drink.
He that believes in me, as the Scripture says,

25. See Hugo Rahner, "On the Biblical Basis of the Devotion," and "The Beginnings of the Devotion in Patristic Times," in *Heart of the Saviour* (note 10, above), pp. 15-35, 37-57. This research was proposed in "Flumina de ventre Christi," *Biblica* 22 (1941): 269-302 and 367-403, and then published in *Symbole der Kirche: Ekklesiologie der Väter* (Salzburg: Otto Müller Verlag, 1964). Certain elements of this explanation are presupposed by but not included in Ratzinger's essay.

26. This incident also gave rise to meditations on the birth of the Church, the New Eve, from the side of the New Adam "sleeping" on the Cross, and on the sacraments of Baptism and Eucharist, symbolized as the water and blood that flowed from his wounded side.

27. H. Rahner, "On the Biblical Basis," pp. 29-30, and "The Beginning," pp. 40-43.

28. According to H. Rahner, the word *koilia* literally means "entrails" in Greek, but would function as a synonym for "heart" in Aramaic. See "On the Biblical Basis of the Devotion," p. 31.

Fountains of living water shall flow
From his bosom [*koilia*].

The evangelist comments: "Now he said this about the Spirit, which those who believed in him were to receive; for as yet the Spirit had not been given, because Jesus was not yet glorified" (John 7:39).

The Ephesian interpretation of this saying supports the conjunction of John 19:24 and John 7:37-39, for it sees *Jesus'* pierced side (or heart) as the source of the "fountains of living water."[29] The Alexandrian interpretation, by contrast, does not link the two; here, it is the *believer's* heart that is the source of living waters. The Fathers who followed the Ephesian reading pursued the many rich associations it suggested with the messianic promise of living water, the Spirit, and consequently with the Paschal Mystery. *Haurietis Aquas* relies upon this tradition when it opens with Isaiah 12:3, "You will draw water with joy from the Savior's fountain," and when it alludes to Zechariah 13:1, "In that day there shall be a fountain open to the house of David and to the inhabitants of Jerusalem for the washing away of sin and of uncleanness."[30] If, as H. Rahner argues, this is the reading intended by the evangelist, then the text bears witness to the expectation that streams of living water — the Holy Spirit — will flow from the heart of the Crucified and Risen Messiah. He reasons that one finds in this patristic tradition the origin of the early medieval devotion that eventually came to focus directly on the Savior's heart (49-50). In his judgment, devotion to the pierced heart is "nothing but devotion to the mystery of Easter," the core doctrine of the Christian faith (49). It is virtually identical with the Easter spirituality proposed by the liturgical movement.

Beyond Haurietis Aquas: *Devotion and Religion of the Heart*

Ratzinger observes that this interpretation was insufficient to sustain the devotion. He asks why the Lord's *heart* should be at the center of the Easter mystery, since the word "heart" does not even appear in the key biblical

---

29. This is the warrant for seeing in Jesus' allusions to what "the Scripture says" references to messianic promise of living water connected with the feast of Tabernacles — Isaiah 12:3; Ezekiel 47:1-12; Zechariah 13:1; Exodus 17:1-7; Numbers 20:7-13. See Ratzinger's exposition in *Jesus of Nazareth*, pp. 244-48.

30. See *Haurietis Aquas* §§3-4.

texts from John 7 and 19. Since worshipers can participate in the *reality* of the Paschal Mystery in the Church's liturgy, is not the "devotional empathizing" associated with the adoration of the Sacred Heart superfluous? (50). In answer, Ratzinger makes the case that a "devotion" that engages the emotions and passions of the human heart is the only worthy response to the passion of the heart of God revealed on the Cross.

The marvel of the Incarnation is that God, whose involvement in human history was described in metaphors drawn from bodily experience by the biblical authors,[31] has in Christ assumed a human nature, complete with a human heart. In the Incarnation of the Son, God has entered "the realm of the flesh, the realm of the passion of the human being" (52). The biblical and patristic sources of the cult of the pierced heart may not trace Jesus' feelings and emotions explicitly to his physical heart, but by virtue of the hypostatic union, his physical heart is a natural symbol of his boundless love. Because of the Incarnation, we can behold the invisible in the visible. This beholding is also an Easter phenomenon, as we see in the Apostle Thomas's encounter with the risen Jesus (John 20:26-29). Thomas needs to see and to touch the Savior's pierced side before he can exclaim "My Lord and my God!" (20:28). We, like him, are invited (in the words of St. Bonaventure) to "look through the visible wound to the invisible wound of love!" (53).[32]

Ratzinger emphasizes that believers need to see, to "behold" silently in a way that "touches," if they are to enter into God's mysteries. An "objective" spirituality based only on participation in the Church's liturgy is not sufficient. "The liturgy itself can only be celebrated properly if it is prepared for, and accompanied by, that meditative 'abiding' in which the heart begins to see and to understand, drawing the senses too into its beholding" (54). It is a mistake, then, to think that the recovery of a spirituality based on the Bible and the Fathers requires us to abandon as obsolete the spiritual practices of the medieval mystics and the ecclesially based piety of modern times. To know the "breadth and length and height and depth" of

31. The God of Israel is living and personal; he enters into a covenant relationship with his people and responds to them with feeling — delight, joy, anger, frustration, indignation, regret, and so on.

32. Bonaventure is cited in *Haurietis Aquas,* §87. Ratzinger adds: "All of us are Thomas, unbelieving; but, like him, all of us can touch the exposed Heart of Jesus and thus touch and behold the Logos himself. So, with our hands and eyes fixed upon this Heart, we can attain to the confession of faith: 'My Lord and my God!'" (54). Undoubtedly, Ratzinger's study of St. Bonaventure's theology contributes much to his appreciation of this mystery.

the love of Christ (see Eph. 3:18f.), it is necessary to engage the heart, the senses, and the emotions. Love needs to see; we need tangible forms such as Jesus' human heart. Since the "hub" of the senses is the heart, a spirituality of the senses is ultimately a spirituality of the heart, "where sense and spirit meet, interpenetrate, and unite" (56).

The Incarnate Word experienced in his human heart the passions of anguish, anger, joy, hope, delight, sorrow, love, grief. He truly experienced these, for "there can be no Passion without passions: suffering presupposes the ability to suffer, it presupposes the faculty of the emotions" (57). Origen grasped this, and even suggested that God suffers, meaning not only that God the Son suffered in his human nature but also that suffering touches God the Father and the Holy Spirit; suffering is the proof of love, even of God's love (58).[33] For Ratzinger, "Incarnational spirituality must be a spirituality of the passions, a spirituality of 'heart to heart.'" "The actual advance registered by the Christian idea of God over that of the ancient world," he affirms, "lies in its recognition that God is love" (58).

Ratzinger believes that the pierced heart of the Savior is a proper and even necessary object of devotion. It is not optional, for it belongs to the core of our faith and draws our hearts into our relationship with God. "The taboo on pathos," he observes, "renders [spirituality] pathological." It has resulted in "the neglect of a meditative, contemplative spirituality in favor of an exclusive, community-based activism," followed by the search for methods of meditation dissociated from the content of Christian revelation (60).

The Drama of the Heart of God

The movement to purify the Church's spirituality by retrieving themes from Scripture and Tradition can find ample evidence of a "heart-centered spirituality [that] corresponds to the picture of the Christian God who has a heart," Ratzinger maintains (61). We find it, for example, in the Song of Songs 4:9 ("You have ravished my heart") and 8:16 ("Set me as a seal upon your heart . . . for love is as strong as death"). Medieval mystics, like the Fathers of the Church, relished these passages that speak of God's passionate love for us and our response. Verses like these are suitable for integrating

---

33. In note 10 on 58, he recalls the saying of St. Bernard of Clairvaux, "*impassibilis est Deus, sed non incompassibilis.*"

"all the passion of human love into man's relationship with God" (61). An even more compelling witness to this biblical theme, however, is Hosea 11:1-9. In this "canticle of the love of God,"[34] the "heart" theme is explicit (62). The prophet depicts the Lord as one who loves his son (the chosen people), and who ought to punish him for his misdeeds, but cannot do it; his *heart* will not let him. His heart turns around and he relents: "my heart recoils within me; my compassion grows warm and tender" (Hos. 11:8). Although the Old Testament mentions God's "heart" some twenty-six times, this "canticle" of Hosea introduces a strikingly new note, namely, the idea that God's heart is so moved by love as to reverse his judgment. His heart "recoils," or "turns around,"[35] creating an interior upheaval in favor of his beloved people (63). For Hosea, "God's merciful love conquers his untouchable righteousness" (64). Here, we see the "Passion" of God's heart that sheds light on the Passion of Jesus.

In the New Testament this "upheaval" in God's heart leads to the Cross, where God, in the person of the Son, experiences rejection. Jesus exchanges places with sinners, offering them his place — the Son's place. "According to Hosea 11, the Passion of Jesus is the drama of the divine Heart"; in fact, "the pierced Heart of the crucified Son is the literal fulfillment of the prophecy of the Heart of God which overthrows its righteousness by mercy and by that very action remains righteous" (64).[36]

Ratzinger contrasts the concern of Jesus' heart with those of our hearts. For us, the heart's task is self-preservation, but Jesus' pierced heart has

truly "overturned" (cf. Hos 11:8) this definition. This Heart is not concerned with self-preservation but with self-surrender. It saves the world by opening itself. The collapse of the opened Heart is the content of the

34. Some years earlier, Ratzinger co-edited a festschrift for Johann Auer, *Mysterium der Gnade* (Regensburg: Verlag Friedrich Pustet, 1975), which included a paper by Heinrich Gross, "Das Hohelied der Liebe Gottes: Zur Theologie von Hosea 11." This essay has clearly influenced Ratzinger's reflections on the question.

35. Ratzinger often refers readers to note 52 of *Dives in Misericordia,* an encyclical by Pope John Paul II on the Mercy of God (1980). This lengthy footnote describes God's covenant fidelity, mercy, and compassion. See the exposition in *Jesus of Nazareth,* pp. 206-7.

36. By appealing to these verses Ratzinger acknowledges the possibility of using the Bible as a whole, reading both Testaments together. Here Ratzinger firmly maintains the legitimacy of doing this, in continuity with the Church's longstanding practice. One must consult the totality of the biblical witness in order to discover these riches (64).

Easter mystery. The Heart saves, indeed, but it saves by giving itself away. Thus, in the Heart of Jesus, the center of Christianity is set before us. It expresses everything, all that is genuinely new and revolutionary in the New Covenant. This Heart calls to our heart. It invites us to step forth out of the futile attempt of self-preservation and, by joining in the task of love, by handing ourselves over to him and with him, to discover the fullness of love which alone is eternity and which alone sustains the world. (69)

The Crisis of Confidence Regarding the Possibility of Knowing Jesus Christ

In preparing the address to a symposium on the Sacred Heart of Jesus that we have just reviewed, Ratzinger's interest in the "spiritual appropriation" of Christology was awakened. He pursued this further when he discovered, in the Christological doctrine of the Third Council of Constantinople, the presence of a similar concern. These two events contributed to the second essay to be reviewed here, "Taking Bearings in Christology."[37] It was actually written in response to an invitation from Latin American bishops who wished to understand the Christological questions emerging from liberation theology. Liberation Christologies tend to rely heavily on reconstructions of the "historical Jesus."[38] Since their concern is to highlight Jesus' solidarity with those who suffer oppression, they view his cruel execution and death chiefly as the price he paid for his liberating praxis, that is, his public protest against injustice. Their prevailing interest in the historical question — "Why did Jesus' contemporaries put him to death?" — leads them to discount or even reject the Church's soteriological affirmation that Jesus freely offered his life to the Father in sacrifice for our sins. Ratzinger sets out an overview of the Church's faith in Christ and his free self-surrender in love as the necessary doctrinal context in which to situate the new questions.

According to Ratzinger's "spiritual Christology," the biblical evidence

37. Ratzinger, *Behold the Pierced One*, pp. 13-46. We will cite page numbers within the text.

38. See the assessment of the Pontifical Biblical Institute (1984) in *Bible et Christologie*, §§1.1.9. For an English translation, plus a commentary, see Joseph A. Fitzmyer, "The Biblical Commission and Christology," *Theological Studies* 46 (1985): 407-44. As prefect of the Congregation for the Doctrine of the Faith, Ratzinger was president of the Pontifical Biblical Commission when this study was produced.

must be read in the Church and appropriated by faith, especially by "participation" in the mysteries of Christ. Without questioning the value of the historical-critical method, he points out its limitations.[39] Insofar as exegetes and theologians rely exclusively on this method, they may begin to think that their scholarly reconstructions establish what is normative for faith in Christ. Believers, faced with the results of these studies, may begin to wonder about the reliability of the gospel testimony regarding the pre-Paschal Jesus, and even about the possibility of knowing and experiencing the risen Christ as an object of personal faith and devotion. The real danger is that the faithful will only be introduced to the "historical Jesus," a man consigned to the distant past, someone whom we can imitate but not encounter in a personal way.[40] Again, once the question of eternal salvation is eclipsed by concern for this-worldly liberation, the traditional understanding of how Jesus' liberating act is mediated is put in question (13-15). Given these developments, theologians were challenged to coordinate the findings of New Testament scholarship with the Church's dogmatic teaching in a new way. In this essay Ratzinger again shows a vigorous interest in sustaining, by means of a new Christological synthesis, a Christ-centered spirituality.[41]

Towards a "Spiritual Christology"

In "Taking Bearings," Ratzinger provides a broad overview of the content of Christology, as held by the faith of the Church, and of the hermeneu-

39. See 42-45. Thesis 7 reads: "The historico-critical method and other modern scientific methods are important for an understanding of Holy Scripture and tradition. Their value, however, depends on the hermeneutical (philosophical) context in which they are applied" (42).

40. In *Jesus of Nazareth*, pp. xi-xxiv, we find Pope Benedict's more recent explanation of the problem.

41. Prior to his appointment as prefect, Ratzinger served as a member of the International Theological Commission from its inception in 1969 until 1979. The commission's documents are not "official teaching," but they provide indications of the considered opinion of approved scholars with respect to these issues. "Select Questions on Christology" (1980), "Theology-Christology-Anthropology" (1983), "The Consciousness of Christ Concerning Himself and His Mission" (1985), and "Select Questions on the Theology of God the Redeemer" (1995). The first three are in *Texts and Documents 1969-1985*, with a Foreword by Joseph Cardinal Ratzinger, ed. Michael Sharkey (San Francisco: Ignatius Press, 1989); the last is in *Communio* 24 (Spring 1997): 160-214.

tical context for grasping it. He insists that the real precondition for knowing Jesus Christ is faith — faith not only as a personal disposition to trust, but also as confession. "The Christian confession of faith comes from participating in the prayer of Jesus" (19). It is the Church that proposes Jesus to us as Messiah, Lord, and Son of God, and we can know him by faith only in and through the Church's tradition and teaching (31-32). Beyond the simple assent of faith, the appropriation of its *meaning* by what may be called a "devotional knowledge" of Jesus Christ and his mysteries is available only to those who participate in his prayer.

This is the common theme that runs through Ratzinger's seven theses.[42] First, the center of Jesus' life and person is his intimate communion with the Father, that is, his prayer. Second, Jesus died praying (Psalm 22); who he is (Christology) and what he does (soteriology) come together on the Cross. Third, the point that interests us here, "Since the center of the person of Jesus is prayer, it is essential to participate in his prayer if we are to know and understand him" (25). Fourth, sharing in Jesus' prayer requires communion with the Body of Christ, the Church, for she is the transcendental "subject" of the tradition "in whose memory the past is present" (31). Fifth and sixth, the dogmatic teaching of the Christological councils faithfully interprets the data of New Testament Christology. And seventh, only faith's hermeneutic is able to provide a synthesis that can both "hold fast the entire testimony of the sources" and transcend "the differences of cultures, times, and peoples" (45). Ratzinger concludes: "Christology is born of prayer or not at all" (46).

Throughout this essay Ratzinger maintains that in order to know and understand Jesus and his mission, one needs to believe in him with the faith of the Church and to enter into relationship with him by participating in his prayer. Just as getting to know anyone well requires a capacity for empathy, so in order to know Jesus through faith a certain prayerful "empathy" is needed. This is achieved by entering into his relationship with the Father, the relationship that is at the center of his identity as the Son.[43] The

---

42. See also his earlier "Theses for Christology," in *Dogma and Preaching*, trans. Matthew J. O'Connell (Chicago: Franciscan Herald Press, 1985), pp. 3-15. German original: *Dogma und Verkundigung* (Munich: Erich Wewel Verlag, 1973).

43. Ratzinger illustrates this with several examples from the Gospels, e.g., the call of the Twelve, the confession of Peter, the Transfiguration, and the Agony in the Garden. He notes that the Fourth Gospel, in a particular way, "draws us into that intimacy which Jesus reserved for those who were his friends" (22).

effort to know Jesus' innermost self through contemplation is "not some kind of pious supplement to reading the Gospels," Ratzinger emphasizes. Rather, "it is the basic precondition if real understanding, in the sense of modern hermeneutics — i.e., the entering-in to the same time and the same meaning — is to take place" (26). This effort is itself a prayer, and as prayer it is an act of love and self-surrender. This is why the theology of the saints, the theology of experience, must complement the theology of the schools (27).

But can we, today, "participate" in Jesus' prayer? Is it possible for us to share in events that are long past, whose exact shape remains unknown to us except through reports of those who interpreted what they understood in light of the Resurrection? How does our contemplation of the "mysteries" of Jesus' life give us access to him? Do we actually encounter the Lord in those events? Here we meet once again the problem, posed this time by biblical scholars, raised by those who questioned devotion to the Sacred Heart. Ratzinger reminds us in "Taking Bearings" that the Church is the living "subject" of our knowledge of Jesus. And in the Church's memory (see John 14:26), "the past is present" (31). For believers, Jesus is not a figure lost in the mists of history; on the contrary, he is our risen Lord, present and living in the Church. We enter into communion with him and into his dialogue of prayer with the Father by participating in the Church's life.[44] The Church is the necessary hermeneutical context for this loving encounter.

Ratzinger finds this theme profoundly reinforced by the Christological achievement of the Third Council of Constantinople (A.D. 680-681),[45] especially by the contribution of St. Maximus the Confessor (d. 662), the champion of the Church's faith against Monotheletism, the heresy that denied Jesus' human will.[46] The Council of Chalcedon (451) had affirmed, against Monophysitism, that "one and the same Lord Jesus Christ, the only-begotten Son, must be acknowledged in two natures,

44. This is nothing to which we have a right, nothing we could achieve on our own (29-30).

45. According to his seventh thesis, its Neo-Chalcedonian Christology "makes an important contribution to a proper grasp of the inner unity of biblical and dogmatic theology, of theology and religious life" (37).

46. Maximus the Confessor taught the mutual "indwelling" *(perichoresis)* of the two natures, and he distinguished the will that belongs to the nature from the "gnomic" will, or *liberium arbitrium* that pertains to the person (39, n. 18).

without confusion or change, without division or separation."[47] Carrying the Chalcedonian doctrine forward, III Constantinople affirms, against Monotheletism, that in Christ there are "two natural volitions or wills and two natural actions, without division, without change, without separation, without confusion."[48] This definition confirms the Church's faith in Christ's human will and therefore his human freedom. His humanity suffers no reduction or "amputation" in being assumed by the Word. Christ's human will is not "swallowed up" by his divine will, as Monotheletism supposed; neither are his two wills opposed, nor simply juxtaposed. Instead, his human will "follows the divine will . . . along a path of freedom," so that they become one in "a form of unity created by love" that corresponds in some way to the Trinitarian unity (39). Remaining two ontologically, they are "one" existentially, in the realm of the Person.[49]

Why does Ratzinger think this doctrine is significant for the "spiritual appropriation of Christology"? He sees that Jesus' human will becomes "one" with the divine will in free obedience. This reveals that "when the human will is taken up into the will of God, freedom is not destroyed; indeed, only then does genuine freedom come into its own" (38). We see this expressed concretely when Jesus, in his hour of "agony" in Gethsemane, prays to the Father, "Not what I will, but what thou wilt" (Mark 14:3). To participate in Jesus' prayer, then, and enter into his relationship with the Father, we too must hand over our will to the Father in a prayer that arises from love. By doing so, we participate in Christ's obedience — "in the pain of this exchange"[50] — and come to know and understand him. The prayer that the Son offers to the Father in and through his human freedom is the source of our own freedom; it opens the way for our prayer, our communion with God, our "divinization."[51] Ratzinger describes as "freedom's lab-

47. Denzinger-Schönmetzer, §302, English translation from *The Christian Faith in the Doctrinal Documents of the Catholic Church,* ed. Joseph Neuner and Jacques Dupuis (New York: Alba House, 1995), §615. Ratzinger comments that belief in the Incarnation means belief that God "actually touches man, and allows himself to be touched by man, in the person of him who *is* the Son" (36).

48. Denzinger-Schönmetzer, §556; Neuner-Dupuis, §635.

49. Another essay in *Behold the Pierced One* elaborates this at some length. See pp. 90-93.

50. Ratzinger, *Behold the Pierced One,* p. 92.

51. Ratzinger ties this in to the Eucharist: "To receive the Lord in the Eucharist, therefore, means entering into a community of being with Christ, it means entering through that opening in human nature through which God is accessible" (90).

oratory" this prayer by which the Christian "enters into the prayer and becomes the prayer of Jesus in the Body of Christ" (42). Only here is a person changed in such a way as to become divine. Here and nowhere else takes place that radical change of which we stand in need "if we are to act according to conscience and make this world a better place." In this "laboratory," the Christian's own will is refashioned, allowing it "to be expropriated and inserted into the divine will" (46).

Consulting these essays from 1978-82, we can see Ratzinger's desire to propose the Church's Christological doctrine in its entirety and to insist that saving faith involves an encounter with a Person, Jesus Christ. As his frequent references to the encyclical *Haurietis Aquas* indicate, he sees the contemporary crisis of belief in Christ as tied in some way to the virtual disappearance of the once-vital practice of devotion to the Sacred Heart of Jesus. He regards this devotion as central to the Church's faith. If it is threatened by developments in liturgical and biblical scholarship, it must be presented afresh, for religion is an affair of the heart, God's heart and our hearts. Devotion to Christ must animate public worship and action on behalf of justice if they are to be authentically Christian. This devotion needs a focus, and a focus already provided in the pierced heart of the Crucified Savior.

The Call to Contemplate God's Love in the Pierced Heart of the Redeemer

Joseph Cardinal Ratzinger quite naturally brought these theological and pastoral concerns to bear on his work when he was appointed prefect of the Congregation for the Doctrine of the Faith in 1981. In this capacity he presided over the Pontifical Biblical Commission,[52] the International Theological Commission,[53] and, from 1986 to 1992, the commission that prepared a *Catechism of the Catholic Church*.[54] It is not difficult to trace in the documents produced by the Congregation and these commissions a certain development of the themes we are examining, but we shall confine our attention to the *Catechism*.

52. See above, note 38. More recently, this commission published *The Interpretation of the Bible in the Church* (1994) and *The Jewish People and Their Sacred Scriptures in the Christian Bible* (2001). Both are available at http://www.vatican.va.

53. See above, note 41.

54. Available online at http://www.vatican.va.

The Catechism *and the Pierced Heart of Jesus*

The *Catechism of the Catholic Church* reflects Ratzinger's preoccupations, especially in the organization and exposition of the Christological chapter. It is striking that the sub-section on the Christological councils, the last of which rejected iconoclasm, concludes with a paragraph on the Sacred Heart. Why is devotion to the Sacred Heart introduced in this context? Although it does not report the teaching of a council, this paragraph is found in the sub-section on the councils. Ratzinger offers an explanation in *Gospel, Catechesis, Catechism: Sidelights on the Catechism of the Catholic Church*.[55] He maintains that the labors of those first seven councils provide "the ultimate foundation for our whole devotion to Jesus." Everything leads up to the *Catechism's* "bold statement" in §478: "Jesus knew and loved us each and all during his life, his agony, and his Passion and gave himself up for each one of us: 'The Son of God . . . loved me and gave himself for me'" (Gal. 2:20). "Only with this statement," Ratzinger claims, "does Christological catechesis become gospel in the full sense of the word." He presses home his point: "Each one of us can and may apply to himself the dramatic personalization that Paul accomplishes in these words. Every man may say: The Son of God loved *me* and gave himself up for *me*."[56] The remainder of paragraph 478 refers explicitly to devotion to the Sacred Heart:

> He has loved us all with a human heart. For this reason, the Sacred Heart of Jesus, pierced by our sins and for our salvation (*cf. Jn* 19:34), is quite rightly considered the chief sign and symbol of that . . . love with which the divine Redeemer continually loves the eternal Father and all human beings without exception.[57]

We may also observe that it is logical to place this text directly after two paragraphs (§§476, 477) having to do with "Christ's true body." The doctrine of II Nicea is reported in §476: because the Word assumed a true

---

55. (San Francisco: Ignatius Press, 1997), pp. 70-71.

56. *Gospel, Catechesis, Catechism*, pp. 70-71. This claim recalls the fourth proposition of the International Theological Commission's study, "The Consciousness of Christ Concerning Himself and His Mission." The fourth proposition, which includes a very stirring biblical defense of this thesis, reflects very well the message Ratzinger continues to proclaim.

57. The final quotation is from *Haurietis Aquas* §54; DS 3924; cf. DS 3812. See also *Catechism* §2669, on the veneration of the Heart of Jesus.

humanity, "the human face of Jesus can be portrayed" in holy images or icons. It is further explained in §477: "the Church has always acknowledged that in the body of Jesus 'we see our God made visible and so are caught up in love of the God we cannot see'" (quoting the Christmas Preface of the Roman Missal). Because God's Son "has made the features of his human body his own," they can be venerated in a holy image.

Although the *Catechism* as a whole seeks to remedy the crisis of faith in Christ, the chapter on Christology addresses it formally. We can see Ratzinger's hand in the opening paragraphs on the need to encounter the Person of Jesus in faith and love (§§422-25) in order to confess him as the Christ, the only Son of God, and "Lord" (§§430-55). His interest in the teaching of the Third Council of Constantinople is reflected in the fact that the summary report of conciliar teaching (§§464-83) includes the post-Chalcedonian councils and elaborates on their significance (§§468-77).[58] The section on Jesus' life and ministry is set out in terms of his "mysteries" (§§512-682), and introduced with an invitation to participate in them through faith and the sacraments (§§512-21, especially §521). And the "mystery" of Jesus' expiatory death (§§599-623) is portrayed in light of his "desire to embrace his Father's plan of redeeming love" (§607) by his free self-oblation (§605). Finally, Part IV of the *Catechism* offers instruction on Christian prayer, highlighting Jesus' own prayer and our ability to enter into it (§§2738-41).

The Pierced Heart of Jesus in *Deus Caritas Est*

Although we can detect the hand and spirit of Joseph Ratzinger rather easily in the work of the commissions over which he presided, and in official documents that he personally wrote and signed, it is only since his election as Pope that we can know precisely what message he himself wishes to communicate to the whole Church. It is, beyond a doubt, the fundamental Christian message that "God is love, and he who abides in love abides in God, and God abides in him" (1 John 4:16). Although Pope Benedict suggests that one reason for choosing this theme is the regrettable association

---

58. In an essay in *A New Song for the Lord: Faith in Christ and Liturgy Today,* trans. Martha M. Matesich (New York: Crossroad, 1996), pp. 3-28, Ratzinger includes his observations on the contemporary importance of these councils.

of God's name with violence and hatred in our time, he clearly intends the encyclical to put forth his positive pastoral program. He wants "to call forth in the world renewed energy and commitment in the human response to God's love" (§1). He proposes the pierced heart of Jesus as an icon of this love at five points in the encyclical.

Pope Benedict first appeals to our human experience of love and its two dimensions, *eros* and *agape* (§7). He observes that since love is a single reality, *eros* and *agape* are not opposed to each other or cut off from each other. In fact, "anyone who wishes to give love must also receive love as a gift." Appealing to John's Gospel, he explains, "one can become a source from which rivers of living water flow (*cf. Jn* 7:37-38)" only by drinking from "the original source, which is Jesus Christ, from whose pierced heart flows the love of God (*cf. Jn* 19:34)." Here the Pope announces a theme to which he will return (§42), namely, that authentic Christian service must be rooted in the experience of Christ's love.[59]

The second point underscores the novelty of the biblical image of God (§§9-10). In biblical revelation, God's love is characterized by *eros* as well as *agape,* but God's *eros* is "totally *agape.*" According to the Prophets, especially Hosea and Ezekiel, God loves the chosen people with a personal, elective, and *passionate* love. As evidence, the Pope appeals to the "canticle of divine love," Hosea 11:8-9. Lamenting the rebellion of his covenant people, God reveals his heart: "How can I give you up, O Ephraim! How can I hand you over, O Israel! . . . My heart recoils within me, my compassion grows warm and tender. I will not execute my fierce anger . . ." (Hos. 11:8-9). The canticle of Hosea allows the Pope to relate the "drama" of God's heart to the Passion endured by his Son:

> God's passionate love for his people — for humanity — is at the same time a forgiving love. It is so great that it turns God against himself, his love against his justice. Here Christians can see a dim prefiguration of the mystery of the Cross: so great is God's love for man that by becoming man he follows him even into death, and so reconciles justice and love. (§10)

The third mention of the pierced heart refers directly to the Incarnation (§12). As Benedict points out, the novelty of the New Testament lies

---

59. In the encyclical, the Pope stays with the "Alexandrian" reading of John 7:37-39.

"in the figure of Christ himself." In Jesus, "it is God himself who goes in search of the 'stray sheep,' a suffering and lost humanity." Jesus' parables of the shepherd searching for his lost sheep, the woman searching for her lost coin, and the father running to meet his "prodigal son," explain his being and his mission. "His death on the Cross is the culmination of that turning against himself in which he gives himself in order to raise man up and save him." The Pope directs our attention to the biblical icon: "By contemplating the pierced side of Christ (*cf. Jn* 19:37), we can understand the starting-point of this Encyclical Letter: 'God is love' (*1 Jn* 4:8). It is there that this truth can be contemplated. It is from there that our definition of love must begin. In this contemplation the Christian discovers the path along which his life and love must move."[60]

The fourth reference provides a Trinitarian perspective (§19). Pope Benedict writes, quoting St. Augustine, "If you see charity, you see the Trinity." By gazing on "the Pierced one (*cf. Jn* 19:37; *Zech* 12:10)," we can recognize the plan of the Father's love — for he sent his only-begotten Son to redeem us. We can also recognize the gift of the Holy Spirit — "given up" on the Cross (John 19:30), breathed forth after the Resurrection (John 20:22), and flowing from the hearts of believers as "rivers of living water" (John 7:38-39). By the interior power of the Holy Spirit the hearts of Christians are conformed to the heart of Christ and animated for service to the world.

Towards the conclusion (§39), the Pope sounds this theme a fifth time: "Faith, which sees the love of God revealed in the pierced heart of Jesus on the Cross, gives rise to love," the love that transforms us, the love that the world needs. He invites his readers "to experience love and in this way to cause the light of God to enter into the world." And in the final section (§42), he recalls the pure, benevolent love of the Virgin Mary. How is such love possible? It is "a result of the most intimate union with God, through which the soul is totally pervaded by him — a condition which enables those who have drunk from the fountain of God's love [the pierced heart of the Savior] to become in their turn a fountain from which 'flow rivers of living water' (*Jn* 7:38)."

---

60. The Pope proceeds to show how this is related to the Eucharist, in which "Jesus gave this act of oblation an enduring presence" (§§13-14).

Jesus of Nazareth

Now that we have identified the themes the Pope favors, and his motives for presenting them, we have a hermeneutical key to his book, *Jesus of Nazareth*. The Foreword and Introduction state very clearly the problem he hopes to address. The gap between the "historical Jesus" and the "Christ of faith" has eroded people's confidence that it is possible to trust the Gospels and to know and encounter the Lord. This crisis in faith has led to a crisis in devotion. "This is a dramatic situation for faith," he writes, "because its point of reference is being placed in doubt: Intimate friendship with Jesus, on which everything depends, is in danger of clutching at thin air."[61] The Pope says it is his "most urgent priority to present the figure and message of Jesus in his public ministry, and so to help foster the growth of a living relationship with him."[62] Anyone familiar with the essays in *Behold the Pierced One* will recall the theses of his "spiritual Christology" and his desire to invite his readers to the "intimate friendship" with the Lord Jesus that is the fruit of faith and devotion, a "friendship" that is learned from the saints and available in the Church.

Pope Benedict XVI, an "apostle" of the pierced heart of Jesus, invites the faithful to accompany him on his "personal search 'for the face of the Lord' (cf. Ps 27:8)."[63] This search has opened the Gospels to him, has helped him defend the possibility of a face-to-face dialogue with the Savior, and has led him to the Cross where he "beholds" the Lord's heart, opened by the soldier's lance, as the wellspring of life and fountain of salvation. He will undoubtedly continue to urge believers to refresh their faith with a "devotional knowledge" of Jesus Christ by contemplating this extraordinary icon of love.

---

61. *Jesus of Nazareth*, p. xii.
62. *Jesus of Nazareth*, p. xxiv.
63. *Jesus of Nazareth*, p. xxiii.

Postscript

RICHARD JOHN NEUHAUS

This admirably thoughtful collection of reflections on the pontificate of Benedict XVI highlights — in the sense of drawing attention to and illuminating — issues that have understandably puzzled both admirers and critics of the current pope. In the immediate aftermath of his election, the much-agitated question was that of continuity: the continuity between Cardinal Ratzinger and Pope Benedict, and the continuity between Benedict and his immediate predecessor, whom I believe history will know as John Paul the Great.

Of course, popes are by virtue of their office keenly attentive to continuity, without which their role as chief shepherd and teacher of the universal Church can be severely jeopardized. This is not to say that the personality and perspective of a pope is completely subordinated to continuity. One thinks, for instance, of the initiative of John XXIII — an initiative that some of his close advisers thought dangerously impulsive — in convening the Second Vatican Council, probably the most influential religious event of the twentieth century and an event without which a book such as this would hardly be conceivable. The council was, among many other things, an invitation to all Christians to make the Catholic Church their business, and a book such as this is a heartening response to that invitation.

And one thinks of the many initiatives of John Paul II, such as his confidence that human freedom grounded in a Christian anthropology could and should challenge the anti-human totalitarian ideology represented by the Soviet Union. In his robust renewal of the Church's appeal to young people — represented by World Youth Day as well as other major projects — and in his articulation of a gospel that "does not impose but proposes" (cf. the encyclical *Redemptoris Hominis*), John Paul brought back to life the missionary mandate and set forth a vision of a universal "culture of life" that established the moral authority of the papacy on the world stage in a measure unprecedented in recent centuries. So the personality and perspective of a pope does matter, and matters greatly.

In addition to the continuity of the papal office, it is well to remember that Joseph Ratzinger was in critical ways the closest collaborator of John Paul throughout almost the entirety of the latter's pontificate. It should be obvious that the depiction of Ratzinger as the hard-line enforcer in contrast to John Paul's charismatic leadership was a caricature, promoted mainly by those who opposed their shared effort to defend and faithfully transmit "the faith once delivered to the saints." Moreover, those who knew Ratzinger personally knew him as a man of great personal gentleness, astonishing erudition, and intense intellectual curiosity.

My own personal encounters with Ratzinger began in 1988 when we invited him to deliver the annual Erasmus Lecture, sponsored by *First Things*. This was followed by a conference of several days involving Catholic, Protestant, and Orthodox theologians. Ratzinger's lecture was on biblical interpretation, and especially memorable in the conference were his exchanges with George Lindbeck, whose very influential *The Nature of Doctrine* had been published a few years earlier. Again and again, participants expressed their pleased surprise at discovering that Ratzinger, far from being the theological "Rottweiler" of implacable and authoritarian assertiveness so often caricatured, was an intense but modest partner in exploring the truth of the Christian tradition and its more effective communication in a world frequently hostile to that truth. Those who have known Ratzinger over the years know him to be a man eager to listen, learn, and candidly respond to questions such as those addressed by the contributors to this volume.

But of course there are significant differences between Benedict and John Paul. On the ecumenical issues treated by some of the contributors, I think it fair to say that Benedict's hopes for Christian unity, at least in the foreseeable future, are somewhat more modest than those suggested by John Paul in his 1995 encyclical *Ut Unum Sint*. Of course the Catholic understanding of the ecumenical destination continues to be full communion understood as unity in doctrine, sacramental life, and ministry. But, before and after becoming pope, Benedict has insisted that this ecumenical possibility partakes of eschatological hope. Our responsibility, he says, is to

pray for and be open to a new initiative of the Holy Spirit that we can neither anticipate nor control. In continuity with John Paul, there is no doubt
that relations with the Orthodox have ecumenical priority, but the patient
and disciplined determination is to deepen conversations with all Christians in the hope of an exchange of spiritual gifts on a common pilgrimage
toward a goal that we cannot now foresee. Above all, the insistence is that
dialogue must be dialogue in the service of truth, not in the service of our
own ecumenical schedules. The only unity pleasing God, and therefore the
only unity we should seek, is unity in the truth. This has been a constant
and emphatic theme in Benedict's understanding of Christian unity.

Ephraim Radner writes about pluralism in the life of the Church, and
Benedict shares an understanding of the mysterious ways in which differences, and even divisions, in the Body of Christ may serve a providential
purpose that is beyond our understanding. This is not to say that we
should resign ourselves to such divisions, but we should recognize that
ours is a preliminary moment in the long history of the Church and that,
through differences and divisions, we may learn from one another, being
led together toward a fullness of truth that none of us now can perfectly
comprehend. Benedict insists that the modesty of this pilgrim hope requires that the Catholic Church be uncompromisingly faithful to the truth
entrusted to her. Only in such fidelity can the Church be, as the Second
Vatican Council taught, the gravitational center of the many gifts of the
Spirit present in the several churches and ecclesial communities.

Another distinction between Benedict and John Paul is evident in the
former's encyclicals, *Deus Caritas Est* and *Spe Salvi,* discussed by Geoffrey
Wainwright. Benedict is very much an Augustinian. In those documents
and others, the repeated references to Augustine, compared with other authoritative voices in the Christian tradition, is striking. While insistent
upon the Christian contribution to civilization and upon the great
achievement that is the synthesis of Hellenic and biblical wisdom in understanding the relationship between faith and reason, Benedict has an
emphatically Augustinian and "realistic" estimate of the possibilities of
history. History does not supply the remedies for the dilemmas of history.
In addition to Benedict's eschatological perspective, Harding Meyer is
surely right that Benedict insists upon a radical and intensely personal relationship with the Lord of history, Jesus Christ, whom Benedict is fond of
describing as "the human face of God."

In this connection, Cheryl Bridges Johns is surely right to accent the ways in which Benedict draws attention to the Holy Spirit and what might be described as the charismatic dimensions of Christian faith and life. Of most particular interest is Sister Sara Butler's treatment of the importance of the Sacred Heart of Jesus in Benedict's thought and piety. This is closely related to his call for a restoration of popular devotions in the life of the Church. While the Council strongly affirmed, and Ratzinger/Benedict strongly affirms, the emphasis of an earlier liturgical movement on the centrality of the Eucharist as the "source and summit" of the Church's life, he has been critical of a certain "minimalism" in postconciliar reforms, leading him to join in calling for a "reform of the reform." It is also in this connection that we should understand his encouragement of the use of the Latin missal of John XXIII as an "extraordinary form" of the Roman Rite.

With respect to these questions and others addressed by the essays in this book, it is evident, I believe, that Benedict is through-and-through a man of the Second Vatican Council. It is as a champion of the council that he insists it is not a moment of rupture that brought into being a pre–Vatican II Church and a post–Vatican II Church, but a Spirit-guided moment of renewal that brings the full riches of the one Catholic Church through time into constructive engagement with the entirety of the Christian movement traveling on its pilgrim way toward the promised Eschaton. As this book helpfully demonstrates, these are the "premises and promises" of the pontificate of Benedict XVI.

Contributors

Sara Butler, M.S.B.T. (Roman Catholic)
Professor of Dogmatic Theology
Saint Joseph's Seminary
Yonkers, New York

Dale T. Irvin (Baptist)
President and Professor of World Christianity
New York Theological Seminary
New York, New York

Cheryl Bridges Johns (Pentecostal)
Professor of Discipleship and Christian Formation
Church of God Theological Seminary
Cleveland, Tennessee

Maximos (Agiorgousis) (Greek Orthodox)
Metropolitan of Pittsburgh
Pittsburgh, Pennsylvania

Harding Meyer (Lutheran)
Former Director and Professor
Institute of Ecumenical Research
Strasbourg, France

Richard John Neuhaus (Roman Catholic) (d. 2009)
Late Editor-in-Chief, *First Things*
New York, New York

Ephraim Radner (Episcopal)
Professor of Historical Theology
Wycliffe College
University of Toronto
Toronto, Canada

William G. Rusch (Lutheran)
Adjunct Professor of Church History
New York Theological Seminary
New York, New York, and
Adjunct Professor of Lutheran Studies
The Divinity School
Yale University
New Haven, Connecticut

Joseph D. Small (Presbyterian)
Director of the Office of Theology and Worship
Presbyterian Church (U.S.A.)
Louisville, Kentucky

Geoffrey Wainwright (Methodist)
Robert Earl Cushman Professor of Christian Theology
The Divinity School
Duke University
Durham, North Carolina